The European Union

New Leadership and New Agendas

The European Union

New Leadership and New Agendas

**Edited by Stephen Alomes, Robert Mężyk
and Sang-Chul Park**

Connor Court

PO Box 7257
Redland Bay QLD 4165
sales@connorcourt.com
www.connorcourt.com

ISBN: 9781922449511

Cover design by Maria Giordano, photo from Istockphoto.

Printed in Australia

CONTENTS

CONTRIBUTORS

Prof. Stephen Alomes is an adjunct professor within the Centre for Social and Global Studies at RMIT University, working mainly on comparative populism. His themed prose poetry collection, *Our Pandemic Zeitgeist*, Ginninderra Press, was published in 2020. Email: stephen.alomes@rmit.edu.au

Dr Remy Davison, formerly Jean Monnet Chair in Politics and Economics (2012–15) within the Monash European and EU Centre, lectures in Politics and International Relations at Monash University. He is a UN Global Conflict Expert, 2010. Email: Remy. Davison@monash.edu

Prof. John Erik Fossum is in the ARENA Centre for European Studies, University of Oslo and Scientific Coordinator of the H2020-funded project, EU Differentiation, Dominance and Democracy. Email: j.e.fossum@arena.uio.no

Dr Sarah Howe researches EU Smart Specialisation Policy and regional responses in Europe and Australia at RMIT University Email: sarahmayhowe@yahoo.com.au

Dr Binoy Kampmark is a Senior Lecturer in Legal and Dispute Studies in the School of Global, Urban and Social Studies at RMIT University and contributing editor to *CounterPunch*. Email: bkampmark@gmail.com

Dr Maren Klein, Dr Chloe Ward and Dr Sophie Di-Francesco Mayot are Research Officers in the European Union Centre of Excellence at RMIT University where **Bradley Davison** is a research assistant, **Campbell Hughes** is a student and **Dr Debbie Long** (who is also a Senior Lecturer at the Wollotuka Institute, University of Newcastle) is a Research Fellow. Email: maren.klein@rmit.edu.au

Dr Robert Mężyk is an independent academic with expertise in law and philosophy. He has been teaching law at the University of Technology Sydney, Australian Catholic University and Western Sydney University. The author of *Die EU und die Finanzkrise*, 2018, he holds a PhD from Humboldt University, Berlin, Masters degrees in law and philosophy from Jagiellonian University, Cracow, and a Magister Legum (LL.M) from Johannes Gutenberg Universität Mainz. Email: robert.mezyk@acu.edu.au

Prof. Sang-Chul Park is a Full Professor of International Business and Trade and International Economic Politics at Korea Polytechnic University. Having worked as a visiting Professor in eight countries in Asia, Europe, and Oceania, he is also Editor in Chief of the *Asia Pacific Journal of EU Studies* (APJEUS). Email: scpark@kpu.ac.kr

Dr Rita Parker is a Europa Visiting Fellow at the Centre for European Studies, Australian National University and an Adjunct Associate Professor, University of Canberra. Her co-edited book (with A. Burke) *Global Insecurity*, was published by Palgrave Press, 2017. Email: Rita.Parker@anu.edu.au

Dr Charles Richardson has been a political analyst in government, media and the private sector. He blogs on world politics at The World is Not Enough. Email: charlesr@ozemail.com.au

Dr André Sammartino is an Associate Professor in Strategy Management and Marketing in the Faculty of Business and Economics, University of Melbourne. Email: samma@unimelb.edu.au

Dr Russell Solomon is a Senior Lecturer in the Criminology and Justice Studies in the School of Global, Urban and Social Studies at RMIT University. Email: russell.solomon@rmit.edu.au

Prof. Gabriele Suder is an Adjunct Professor in GUSS, RMIT University and a Professorial Fellow in the Melbourne University Business School. She co-edited (with Monica Riviere and Johan

Lindeque) *The Routledge Companion to European Business*, 2019. Email: gabriele.suder@rmit.edu.au

Dr Perparim Xhaferi has researched the role of the European Union and other regional and international powers in the Balkans, with a focus on Albania which is included in his recent book, *Albania: Escaping the East, Aspiring for the West* (Connor Court, 2020). He currently works for RMIT University in risk and compliance and is a member of the European Studies Association Australia and New Zealand (ESAANZ). Email: rimi.xhaferi@rmit.edu.au

1

INTRODUCTION: THE EUROPEAN UNION
IN A TROUBLED WORLD

Stephen Alomes, Sang-Chul Park and Robert Mężyk

In the global century the European Union must address the challenges of our times. As an evolving new federation, although not a unitary state, it faces additional stresses, although ones not unfamiliar to many older nations, as we all face a major disease pandemic and a global climate crisis.

The European Union – New Leaderships and New Agendas addresses the complexities, the federal, legal, economic and political tensions, and several local and regional experiences, which shape the European Union as it enters the third decade of the 21st century. The book explores the myriad challenges to the European Union project as a potential great federal nation, including the UK's Brexit departure (despite Scotland's dissent) and protest parties and movements and rhetorical invocations, suggesting 'Frexit', 'Grexit' and other departures. Critiques of the EU come from Marine Le Pen in France and the 'illiberal democracies' further east, from Italian 'sovereigntism' and include the Mediterranean critiques of EU economic and immigration policy. Debates over debt and the Euro, the impact of the Global Financial Crisis and now the responses to the global Covid-19 pandemic continue the

1

theme of crisis. Euroscepticism persists, despite the evolving government institutions of a nation, including the European parliament and the Euro common currency, and the invented traditions of an imagined national community through the European flag and Europe Day.

The studies in *The European Union – New Leaderships and New Agendas* reflect the interest in the EU and its complications from scholars in Australia, New Zealand and Asia. At a time of global stresses and strains, mirrored in the EU, the chapters address these ongoing uncertainties and the demands for new agendas and leadership. Seventy years after the formation of the European Coal and Steel Community (1951) and then the European Community (1957) the evolving European Union lives in uncertain times.

That growing research interest in the European Union in the Asia-Pacific region contributes to the explanation and illumination of contemporary problems, some European and many shared with the countries of Asia-Pacific and the Americas. Researchers, working under the larger umbrella of EUSAAP, the European Union Studies Association of Asia and the Pacific, and more specifically Australasian researchers working with the new association ESAANZ, the European Studies Association of Australia and New Zealand, have come together to develop the analyses. Research is advancing in specialist centres including the European Union Centre of Excellence at RMIT University, which hosted the major international conference in late 2019 addressing the difficulties and opportunities faced by Europe in a time of transition. Held under the auspices of EUSAAP and with the support of New Zealand and the EU Centres at the ANU, of Swinburne University of Technology and the Contemporary European Studies Association of Australia, it presented several exciting analyses. This book is a manifestation of the fruits of the efflorescence in EU studies.

In the opening chapter, 'The crisis to end the European Union or

'Next Generation EU? Covid-19 and the European Union', Maren Klein and her co-authors, most based at the EU Centre of Excellence at RMIT University, Melbourne, seek to delineate a European Union facing over a decade of crises which threaten its cohesion and effectiveness, from economic crises to the health and economic implications of the global pandemic. Studies by Binoy Kampmark and Stephen Alomes address European-Australian connections. Considering one of the great challenges of today, global refugee movement and First World nations' policies towards refugees, Binoy Kampmark analyses the influence of Australian conservative refugee deterrence policies on European refugee policies, especially after the great waves of 2015. Differently, Stephen Alomes explores two contemporary political tendencies in comparison and contrast terms, with a focus on France and Australia: the appeal of leadership in our media age and distinct, including political party uses, of Centre and Right populism, from Emmanuel Macron's *En Marche* to Australia's Liberal-National parties.

Regional variations are important with the EU expansion east, including the former countries of the Soviet bloc. Part of that story, as with development policies regarding the South of Italy, is one of an economic transition from command economies and old technology to competitive activities in a global world. Sarah Howe pursues the concept of 'smart specialisation' and the movement from concept to implementation in Hungary given the many obstacles, from historical attitudes to the 'illiberal democracy' of the Fidesz government under Viktor Orbán. In a different regional study, as tensions over identities, borders and states continue in the Balkans, Perparim Xhaferi elaborates the cross-sectional complexities of Albanian history including aspirations for a Greater Albania.

While the symbols, history, politics and shared identity of nations, including the European Union, may have the highest profiles, other underlying realities are worked out in the words and policies expressed in law. In a federal state, the law is central to its workings, a key factor pursued by Robert Mężyk and by Russell Solomon and John Erik Fossum.

Today, the cohesion and functioning of the European Union is threatened by the non-compliance of the 'rogue states' of Poland and Hungary, whose conservative governments refuse to abide by European laws and threaten the rule of law in the community. Given this conflict, Robert Mężyk investigates legal options under international law for the EU to counteract the behaviour of a rogue member state. Rita Parker assesses internal and external threats to Europe's future security, including racism and the arrival of refugees. She reviews the evolution of the EU in history, from the Cold War to contemporary security questions, including Brexit, NATO and European relations with the several major powers. She recognises the influence of populism amongst contemporary uncertainties including the looming spectre of climate change. She relates the changing face of security in Europe to the ways in which it has enabled or inhibited the European Union project.

Trade or intercourse between nations is both a force for cooperation and also of tension and conflict, both within the EU and on the world stage, a subject addressed by Davison and Park. Sang-Chul Park demonstrates how the trade conflicts between the two super-powers, the US and China, indirectly impact on the EU economy. From the global financial crisis until the tensions of the Trump trade war with China, the global free trade system has been under threat, with forces engendering negative growth. The study explores how the third major trading bloc, the EU, has responded to the negative impacts of the trade war between the G2.

When UK Prime Minister Boris Johnson declared - in his eccentric and theatrical way, imbued with flag-waving populism - 'Let's get Brexit done!' he seemed to suggest that leaving the EU would be simple, a clean break. However, as Remy Davison demonstrates, one future scenario of a free trade treaty with Australia may be complex and difficult to achieve. He analyses the potential stumbling blocks which demonstrate the complexification of future Australia-UK and Australia- EU free trade agreements.

Taking up legal themes which mirror aspects of Davison's economic analysis, Russell Solomon and John Erik Fossum consider the UK process of 'dejuridification' after its many years as a member of the European Union. They demonstrate that the EU legal legacy is likely to endure and European legal conventions may have a continuing influence within British law.

Gabriele Suder and André Sammartino are concerned to understand several complex linkages within and beyond the EU borders in their study on 'De-integration in a regionalised world: The meaning of Brexit for multinationals' cross-border strategy across Australia and Europe'. They address multi-factorial behaviour within the microcosms of the corporate sector as well as the macrocosms of nations and trading blocs. Focusing on how Brexit is reshaping the regionalisation strategies of multinationals across Europe and Australia, they show how regionalisation is now displaying aspects of 'deglobalisation'.

Charles Richardson takes up the contemporary political debate on popular disillusionment with politics, sometimes termed a 'democratic deficit' or associated with populism. He finds the problem in the relationship between the EU executive and the European parliament and suggests drawing on older traditions associated with the evolution of parliament in the UK.

Europe's challenges are international as well as internal. As China rises to compete with both America as a superpower and, in trade, with the USA and with the EU as a major trading bloc, the world faces multiple stresses: globalisation, trade wars, populist discontents with government and larger political structures, and the twin spectres of Covid-19 and climate change. The European Union shares with other nations the need for new agendas and new leadership to respond to what may be the biggest challenge, a shared global reality, as expressed in the old Chinese curse, 'May you live in interesting times'.

2

THE CRISIS TO END THE EUROPEAN UNION OR 'NEXT GENERATION EU'? – COVID-19 AND THE EUROPEAN UNION

Maren Klein, Chloe Ward, Bradley Davison, Sophie Di-Francesco Mayot, Debbi Long, Campbell Hughes

Keywords: Polycrisis, COVID-19, Future of the EU, Rule of Law Conditionality, Solidarity

Abstract

The European Union is no stranger to crisis and has managed to evolve and grow through them. The 2010s have been a decade of interrelated 'polycrisis', raising the question of the European project, especially after the United Kingdom's withdrawal from the Union. The emergence of severe acute respiratory syndrome coronavirus 2 (SARS-CoV-2) and the resultant COVID-19 pandemic acted as the trigger of a further multifaceted crisis: health, socio-economic but also touching on issues of the institutional set-up of the EU and European policy-making processes in the face of multiple cleavages. This chapter explores the crises of the last decade, the cleavages which have arisen from these crises, how those cleavages have influenced the EU's handling of the COVID-19 crisis, and considers the opportunity of change this latest crisis offers the EU by advancing targeted solutions addressing the fundamental policy problems at stake.

Introduction

The European Union (EU) is no stranger to crises and so far has continued to evolve despite setbacks, most significantly the United Kingdom's withdrawal from the Union, Brexit. The emergence of the COVID-19 pandemic in 2020, though, has shifted the focus back on the question of the European Project's foundations and the shape of its future.

Even though Brexit seemed to have engendered a renewed sense of unity among the remaining 27 member states, the impacts of the preceding crises were manifested in widespread Euroscepticism, populism, and a general dissatisfaction with the EU and its institutions. Brexit also highlighted the cleavages which have developed in the wake of the crises of the last decade. To counter these developments, the EU had planned to commence the second phase of the Debate on the Future of Europe, the Conference on the Future of Europe, in early 2020. But the emergence of severe acute respiratory syndrome coronavirus 2 (SARS-CoV-2) and the disease caused by the virus, COVID-19, put a stop to this venture. It has also changed many of the EU's immediate priorities, making the future of the EU looking quite different to what had been reasonably expected only 12 months earlier. Since COVID-19 struck the EU in early 2020, the Union has been going through continuing crises: an initial health crisis and its attendant socio-economic crisis, and a resurgent health crisis. Finally, at the end of the year, a political crisis emerged with its roots in the only partly resolved crises of the decade, touching on issues of solidarity and sovereignty but also European policy-making processes and values more broadly.

Seeds of EU discontent: the decade of polycrisis

Since its inception nearly 70 years ago, the European Union, including its precursors, has been no stranger to challenges and crisis but, despite its problems, has managed to advance integration while broadening membership considerably (Dinan 2019, 491-492; Zeitlin, Nicoli, & Laffan 2019, 963-964). Initially, support for the EU and its institutions was high, based on rational utilitarian considerations, i.e. increasing member state benefits through effective economic policy solutions rather than support for EU values (Schweiger 2020, 161).

However, this support has dwindled, in particular in the last decade, a particularly turbulent decade for the European project with multiple crises and challenges across policy areas, including the continuing Eurozone crisis, the deleterious economic consequences of the Global Financial Crisis and then the great refugee/immigrant waves of 2015. All would impact on the EU, weakening cohesion. In 2016 Jean Claude Juncker, the then President of the European Commission, went as far as describing the EU in a speech to the Hellenic Federation of Enterprise in Athens as being in a 'polycrisis' (Juncker 2016a) Later the same year, in his State of the European Union address, he described the EU as going through an 'existential crisis' (Juncker 2016b).

Increasingly complex multi-level governance structures and constraints on the EU's ability to initiate effective policy solutions, resulted in what has been termed 'muddle through' solutions (Hughes 2019, 15) to external and internal challenges, sometimes with unintended consequences necessitating further reform at a later stage. Such an approach has economic and political costs. Policy failures can impact severely on EU citizens and member states with disastrous socio-economic consequences. Negative outcomes in turn can influence perceptions of the EU and support for the European project. This is significant, given that one of the reasons for EU citizens' support was the EU's utilitarian benefits rather than affective belonging. The second issue is that this approach creates the perception of the EU in constant crisis with the need for constant reforms. This perception undermines popular support for European integration.

2.1 Eurozone crisis

The Eurozone crisis has been one of the major crises to dominate the EU policy landscape for much of the 2010s and with far-reaching and long-lasting impacts. Even a decade after its eruption, it has not been completely resolved and continues to affect the EU. It has brought to the fore the political and economic divides between the core – the stronger economies of the north – and its two peripheries, the weaker southern and eastern European economies, with a prominent role for the Visegrad group, i.e. the Czech Republic, Hungary, Poland and Slovakia, (Celi et al. 2020, 412-413; Schweiger 2020, 163-165).

The austerity measures and strict conditionality of the bailout imposed on the member states which required EU assistance have affected some member states more profoundly than others, leading to persistent negative impacts on national economies, affecting infrastructure spending on health systems for instance, and high levels of unemployment. Trust in the EU has declined considerably since the start of the Eurozone crisis (Schweiger 2020, 163). This has contributed to populism and Euroscepticism, as can be observed in Italy (Brunazzo & Mascitelli 2020, 27-29).

2.2 Migration crisis

The second major crisis of the decade was the so-called migration or Schengen crisis in 2015. Fleeing violent conflict, persecution and extreme poverty, a large number of refugees and migrants predominantly from the Middle East and North Africa, the so-called MENA region, or, in this case, the MENAP region which includes Afghanistan and Pakistan—tried to reach the EU via its frontline countries.

This highlighted the deficiencies of the EU's migration system, of which the Dublin Regime forms part. The EU's system is an externalisation system, i.e. one that prevents migrants from entering the territory or legal jurisdiction, making them legally inadmissible. The Dublin rules stipulate that the member state through which an asylum seeker first entered the EU will be the one responsible for processing the claim (Hassouri, 2018, s. Externalization Policies and Key Countries in the MENA Region).

As during the Eurozone crisis, the impact on member states was asymmetrical. Greece and Italy, two of the countries hardest hit by the Eurozone crisis, were also hit hard by the migration crisis due to being external border countries. The EU's solution, a quota system to distribute migrants across the various member states, was strongly opposed by the Central and Eastern European countries. The Visegrad group categorically refused to comply with a compulsory migrant quota, thus deepening the divisions in the EU but also highlighted the fact that the EU was incapable of enforcing its own rules.

This refusal is best understood on the background of the gap in the levels of economic development and social cohesion in Central and Eastern European member states, especially in rural areas. Economic integration in these countries has slowed since the GFC; wages remain low, there is a high level of poverty, and until the advent of the COVID-19, there was a high level of outmigration of younger people to wealthier member states.

2.3 Democratic backsliding

Since their accession, the Central and Easter European countries have been transitioning their political systems and economies from control to democracy and market economies with varying degrees of success. However, it appears that some countries have reversed course and are moving towards authoritarianism again. The so-called democratic backsliding of certain Central and Eastern European countries, particularly apparent in Hungary and Poland, the two EU member states showing the strongest trend towards a return to a political and economic nationalistic focus with authoritarian tendencies (Schweiger 2020, 165-166), is a case in point.

Both countries have been accused of breaches of the EU rule of law and EU values. In 2018 in response to these breaches, Article 7 of the Treaty on European Union procedures (clear risk of serious breach of the EU's values) was initiated against both countries: the European Parliament (EP) initiated an Article 7 of the Treaty on the European Union procedure (clear risk of serious breach of the EU's values) against Hungary (September 2018). The European Commission (EC) opened a rule of law Article 7 against Poland (December 2017) for undermining the rule of law in the country; this was followed by a hearing in June 2018, and a new infringement notice was launched in April 2019 in relation to further Polish proceedings against its judiciary (Hughes 2019, 16-17). The European Court of Justice handed down two rulings in relation to changes to Polish law on the ordinary courts organisation, in relation to lowering the retirement age of ordinary court judges, giving the Minister of Justice capacity to decide on the prolongation of judges' service without clear criteria, and different retirement age depending on gender, on 24 June 2019 and 5 November 2019, determining that those changes were contrary to EU law (European Commission 2019). None of these proceedings have yet resulted in any direct consequences. However, in 2018 the EU decided to develop a mechanism that would allow the Union to suspend disbursement of funds to countries engaged in breaches of EU law, the so-called rule of law conditionality. The rule of law conditionality is one further tool in the EU's tool kit to address serious breaches of EU law. To invoke the rule of law conditionality two preconditions need to be present: breaches of the principle of the rule of law must have been detected, and the breaches affect or seriously risk affecting the sound financial management of the EU budget or the protection of the financial interests of the EU. Examples of breaches include cases of corruption and fraud, but also breaches of fundamental values such as freedom, democracy, equality and respect for human rights including the rights of minorities. The decision to suspend funds would need to be taken by the European Council 'acting by a qualified majority on the proposal of the European Commission' (European Parliament 2020a).

2.4 Brexit

The largest blow to the European project was 'Brexit'. Much in the same way as the challenges and crises, the question of future of the European Union is as old as the European Union (and its predecessors) itself. However, after more than 50 years of existence and various rounds of enlargement, a collapse of the EU seemed unlikely. The UK's withdrawal highlighted that the 'ever closer union' was neither inevitable, nor a foregone conclusion but an active choice.

Brexit and the real costs of departure seemed to have rekindled a strong sense of unity and cohesion in the remaining 27 member states. This may be explicable by the fact that in some ways, the EU provides a stable and secure environment for the member states in the global world order. None of the EU countries has been a major geopolitical player since World War 2 and as Dinan argues 'the more rule-based and institutionally bound the international regime; the more secure its members—especially its small members—feel' (Dinan, 2019, 495).

At the end of 2019, with a new European Commission and Commission President, a forward-looking program that included a serious – though not uncontested – focus on European sustainability, EP elections that did not result in the right-wing populist landslide that had been expected, the EU seemed set to start a new chapter as the EU 27. The two major concrete challenges to be tackled in 2020 were finalisation of Brexit and achieving agreement on the 2021-2027 multiannual financial framework (MFF) which was still outstanding.

Also planned to start in 2020 was the two-year Conference on the Future of Europe, a forum intended to provide a grassroots-driven opportunity to engage in a debate on the EU's priorities and how to improve the functioning of the EU institutions and their capabilities (Dinan 2019, 500; Didili, 2020; European Parliament 2020b).

Then the novel corona virus emerged.

COVID-19 in Europe

3.1 Brief timeline of initial SARS-CoV-2/COVID-19 developments

One of the reasons for the devastation wrought by COVID-19, is the speed and severity of the spread. The other is that the world was not prepared, even though the pandemic should not have come as a surprise (Renda & Castro 2020, 2-3). In 2019 alone, a number of reports warned of the threat of a virulent respiratory pathogen pandemic. This was the scenario in which the EU and member states found themselves at the beginning of the year, unprepared for a pandemic but in particular unprepared for the speed with which the pandemic spread across Europe: case numbers increased by 66,000 % between 24 February and 24 March (Maurice et al. 2020, 2). It is worth bearing in mind that it did not even take three full months from the first mention of the virus to Europe becoming the epicentre of the pandemic. Unlike South East and North East Asia which had experienced SARS and MERS earlier in the century, Europe had no recent experience of epidemics.

The World Health Organization (WHO) became aware of reports of cases of 'viral pneumonia' in Wuhan on 31 December 2019. On 9 January 2020, WHO reported Chinese advice that the outbreak was caused by a novel coronavirus. On 19 January, the WHO disseminated advice of evidence of limited human-to-human transmission (WHO 2020a).

Cases of the disease outside China were reported in Thailand on 13 January 2020, and in Japan on 16 January 2020. The first case in the USA was reported on 21 January, the same day the WHO publicised its conclusion that human-to-human transmission was occurring, citing infections among health care workers as evidence. France was the first European country to report three confirmed cases on 24 January, all in travellers from Wuhan. On 29 January, the United Arab Emirates reported the first cases in the WHO Eastern Mediterranean Region (WHO 2020a).

On 30 January, the WHO determined that the novel coronavirus outbreak constituted a public health emergency of international concern (PHEIC). At that time 98 cases and no deaths across 18 countries had been recorded outside China. Four countries outside China, Germany, Japan, the United States of America, and Vietnam, had evidence of human-to-human transmission. The WHO assessed global risk as high, and for China as very high (WHO 2020a). Trade and tourism, and the associated people movement, exported the virus to Europe.

Case numbers continued to grow globally but most rapidly in Europe during February and March, with a major outbreak in Italy. On 11 March 2020, the WHO declared COVID-19 a pandemic, voicing its concern regarding levels of spread and severity of the disease but also the alarming levels of inaction globally. On 13 March 2020, the WHO declared Europe the epicentre of the pandemic with more reported cases and deaths than the rest of the world combined, apart from China (WHO 2020a).

3.2 The health response: too little Europe?

COVID-19 struck the EU in early 2020. As with the Eurozone and the migration crisis, the Union's own and member states' initial response to the health crisis, seemingly driven by national interests, reignited doubts about the viability of the European Project.

Despite detection of the first coronavirus cases in Europe in late January, it seemed that decisive action was first taken by member states almost a month later.

Faced with the possibility of a collapse of their individual health systems, the member states resorted to uncoordinated national responses, with little regard to the impact of their measures on the EU as a whole or on other member states: Italy was left to fend for itself while France and Germany placed embargoes on medical supplies in early March (Bayer et. al. 2020; France 24 2020) and only rescinded these measures after facing action by the EU. Other examples include unilateral border closures, disrupting pandemic management, supply chains and the economy more broadly.

In a situation that would have benefited from a consolidated co-ordination effort, it seemed national interest overrode any common interests, while the EU and its institutions seemed to be missing in action.

While the unilateral actions of the member states dominated the agenda and the media, within the framework of EU competencies, institutions had in fact started to act earlier than the member states, starting with the ECDC's (European Centre for Disease Control) first threat assessment on 9 January, a time when information concerning the virus was scant. The European Commission's health security committee held its first coronavirus teleconference on 17 January, however, only half of the member state health representatives attended (Boffey et al. 2020). The EU Council activated the EU integrated political crisis response mechanism (IPCR) level 2 (information sharing) on 28 January (Goniewicz et al 2020, s. 4). The Commission held a press conference on 29 January to send a clear message to the EU to prepare. However, the message was lost in the attention focused on Brexit (Boffey et al. 2020). While these actions provide evidence that the EU acted, it also reinforces the uncoordinated nature of the approach and the general unpreparedness of EU institutions.

The Centre for European Reform observed that 'the EU's initial reaction was slow and rather haphazard' (Gostyńska-Jakubowska & Scazzieri 2020, 1). The lack of preparedness is perhaps best illustrated by the well-documented inability of the EU to respond to Italy's urgent request for critical medical equipment including Personal Protective Equipment (PPE) via the EU's Civil Protection Mechanism of European solidarity in disasters because stocks had been depleted, and the EU was unaware of the situation. Even more damning, until 23 February PPE had been shipped to China in an effort to contain the outbreak there (Boffey et al. 2020). The EU's initial response did not seem to live up to von der Leyen's ideal of 'more Europe'.

It took until the beginning of March when the full scale of the epidemic began to emerge that the EU started acting decisively on a European basis: the Commission set up a crisis response team of commissioners to cover such diverse areas as health, economy and borders. The Council meanwhile triggered the full activation of the EU's integrated crisis response mechanism for a political level response in crisis situations.

Long (2020) argues that while some of the criticisms levelled at the EU, especially regarding the availability of equipment, were valid, others involved areas outside the EU's mandate in the area of public health. The legal framework of the EU in line with the principle of subsidiarity clearly sets out that public health is the competence of the member states, which finance, coordinate and manage their own health systems. As set out in Article 168 of the Treaty on the Functioning of the European Union (TFEU), the EU's role is to support, complement, or supplement member states' actions (European Commission 2020a). The Lisbon Treaty, while upholding the principle of subsidiarity, provides the EU with the ability to 'adopt incentives designed to protect and improve human health and in particular to combat the major cross-border health scourges, measures concerning monitoring, early warning of and combating serious cross-border threats to health' (Tsolova 2010). COVID-19 fits the description of a serious cross-border threat and thus offers the EU a role in the pandemic response; the reality of that role lies in coordination, flow of supplies, monitoring and research, and does not provide the authority to enforce most of the COVID-19 responses as recommended by the WHO (WHO 2020b) such as reporting of case incidences, responses to infection, and infection prevention and control, These are clearly member state competencies.

3.3 The socio-economic response: developing solidarity?

The initial discussions on how to approach and mitigate the socio-economic impact of the pandemic on the member states seemed to follow the path taken in the Eurozone crisis, reinforcing the perception of a lack of European solidarity along the north-south divide. Coupled with the seeming lack of solidarity and unilateralism in the health crisis response, the spectre of an existential threat to the EU arose, spurring a concerted effort in the economic sphere to mitigate the socio-economic fallout of the pandemic.

Initial deliberations around recovery measures resurrected old grievances. In March 2020, a number of member states including France, Italy and Spain argued that the symmetric exogenous shock of the pandemic was asymmetric in its impact, affecting some member states much more severely than others. To address these asymmetric impacts, they proposed corona bonds, a type of mutualised debt shared by all member states and issued by the European Investment Bank, as an economic support mechanism (*What are 'corona bonds' and how can they help revive the EU's economy* 2020). The argument was that mutualising the debt was based on principles of equity and solidarity. Northern European nations, headed by the Netherlands, opposed the measure, insisting on the use of the European Stability Mechanism (ESM) as the tool to finance the recovery. Germany's resistance at a Eurogroup meeting in March resulted in the corona bonds proposal being scrapped. Instead, three broad interim measures were agreed on in April: a European Investment Bank fund of €200 billion accessible to companies impacted by the pandemic; a €100 billion temporary loan instrument to support short-time working schemes (SURE); and loans of up to two per cent of any member state's economic output available under the ESM to cover emergency health costs. Use of the ESM as one tool in the COVID-19 recovery measures was a fraught undertaking, evocative as it was of the punishing conditionality enforced in the bailout measures of the Eurozone crisis. To southern European member states the EU's economic response was a test of European solidarity with implications for national politics (Tooze 2020).

By May, a Franco-German compromise paved the way for the Commission's recovery instrument, proposing €500 billion in grants and €250 billion in loans to aid the recovery on top of an increased EU budget. It appeared the EU had learned some lessons from previous crises, negotiating – figuratively and literally – its way through the asymmetric socio-economic impact of the symmetric pandemic shock. The financial rescue package, dubbed Next Generation EU (NGEU), was tied to the EU's next multiannual financial framework (MFF) for the period 2021-2027. The MFF offered not only badly needed funds for the worst hit economies but incorporated it in such a way as to achieve the current Commission's flagship project, the European Green Deal with its goal of a climate neutrality by 2050 and setting the EU on the path to sustainability. Coupled with the MFF of just above €1074 billion, the stimulus package would come to €1.8 trillion. In her speech unveiling the recovery tool, Commission President von der Leyen referenced the forward-looking nature of the package but, more importantly, acknowledged the asymmetric conditions across the member states and the need to ensure fair and inclusive outcomes via specific instruments within the package (European Commission 2020b).

At the European Council summit in July 2020, after lengthy negotiations among the member states, the MFF 2021-2027 and the NGEU recovery fund were agreed on in draft form. The package included the provision for a rule of law conditionality linked to the disbursement of EU funds, enabling the EU in tightly defined cases of violations of EU principles and values to stop disbursement of funds to member states. This was one of the two main issues of contention in the various rounds of consensus-seeking negotiations on the details of the two packages between the Presidency of the EU and the European Parliament as Parliament considered the Council's initial proposal as too weak. The other issue of contention was funding available for a number of EU flagship programs which had seen amounts reduced in the European Council summit negotiations. After months of negotiations, compromise was reached on both counts in early November 2020.

The next phase of negotiations brought a setback. While the rule of law conditionality had been provisionally agreed on within the framework of the MFF on 5 November 2020 (European Parliament 2020c), Poland and Hungary, opposed to it, withheld their consent for the Own Resources Decision as a means to stop the inclusion of the rule of law conditionality in the MFF. The Own Resources Decision sets out where the revenue for the MFF comes from and, unlike a number of other decisions in the MFF negotiations process which can be decided by qualified majority—the inclusion of the rule of law mechanism being one of those—the Own Resources Decision requires unanimity. The veto effectively meant the MFF 20210-2027 and the NGEU were in limbo.

Timelines for negotiations were tight as the MFF 2014-2020 was about to expire at the end of 2020 and approval processes for the adoption of multiannual frameworks are lengthy. Finally, after nearly a month of negotiations, during which the possibility of starting 2021 with an emergency budget and a delay in the distribution of recovery fund moneys had been contemplated, comprise was reached. While the text of the rule of law conditionality remains unchanged, it will not come into force until Hungary and Poland are able to challenge the legality of the measure in the European Court of Justice. Per se not a major breakthrough on the political front, the compromise clears the way for the adoption of the budget and recovery fund: despite the need for the European Parliament's approval of the MFF 2021-2027 and NGEU, and national parliaments consent to the implementation of the package, no further obstacles are expected (Bayer 2020).

3.4 Member state positions: solidarity or sovereignty?

Hungary's and Poland's refusal to agree to the Own Resources Decision would not have come as a surprise given the tensions around what the other member states see as the two countries' democratic backsliding. Both countries' ruling parties, Hungary's Fidesz – Hungarian Civic Alliance, and Poland's Law and Justice Party (Prawo i Sprawiedliwość, PIS), represent conservative populist authoritarian orientations: in Hungary embodied by Fidesz president's, Viktor Orbán, 'illiberal democracy' and in Poland by the government's reforms of the judiciary and media laws, coupled with 'moral' conservative policies on abortion and homosexuality. Both countries had voiced their opposition to the rule of law conditionality repeatedly and indicated that inclusion of the mechanism would lead to their non-approval of the package (Hungary's Orbán threatens EU budget veto over rule-of-law 2020). The EU had held out hope that this would remain rhetoric to appease the domestic arena - being net beneficiaries of EU funds at a time of severe impact of the second wave of COVID-19 would outweigh their opposition.

Both countries have longstanding objections to being subjected to EU rules, arguing they impinge on their national sovereignty. In relation to the rule of law conditionality in the MFF 2021-2027, Poland's justice minister is reported to have claimed: 'This is an issue that will determine if Poland is a sovereign subject in the EU community, or it will be politically and institutionally enslaved. ... It's not about a rule of law ... but about political and institutional slavery' (Herzsenhorn & Bayer 2020). Other government ministers made similar comments. Michał Wójcik, a member of the Chancellery of the Prime Minister and the ruling party, reportedly stated that the party would not 'trade sovereignty for any amount of money ... the policy of the bowed head is over' (Solidarity Poland opposes 'trading sovereignty' for EU money 2020).

These comments underscore the concept of EU membership set out by Polish Prime Minister Morawiecki in 2018:

> Europe should be strong in order to better defend our interests, yet European sovereignty cannot mean building the Union at the expense of the strength of the Member States, because the strength of the sovereign Europe comes from the strength of the Member States (Morawiecki 2018).

Hungary's Justice Minister Judit Varga was more circumspect, claiming concern related to there being neither clear, objective criteria nor definition of the principles of the rule of law, therefore the rule of law was not suitable to be used as a sanctioning mechanism (Herszenhorn & Bayer 2020). However, she also made the point that:

> At the time of its accession to the EU in 2004, Hungary did not say yes to a federalist Europe, or to globalism and espe-

cially not to the United States of Europe, but to a mutually supportive and respectful alliance based on strong nation-states (Justice Minister: Hungary Fighting for Europe, Not Against 2020).

Poland's and Hungary's position vis-à-vis the MFF and the recovery fund has essentially brought the negotiations for a recovery tool to address the very real socio-economic impact and institutional shortcomings laid bare by the pandemic to a standstill. More importantly, it seems to have stymied the EU's attempt to address the perceived solidarity deficit which has led to high levels of Euroscepticism in southern member states such as Italy (Brunazzo & Mascitelli 2020, 27-29) and increasingly Spain (Dennison & Zerka 2020, 5).

Leaving aside the performances and theatrics on the political stage – it is drawing a long bow painting the rule of law conditionality as an attack on member state sovereignty – it is worth noting that the both countries' grievances focus on the same populist issues that led to Brexit: sovereignty and migration, although in Poland's case in particular there is also the issue of the Polish government's opposition to recognising LGBT rights. The two countries' veto also puts a spotlight on the complexities of EU decision making and Euroscepticism intertwined with the concept of solidarity and/or sovereignty.

Solidarity deficit and/or sovereignty deficit: too little EU or too much EU

Solidarity is one of the fundamental values of the EU as articles 2 and 3 of the Treaty on European Union set out. Article 3.3 sets out solidarity as one of the fundamental principles of the internal market which has as its aims (among others) promotion of 'economic, social and territorial cohesion, and solidarity among Member States.' Yet, when Italy requested assistance for its COVID-19 emergency, it took the EU some time to provide some concrete actions of solidarity. That poses the question of what solidarity looks like in the EU and how to achieve it.

There is no single definition of solidarity because it is contextual. Very broadly, solidarity generally contains an idea of the cohesion of a particular community which may encompass certain obligations by group members. It describes a relationship between an individual and a community, or individual interest and common good (Scholz 2015, 725).

The EU has its origins in a rational political construct, enmeshing nation states via their economies to ensure unity and peace. Therefore, unlike solidarity among groups sharing certain values, there is no 'natural' solidarity based on emotional/moral and historical ties of belonging (Cohen & Sabel 2003, 351-354). While this type of solidarity may be found within the member states, it is unlikely to exist to the same extent across member states. This does not rule out the existence of an emotional/moral European solidarity in a subset of EU citizens, however, such a type of emotional solidarity is more likely to have developed as a side-effect of the more structurally based solidarity (Bertoncini 2020, 2-4).

Solidarity in the EU can be described as contractual, as it is, first and foremost, based on legal agreements, in treaties, policies and tools, which delineate member state and EU supranational competences. Member states keep their sovereignty but negotiate areas in which they transfer some of their sovereign rights to the EU, thus contributing to solidarity among the member states. However, decision-making in the EU involves multiple governments with heterogenous goals and preferences – some of which are influenced considerably by domestic political rationales (see Putnam (1988) on two level game theory) – resulting in political compromise and lowest common denominator decisions which may not satisfy all of the actors involved (Jones et al. 2017, 1014).

Further, while some of these solidarity tools were developed in long and comprehensive negotiations, others were developed in response to crisis situations which can lead to suboptimal outcomes and unintended consequences as the various crises and their fallout illustrate.

This then has led to the emergence of two types of Euroscepticism: one that believes the EU and its institutions do not provide equitable solutions to all member states and the second that feels that the EU interferes too much in the internal matters of sovereign nation states.

These positions are not new, though, and they are not intrinsically linked to the COVID-19 pandemic. In fact, in 2001 Timothy Garton Ash commenting on the EU's preparations for the Treaty of Nice – signed on 26 February 2001 and entered into force on 1 February – 2003, stated:

> More legitimacy, it is suggested, will come from more 'transparency' of European institutions. Or from more democracy. Or through the EU visibly doing more things closer to the experience of ordinary people: .... Or through it doing less of the intrusive regulation of everyday life that irritates people all over Europe (Garton Ash 2001, s. 7).

Euroscepticism in various forms has been part of the realities of the European Union for decades. To date, the Union has been able to reach a democratic compromise, but the question now is whether in a more nationalistic and nativist world, there is a will to reach compromise.

Wither EU?

Facing one of its greatest health and economic crises, Covid-19, what is the future of the European Union in troubled times? COVID-19 has illustrated that despite all its faults – bureaucratic, slow, haphazard, nationalistic, lacking solidarity and being driven by nationalistic member state interest – the EU is capable and, even more important, willing to engage in a massive and timely effort to address the crisis, to be undogmatic, innovative, inventive and forward-looking ensure a whole-of-EU recovery.

Comparing the effectiveness of individual member state and EU responses, it should be clear by now that member states in isolation cannot achieve more or handle a crisis better by going it alone. In the EU the sum of the parts is far more effective than the parts acting alone.

Is Eurosceptic Timothy Garton Ash (2001, s. 5) still right: 'unity impossible, collapse improbable'?

If the EU can weather its current health, economic and political crisis and achieve a sustainable and future-oriented recovery from the pandemic it will 'not only have proved its resilience and the relevance of coordinated public action, but will also have paved the way for far-reaching institutional and political changes (Vitrey & Lumet 2020, 8).'

As John F. Kennedy (1959) said: 'Along with danger, crisis is represented by opportunity'.

References

Bayer, L (2020), 'EU leaders back deal to end budget blockade by Hungary and Poland', *Politico*, 10 December 2020, https://www.politico.eu/article/deal-reached-to-unblock-eu-budget-and-recovery-fund/.

Bayer, L, Deutsch, J, Hanke Vela, J & Tamma, J, 'EU moves to limit exports of medical equipment outside the EU', *Politico*, 15 March 2020, https://www.politico.eu/article/coronavirus-eu-limit-exports-medical-equipment/.

Bertoncini, Y 2020, *European Solidarity in Times of Crisis: A Legacy to be Deepened in the Face of Covid-19*. Fondation Robert Schuman, 31 October 2020) https://www.robert-schuman.eu/en/european-issues/0555-europe-an-solidarity-in-times-of-crisis-a-legacy-to-be-deepened-in-the-face-of-covid-19.

Boffey D, Schoen, C, Stockton, B & Margottini, L,(2020) 'Revealed: Italy's call for urgent help was ignored as coronavirus swept through Europe', This is Europe, *The Guardian*, 15 July, https://www.theguardian.com/world/2020/jul/15/revealed-the-inside-story-of-europes-divided-corona-virus-response.

Brunazzo, M & Mascitelli, B (2020), 'At the origin of Italian Euroscepticism', *Australian and New Zealand Journal of European Studies*, vol. 12, no. 2, 18-31.

Celi, G, Guarascio, D & Simonazzi, A (2020), 'A fragile and divided European Union meets Covid-19: further disintegration or 'Hamiltonian moment'?' *Journal of Industrial and Business Economics*, vol. 47, no. 3, 411-424.

Cohen, J & Sabel, CF (2003), 'Sovereignty and Solidarity: EU and US', in J. Zeitlin & DM Trubek (eds), *Governing work and welfare in a new economy: European and American experiments*, Oxford University Press, Oxford, 345-375.

Consolidated versions of the Treaty on European Union and the Treaty on the Functioning of the European Union (TFEU) *Official Journal C 326*, 26/10/2012 P. 0001-0390. https://eur-lex.europa.eu/legal-content/EN/TXT/?uri=celex%HYPERLINK "https://eur-lex.europa.eu/legal-content/EN/TXT/?uri=celex%3A12012E%2FTXT.

'Coronavirus: France to requisition face masks for use by health professionals, those infected', *FRANCE 24*, 3 March 2020, https://www.france24.com/en/20200303-coronavirus-france-to-requisition-face-masks-for-use-by-health-professionals-those-infected.

Dennison, S & Zerka, P (2020), *Together in trauma: Europeans and the world after covid-19*, European Council of Foreign Relations, https://ecfr.eu/publication/together_in_trauma_europeans_and_the_world_after_co-vid19/.

Didili, Z, 'Conference on the Future of Europe postponed', *New Europe*, 19 April 2020, https://www.neweurope.eu/article/conference-on-the-future-of-europe-postponed/.

Dinan, D (2019), 'Debating Europe's future.' *Irish Political Studies*, vol. 34, no. 4, 490-506.

European Council of the European Union (2020), The Council of the EU, Qualified Majority, https://www.consilium.europa.eu/en/council-eu/voting-system/qualified-majority/#.

European Commission (2019), European Commission statement on the judgment of the European Court of Justice on Poland's Ordinary Courts law, https://ec.europa.eu/commission/presscorner/detail/en/STATEMENT_19_6225.

European Commission (2020a), EU Health Policy, European Commission, https://ec.europa.eu/health/policies/overview_en.

European Commission (2020b), *Europe's moment: Repair and prepare for the next generation*, https://ec.europa.eu/commission/presscorner/detail/en/ip_20_940.

European Parliament (2020a), Rule of law: new mechanism aims to protect EU budget and values, https://www.europarl.europa.eu/news/en/headlines/eu-affairs/20201001STO88311/rule-of-law-new-mechanism-aims-to-protect-eu-budget-and-values.

European Parliament (2020b), *Conference on Future of Europe should start 'as soon as possible in autumn 2020'*, European Parliament, https://www.europarl.europa.eu/news/en/press-room/20200615IPR81226/conference-on-future-of-europe-should-start-as-soon-as-possible-in-autumn-2020.

European Parliament (2020c), Proposal for a Regulation on the Protection of the Union's Budget in Case of Generalised Deficiencies as Regards the Rule of Law in the Member States, https://www.europarl.europa.eu/legislative-train/theme-new-boost-for-jobs-growth-and-investment/file-mff-protection-of-eu-budget-in-case-of-rule-of-law-deficiencies.

Garton Ash, T (2001), 'The European Orchestra', *New York Review of Books*, vol. 48, n. 8, 60-67.

Goniewicz, K, Khorram-Manesh, A, Hertelendy, AJ, Goniewicz, M, Naylor, K & Burkle, FM (2020), 'Current response and management decisions of the European Union to the COVID-19 outbreak: a review', *Sustainability*, vol. 12, no. 9, 3838. https://doi.org/10.3390/su12093838.

Gostyńska-Jakubowska, A & Scazzieri, L (2020), The EU needs to step up its response to the COVID-19 outbreak, Centre for European Reform, https://www.cer.eu/sites/default/files/insight_AG_LS_23.3.20.pdf.

Hassouri, P (2018), 'Building Fortress Europe', *The Cairo Review of Global Affairs*, https://www.thecairoreview.com/essays/building-fortress-europe/.

Herszenhorn, DM & Bayer, L, 'EU in crisis over Hungary and Poland's €1.8T hold-up. Budget and coronavirus recovery fund blocked in rule-of-law wrangle, *Politico*, 16 November 2020, https://www.politico.eu/article/eu-in-crisis-over-hungary-poland-budget-hold-up/.

Hughes, K (2019), 'Europe's Future in the Face of Systemic Challenges', in Hughes, K. (ed). *The Future of Europe: Disruption, Continuity and Change.* Scottish Centre of European Relations Edinburgh, https://www.scer.scot/database/ident-10675.

'Hungary's Orbán threatens EU budget veto over rule-of-law', EURACTIV. com with AFP, 9 November 2020, https://www.euractiv.com/section/justice-home-affairs/news/hungarys-orban-threatens-eu-budget-veto-over-rule-of-law/.

Jones, E, Kelemen, RD & Meunier, S (2016), 'Failing forward? The Euro crisis and the incomplete nature of European integration', *Comparative Political Studies*, vol. 49, no. 7, 1010-1034.

Juncker, J-C (2016a), 'State of the union 2016: Towards a better Europe— a Europe that protects, empowers, defends, European Commission', https://ec.europa.eu/commission/presscorner/detail/en/SPEECH_16_3043.

Juncker, J-C (2016b), Speech by President Jean-Claude Juncker at the annual general meeting of the hellenic federation of enterprises (SEV), European Commission, https://ec.europa.eu/commission/presscorner/detail/en/SPEECH_16_2293.

'Justice Minister: Hungary Fighting for Europe, Not Against', *Hungary Today*, 16 November 2020, https://hungarytoday.hu/justice-minister-hungary-fighting-europe-against-budget-rule-of-law/.

Kennedy, J. F. (1959). Remarks at the Convocation of The United Negro College Fund, Indianapolis, Indiana, April 12, 1959, John F Kennedy Presidential Library and Museum, https://www.jfklibrary.org/archives/other-resources/john-f-kennedy-speeches/indianapolis-in-19590412.

Long, D (2020), 'Mixed Mandates: COVID-19 and multi-level governance', *EUCE News and Blogs*, 27 April 2020, https://www.rmit.edu.au/news/eu-centre-news/mixed-mandates.

Maurice, E, Bloj, R, Buzmaniuk, S, Antonini, C & d'Angelo, C (2020), *Covid-19: European Responses, a Complete Picture.* Fondation Robert Schuman, https://www.robert-schuman.eu/en/doc/actualites/covid19-26032020-en.pdf.

Morawiecki, M (2018), Address to the European Parliament, Chancellory of the Prime Minister, https://www.premier.gov.pl/en/news/news/prime-minister-mateusz-morawiecki-respecting-national-identities-is-the-foundation-for.html.

Putnam, RD (1988), 'Diplomacy and domestic politics: the logic of two-level games', *International organization*, 427-460.

Renda, A & Castro, RJ (2020), *Chronicle of a Pandemic Foretold*, CEPS Policy Insights No 2020-05, https://www.ceps.eu/wp-content/uploads/2020/03/CEPS-PI2020-05_Chronicle-of-a-pandemic-foretold.pdf.

Scholz, SJ (2015), 'Seeking solidarity'. *Philosophy Compass*, vol. 10, no. 10, 725-735.

Schweiger, C (2019), 'The European Union' in K Larres & R Wittlinger (eds), *Understanding Global Politics: Actors and Themes in International Affairs*, Routledge, London and New York, 160-171.

'Solidarity Poland opposes 'trading sovereignty' for EU money', *Polandin*, 17 November 2020, https://polandin.com/50836318/solidarity-poland-opposes-trading-sovereignty-for-eu-money.

Tooze, A, 'Corona bonds and Europe's North-South divide', *Social Europe*, 13 April 2020, https://www.socialeurope.eu/corona-bonds-and-europes-north-south-divide.

Tsolova, S (2010), 'The Treaty of Lisbon and public health in the EU', *The European Journal of Public Health*, vol. 20, no. 4, 475-475, https://doi.org/10.1093/eurpub/ckp235.

Vitrey, A & Lumet, S (2020), *Multi-annual financial framework and Next Generation EU, Review of an unprecedented, tumultuous European budgetary chapter*, Fondation Robert Schuman, https://www.robert-schuman.eu/en/doc/questions-d-europe/qe-575-en.pdf.

'What are 'corona bonds' and how can they help revive the EU's economy?' *Euronews*, 26 March 2020, https://www.euronews.com/2020/03/26/what-are-corona-bonds-and-how-can-they-help-revive-the-eu-s-economy.

WHO (2020a), *Timeline of WHO's response to COVID-19*, World Health Organization, https://www.who.int/news/item/29-06-2020-covidtimeline.

WHO (2020b), *Strategic preparedness and response plan*, https://www.who.int/publications/i/item/strategic-preparedness-and-response-plan-for-the-new-coronavirus.

Zeitlin, J, Nicoli, F & Laffan, B (2019), 'Introduction: the European Union beyond the polycrisis? Integration and politicization in an age of shifting cleavages', *Journal of European Public Policy*, vol. 26, no. 7, 963-976.

3

TURNING BACK BOATS: AN AUSTRALIAN EXAMPLE IN EU REFUGEE POLITICS

Binoy Kampmark

Keywords: Refugees, Boat arrivals, Populism, European Union, Australia

Abstract

Australia provides a singular example of refugee processing. To refugee NGOs, the approach has been seen as cruel and unproductive; according to the country's major political parties it has been deemed a necessary deterrent against people smuggling rackets (known as the 'business model') and preventing deaths at sea. Central to the policy is Operation Sovereign Borders, a military-grade approach deploying naval assets against undocumented boat arrivals. This involves both turning back unwanted arrivals and transferring arrivals to offshore processing centres on Papua New Guinea's Manus Island and the island state of Nauru. In the European Union context, parallels have emerged suggesting the persuasive strength of the Australian example. This chapter considers the influence of the Australian precedent and cognate approaches in the populist politics of the current European Union to irregular migrations. Growing reservations about the mobility principle and the breakdown of any unified front in dealing with refugee and asylum arrivals within the EU is considered. Recent examples of boat 'turn backs' in the Mediterranean are examined as showing examples reminiscent to Australia's own approaches.

Introduction: The *Tampa* Precedent

In August 2001, Australian Prime Minister John Howard demonstrated to the world what his country's elite soldiers could do. Desperate, close to starvation and having been rescued at sea from the *Palapa I* in the Indian Ocean, refugees and asylum seekers on the Norwegian vessel, the MV *Tampa*, were greeted by the 'crack' troops of the Special Air Services. A bitter, politicised standoff ensued. The Norwegian vessel had initially made its way to the Indonesian port of Merak, but then turned towards the Australian territory of Christmas Island. Howard, needing a boost in flagging polls which suggested that he would lose the next election, saw an opportunity centred on national security entailing 'a highly politicised and militarised response to the 'problem' of unauthorised maritime arrivals' (Tavan 2019). A rhetorical strategy was thereby adopted, stressing themes of invasion, the purportedly immoral nature of the arrivals and the grave threat they supposedly posed to border integrity (McMaster 2001; Marr & Wilkinson 2003; Crock and Saul 2002).

Australian authorities proved less than accommodating to the arrival of the vessel. Threats to the container ship's captain were issued: if Arne Rinnan refused to change course entering Australia's territorial sea, he would be liable to prosecution for people smuggling. The vessel was refused docking at Christmas Island. The measure was audacious, potentially breaching the UN Convention on the Law of the Sea ('UNCLOS') and a range of humanitarian instruments. According to article 92 of the Convention, vessels on the high seas are subject to the exclusive jurisdiction of the flag state, otherwise known as the country of registration. Absent consent from that state, states have no right to intercept and turn back the boats on the high seas, subject to the exceptions outlined in UN-CLOS. A right to visit is present regarding stateless vessels, but this does not generate powers of arrest or interdiction.

As was remarked a few years later by Mary Crock (2003), 'The stand taken by Australia in August 2001 set a precedent that, if followed by other refugee receiving countries, could only worsen the already deplorable problems facing asylum seekers in the world today.' In 2018, authors of a study comparing Australian and European responses to the refugee crisis would similarly warn that the pioneering approach by Australia should not be followed by Europe 'nor anyone else' (Minns, Bradley& Chagas-Bastos 2018, 16). What this tended to overlook was that the Australian 'approach' already had its genesis in policies adopted in 1981 by the Reagan administration of the United States towards Haitian asylum seekers, based on 'maritime interdiction and deflection, long-term administrative detention, and offshore asylum processing' (Crisp 2019, 172; Ghezelbash 2018).

Daniel Ghezelbash suggests that refugee polices formulated by Australia, and prior to that the United States, have been disseminated into the refugee policy mainstream, focusing on 'legal transfer', 'policy transfer' and 'diffusion' (Crisp 2019). The adoption of such approaches is based on matters of efficiency, which alleviates the need to formulate a unique response; prestige, where a state embraces the policy of another once it has acquired legitimacy; and traditional coercion, where pressure is exerted on 'less economically developed neighbours to implement harsh border control measures as a buffer against irregular migration (Ghezelbash 2018 22).

Australia's peculiar status in terms of responding to refugees was most explicitly noted by US President Donald Trump, in what became a notorious phone call with then Australian Prime Minister Malcolm Turnbull regarding a previous refugee exchange struck with the Obama administration. The terms of the agreement involved Canberra accepting refugees from Central America in exchange for 1,250 refugees detained on Nauru and Manus Island, Papua New Guinea. Turnbull's boastful words are worth recalling: 'If you try to come to Australia by boat, even if we think you are the best person in the world, even if you are a Nobel-Prize-winning genius, we will not let you in' (March Aug 4 2017). Trump, despite damning the Australian-US agreement , was impressed by Canberra's cold response. 'That is a good idea. We should do that too. You are worse than I am' (March Aug 4 2017). As that exercise shows, idiosyncratic and cruel considerations have come to dominate this field.

Turning Back the Boats

The actions of August 2001 catalysed a different approach in the field of refugee policy. Heavy-handedness replaced careful bureaucratic consideration; populist manipulation took the place of pondered legal assessments. While boat turn-backs were not officially stated as the policy of the Howard government, it became a central feature of the Abbott government from 2013. That same year, the Abbott government was elected to office on the express platform of a 'stop the boats' policy in the aftermath of increased irregular arrivals under both the Gillard and Rudd Labor governments. Operation Sovereign Borders (OSB) militarised the nature of combating 'illegal arrivals', including imposing blanket secrecy in disclosing matters connected with 'operational matters'. This point was explicitly stated by immigration minister Scott Morrison at a media briefing on 23 September 2013 (Morrison 2013). 'This briefing is not about providing shipping news to the people smuggler – it's about what the government is going to do in this operation to stop those people coming to Australia on those boats and deliver on our mandate achieved at the recent elections to implement policies that will stop the boats' (Morrison 2013).

The operation was given a further military accent by the appointment of a defence force general, an addition deemed essential by Abbott during his election campaign. Abbott's rhetorical approach twinned the arrival of refugees outside acceptable channels to invaders requiring military repulsion. Bureaucratic expansion also followed in step, with the creation of a new entity known as the Australian Border Force, one coming with its own complement of uniforms, ceremonial regalia and militaristic culture (Public Eye 2016).

Such developments offer some parallels with the European Union's approach to increased irregular arrivals, primarily through the Mediterranean. As the think-tank and London-based Overseas Development Institute reasons, 'high-income countries have influenced each other's policies, and consciously cultivated or indirectly fostered negative developments in lower-income states' (Hargrave & Pantuliano, September 2016, 1).

Three lines of reasoning in this discussion are central. The first is a case of striking parallels worthy of mention, be it through operations conducted by Frontex, the rough equivalent of the ABF, and practices regarding interdiction and transfer. The behaviour of personnel engaged with Frontex operations and those of Australia's border protection apparatus have drawn similar accusations from refugee advocates: a lack of transparency, policed secrecy, and an uneven observance of international humanitarian law. In terms of specific examples, the naval refugee policy of Italy's former interior minister Matteo Salvini, adopted towards specifically singled out vessels operated by charities, suggests a policy transfer of sorts from the Australian turn-back policy and outsourcing of obligations regarding the UN Refugee Convention (Pannonhírnök 2018). Finally, a measure of how popular Fortress Australia policies have been in Europe can be gathered by the reception given to the ideas of Abbott himself, architect of Operation Sovereign Borders, most notably by Hungarian Prime Minister Viktor Orbán. In Orbán's praise of Abbott, we see an eliding of concepts: border security, nationalism, race and demography (Orbán 5 September 2019).

Parallels and similarities

The EU responses adopted since 2014 suggest various inspirations from the Australian model. This was encouraged by the dramatic influx of migrants and refugees in 2015, propelled by continuing conflicts in Syria, Afghanistan and Iraq and sharply, if cruelly defined, by the death of Aylan Kurdi, a young Syrian boy whose body was found on a Turkish beach after a failed effort to reach Greece (Spindler 2015). The operational language, for instance, is similar. Operation Triton, which replaced the Italian Mare Nostrum search-and-rescue mission, had a specific focus on border security and migration control supported by a military operation, the European Union Naval Force Mediterranean ('EUNAVFOR Med'). For critics, it shifted the burden of rescue to merchant vessels (BBC 2014). Operation Sophia aims to combat smuggling and trafficking through the Central Mediterranean. Its purpose includes measures to identify, capture and dispose of smuggling vessels. Joint Operation Poseidon, involving 23 EU and Schengen countries, targets irregular movements in south-eastern Europe, particularly along Greece's sea and land borders (Frontex 2016). Such operations have seen the interception and return of vessels to Turkish territorial waters (Umurbilir 2015). Australia's own practice has been to adopt tow-back practices, pushing unwanted vessels back into Indonesian waters (Lloyd 2014).

The process of outsourcing modes of deterring arrivals through passing on processing and prevention to Niger, Libya and Turkey (Andersson & Keen 2019) is resonant of the Australian formula of using Pacific detention bases ostensibly run by sovereign states but financed by the Australian federal budget. Some of these appeal to what has been deemed a broader nativist sentiment. Despite Australia being an immigrant society, the policy adopted to refugee processing and deterrence has found support in various political quarters in Europe. This has also been helped along by the sheer scale of population displacements occasioned by the Syrian and Libyan civil wars, and broader political instability in Africa. In these instances, the categories of irregular migration (refugees, asylum seekers and economic migrants) have tended to be conflated. The approach has also lacked uniformity, a point of contention that has created a rhetorical space for exploitation by Australian politicians keen to internationalise Canberra's border protection program.

A case in point was the visit by a cross-party Danish delegation to the Nauru detention centre in August 2016. While the cross-section of Danish politicians hailing from the Endhedslisten Red-Green alliance to Martin Henriksen of the far-right Danish People's Party seemed exercised by the problematic nature of the treatment of refugees on Nauru, much speculation arose as to why they had deigned to visit the facility in the first place (Farrell 2016). The simple answer: the search for refugee policy alternatives for Europe in general and Denmark in particular.

Australian refugee policy has proven a subject of considerable interest, seen as a model for critique and imitation; it is also advertised in other countries as a worthy, popular solution to the problem of irregular arrivals, a point that the Australian government continues to advertise to various countries (Nethery, Rafferty-Brown & Taylor 2013). This has seen diplomats from Canberra attempting to 'sell' the OSB model to European governments and even the staff of the UNHCR (Crisp 2019). Despite the EU's insistence that it does not do so there is a strong suggestion that policies of the harsher sort against refugees have been adopted in line with those developed in Canberra (Loewenstein 2018). The salient point here, according to Jeff Crisp of Oxford's Refugee Studies Centre, is that the message is more subtle when shaped in the offices of the European Commission (Loewenstein 2018). Like Australia, the EU has also created a framework of turning back boats, similarly using the language of breaking the 'people smuggler model'. As Richard Lindsay, head of the security policy department of the Defence and International Security Directorate of the Foreign and Commonwealth Office explained in 2016 to the House of Lords, search-and-rescue matters are in themselves inadequate and inappropriate in lacking intelligence, surveillance and reconnaissance activities (Lindsay, 2016). The jump, then, to a more militarised, security-oriented approach, one that relegates the importance of refugee rights while stressing trafficking networks, is duly made.

Under a March 2016 agreement between the EU and Turkey, all 'new irregular migrants' crossing from Turkey into the Greek islands are to be returned to Turkey, a process that includes turning back vessels and, to use language popularised by Australian governments, breaking 'the business model of the smugglers' while offering 'migrants an alternative to putting their lives at risk' (European Council 2016). The language seems more moderate than that of Australia's turning back policy, in so far as any relevant international and EU law protections are said to be abided by during the process. Turkey is required to take 'any necessary measures' to prevent irregular migration through new sea or land routes to the EU. In return, the EU agreed that '[f]or every Syrian being returned to Turkey from Greek islands, another Syrian will be resettled from Turkey to the EU taking into account the UN Vulnerability Criteria (European Council 2016). On the substantial and sustainable reduction of irregular crossings between Turkey and the EU, a Voluntary Humanitarian Admission Scheme was to be activated for Syrian refugees in Turkey. Italy has also made specific arrangements with Libya via a 2017 memorandum of understanding negotiated by Marco Minniti ostensibly in the field of security and cooperation to stem illegal immigration. Emphasis was placed on completing 'the system of border control in Southern Libya' and adapting and financing 'reception centres' with trained Libyan personnel 'to face the illegal immigrants' conditions' (Odysseus Network 2017).

The European Union border and Coast Guard Agency, Frontex, furnishes a close comparison to the Australian example in its approach to arrivals, coordinating a number of joint missions to intercept and return boats and overall organisational management. Established in 2004 and being one of the European bodies funded in the face of increased irregular arrivals it will have a budget worth 11 billion euros over 2021-2027 (European Court of Auditors 2020). The language used by Frontex to describe its mission is carefully chosen: humanitarian purposes are stressed, as are objects of security. In many ways, it sits in a similar orbit to the functions of the Australian Border Force, the Royal Australian Navy and the overall purpose of Operation Sovereign Borders. Frontex, however, strings together elements of security, surveillance and border control in a manner more subtle than its Australian equivalent. Operation Triton, dealing with migratory flows in the central Mediterranean is described as follows: 'While the primary focus of Operation Triton [...],launched in November 2014, is border control and surveillance, search and rescue remains a priority for the agency. Since the beginning of the operation, Frontex vessels and aircrafts have regularly been redirected by the Italian Coast Guard to assist migrants in distress' (Frontex October 10 2016). The organisation's assessment of Operation Themis (Frontex, Main Operations 2018) also suggests a form of securitisation at play: 'Reflecting the needs of the Italian authorities, as well as the priorities of Frontex, Operation Themis also has a significant security component, include collection of intelligence and other steps aimed at detecting foreign fighters and other terrorist threats at the external borders.'

Prior to the European Parliamentary elections in 2019, the European Parliament adopted the Commission's proposal to add 10,000 border guards to the Frontex operation by 2027 (European Commission 2019). In 2020, recruiting for the European Border and Coast Guard standing corps began in a manner resonant of the Australian Border Force: upwards of 700 candidates were sought, a measure deemed by Frontex Executive Director Fabrice Leggeri 'a true transformation of our agency. For the first time, Frontex will have its owned uniformed service, working under the banner of the European Union.'

Frontex and the Operation Sovereign Borders platform share a similar approach to information on matters touching on rescue and processing. This has led to accusations of human rights abuses (Correctiv 2019). Australian authorities, for comparison's sake, employ what is described as 'enhanced screening' at sea to determine asylum claims, a process deemed expedient and inaccurate (Andrew & Renata Kaldor Centre for International Refugee Law, 7 July 2014). Such screening involves the use of inadequate teleconferences and interviews on the vessel conducted by Australian officials with insufficient opportunities on the part of asylum seekers to articulate their grounds for protection. Doing so 'raises a real risk of refoulement [the transfer or return of individuals to a jurisdiction where they would be at risk of harm, persecution, torture, ill treatment of other serious human rights abuses], in breach of Australia's obligations under international refugee and human rights law, including the 1951 Refugees Convention, 1948 Universal Declaration of Human Rights, and the 1966 International Covenant on Civil and Political Rights' (Andrew & Renata Kaldor Centre for International Refugee Law, 7 July 2014). The UNHCR has similarly argued that its own 'experience over the years with shipboard processing has generally not been positive', as it is rarely able to 'afford an appropriate venue for fair procedure' (UNHCR 7 July 2014).

Frontex's operations remain similarly opaque to their Australian equivalents despite claiming to observe human rights in discharging their functions (Report München 2019). A lingering concern centres on European border surveillance vessels which deliberately avoid areas where refugee vessels capsize (Correctiv 2019). The group has made various assertions: that access to logs on consultation between governments on migration policy is not open, as are the situational and operational reports of Frontex. The same goes for data and ship movement and locations. There is also an absence of legal arguments in response to investigations by journalists (Report München 2019). Secrecy is justified on the basis that people smugglers would otherwise know the strategy and tactics of Frontex if movements were disclosed, a point also iterated by former Australian immigration minister, Scott Morrison on revealing details pertaining to Operation Sovereign Borders (Morrison 2013).

Populist Exploitation

Politicising irregular arrivals was, and continues to be, a central feature of Australian refugee policy. It is a lesson that has not been lost in the European debate. The turn back the boats platform has become something of an inspiration for a range of European politicians, among them Germany' Minister of the Interior Horst Seehofer, and Austria's Sebastian Kurz, not to mention representatives in Poland, Hungary, the Czech Republic, and Slovakia (Mével 2019). They form a collective of hardened populists who are taking the issue of regulating the processing of refugees away from the centralised assumptions of the EU polity towards the universal right to asylum.

Kurz has openly entertained ideas of embracing a variant of the hardened Australian border protection model. In an interview with *Die Presse* (5 June 2016), he opined that, 'The Australian model of course cannot be completely replicated but its principles can be applied in Europe' (Ultsch 2016). In this, Kurz saw a historical consistency rather than a harsh precedent, stretching back to the early 20th century which saw the detention of arrivals who reached Ellis Island before making their way to New York. The current policy, in his view, had been responsible for the unnecessary stirring of hopes for those embarking upon perilous journeys, often resulting in drowning. The naval military nature of Operation Sovereign Borders also impressed, deployed as a 'border protection operation' to intercept refugee boats, including the return of individuals to countries of origin and the creation of a Pacific detention system. Seehofer has also encouraged the adoption of similar models. 'We must help our European partners even more in patrolling the EU's external borders; we have left them alone for too long' (Deutsche Welle, 7 Oct 2019).

The logistical and operational mechanics of refugee and migrant vessels the Mediterranean evince resonances between the Australian turn-back the boat polices with those of a dysfunctional European front. In 2018, Italy's response to the migrant rescue ship, MV *Aquarius*, was an occasion to draw parallels with the detention and ultimate moving on of the Tampa in 2001 off Christmas Island. The charity ship, carrying some 629 African refugees, found all Italian ports closed to it under the express directions of the populist leader of the Lega, Matteo Salvini (BBC 2018). Italy's then new deputy prime minister and minister for the interior was intent on politicising the matter of refugee arrivals, having declared that Italy had to cease being the 'refugee camp of Europe' (BBC 2018). Salvini had, at first instance, pressed Malta to accept the human cargo, but only got an offer of assistance with air evacuations. 'The good God,' he quipped, 'put Malta closer to Africa than Sicily.' The result was initial diplomatic inertia, followed by a growing humanitarian crisis, and a Spanish offer to accept the vessel.

For Salvini, the Australian 'stop the boats' mantra and the seal-the-borders approach of Hungary's Viktor Orbán, were examples worthy of emulation (Pannonhírnök 2018). Detaining and repelling such vessels as the *Aquarius*, as with the case of the *Tampa*, was calculated for maximum political bruising, playing to Salvini's populist Lega party. The rebadged far-Right Lega Nord party capitalised, along with the progressive Five Star Movement, on Prime Minister Giuseppe Conte's failure to form a government in May 2018.

Targeting the *Aquarius* also served another symbolic purpose. The vessel's owner, the European-based non-governmental organisation SOS Méditerranée, had filled a vacuum in the conduct of rescue operations in the Mediterranean. According to the NGO, there was 'no adequate rescue mission in the Mediterranean Sea to help migrants and refugees in distress in an efficient, appropriate and lasting manner' (SOS Méditerranée 2018). This – and here the similarities in Australian political rhetoric are striking - aggravated Salvini and his supporters for purportedly feeding a people smuggling business model (O'Grady 2018).

The process was repeated with equally dramatic effect on 14 June 2019, this time in response to the German NGO-owned *Sea-Watch 3*, which had picked up 53 migrants off the Libyan coast two days prior. It proceeded towards Italy, claiming Libya to be an unsafe destination to dock (Squire 2019). *Sea-Watch 3*, finding its way barred to all Italian ports, sought legal relief in the European Court of Human Rights to disembark their human cargo. It failed, prompting the vessel's captain to enter the port of Lampedusa on 29 June in defiance of an Italian-wide port closure to refugee vessels citing 'the rights of the rescued people to be disembarked in a place of safety' (APR 2019). The Italian authorities subsequently availed themselves of a European Council Directive (2002) in prosecuting Captain Carola Rackete, for being involved in the 'facilitation of unauthorised entry, transit and residence' into the EU (Squire 2019).

With Salvini at the helm of internal security, plans were drawn up to limit irregular migration by shifting the onus of evaluating asylum applications to countries of origin or transit, stemming migrant flows at external borders, targeting international trafficking utilising the assistance of other EU states, and establishing detention centres in all of Italy's 20 regions (Di Maio & Salvini 2018). The standout feature here was the suggested abolition of the Dublin Regulation obliging countries on the border of the EU to host arrivals (Robertson 2018).

The EU response to Salvini's position proved incoherent, marked by disunity. The meeting in direct response to his rattling stance resulted in a weak agreement promising little to resolve the humanitarian crisis. Terms such as 'regional disembarkation platforms' and 'controlled centres' featured, with the intention being the disruption of the movement of peoples from Libya itself (Marmouyet 2018).

An Australian in Europe: Tony Abbott

The 'turn back the boats' message has not merely focused European policy on the issue of irregular arrivals and what happens at sea; it has also served an indigenous, local purpose. The program fits in what has been described as a particular nativist construction of European identity (Loewenstein 2018). As Sasha Polakow-Suransky (quoted in Loewenstein 2018) puts it, individuals of the political right deemed 'defenders of a nativist nanny state' insist that they are 'defenders of social benefits only for the native born.' Such a strategy has drawn in ex-Communists and social democrats into their orbit. 'These politicians are seeking ways to protect their comprehensive safety nets and avoid sharing with newcomers.'

One of the most significant figures to warn European governments to embrace tougher border control measures from a cultural-demographic perspective is Australia's former Prime Minister, Tony Abbott. In 2016, the maverick conservative former Australian prime

minister apprised a gathering of European conservatives at Lobkowicz Palace in the Czech capital that Europe and Western civilisa-
tion was under attack and needed to heed the urgings of France's
Marshal Ferdinand Foch during the First World War: 'my centre
is giving way, my right is in retreat; situation excellent. I shall attack' (Abbott 7 September 2016). He appreciated 'that people from
Africa and the Middle East have every reason to seek a better life
- but they have no right to demand that Europe should provide it
to them.' Some deterrence was required, something moving beyond
mere crisis management for, 'So long as people think that arriving
in Europe means staying in Europe… they will keep coming.' It followed that those 'in no immediate danger have to be turned back at
Europe's borders.'

As he had pronounced with severity when in office, 'Effective
border protection is not for the squeamish, but is absolutely necessary to save lives and to preserve nations.' The humanitarian element in the policy would be to stop boats to save lives. European
leaders could do well to heed the Australian precedent; 'for more
than two years now, there have been no illegal arrivals by boat in
Australia and the drownings have stopped' (Abbott 7 September
2016). Focusing on preventing such arrivals and drowning inci-
dents enabled policy makers to focus on the refugee intake while
defying people smugglers.

In 2019, the following warm words were mentioned by Hungary's Prime Minister Viktor Orbán to Abbott at the Third Budapest
Demographic Summit on 5 September. 'I extend a special welcome
to Australia's former prime minister. It is in part due to his tough
policy that we regard Australia as a model country. We especially
respect it for the brave, direct and Anglo-Saxon consistency which
it has shown on migration and defence of the Australian nation'
(Orbán 5 September 2019).

Orbán, as with some of his European colleagues, is transfixed by the theme of demographic vanishing. 'It's not hard to imagine that there would be one single last man who has to turn the lights out.' At the summit, he noted 'the spiritual foundations of Hungary's family policy'. The implications of demography, in his view, were unavoidable: 'human life is finite; and that just as we enter life, so we must leave it'. With certain resignation, he noted the need to have more gatherings with the demographic theme, in part to return his country to a state of model, diligent procreation. Woodpeckers, he surmised, had to be taught how to peck wood again. Christianity had to 'regain its strength in Europe' (Orbán Sep 5, 2019). Such a view marked central divisions within Europe about norms of democratic pluralism. For the Hungarian prime minister, the idea that democracy could ever be exclusive and openly 'liberal' and open had to be challenged; 'Christian democracy' and 'illiberal democracy' were equally valid concepts (Orbán 2020).

Orbán's welcome and admiration for Abbott was very much in keeping with a strongman mythology: inherent toughness, a special attention to border security, and praise for appropriate racial stock – the indomitable, pragmatic character that would not bow down to other 'ethnic' elements in the populace. The irony, of course, is that Australia's unsparing anti-refugee policy has the support of a good many nationalities keen to ensure that yesterday's immigrants prevent today's boat arrivals.

Abbott, for his part, wrote gushingly of the Hungarian leader a few days after his Budapest meeting, seeing him as the prominent personality behind the Visegrád group (Poland, Hungary, the Czech Republic and Slovakia) who had valiantly rallied, along with Brexiteers in the United Kingdom, against the European Union and its more intrusive expectations. Orbán 'has not only transformed the economy but was the first European leader to cry 'stop' to the peaceful invasion of 2015 and is now trying to boost Hungary's flagging birth rate' (Abbott 14 September 2019).

The effusive admiration for Orbán shares a few common characteristics with muscular approaches to border control and regulation; he is an authoritarian figure holding the banner of threatened civilisations; he articulates the central demographic threat posed by the Great Replacement theory, an ethno-nationalist proposition warning against the gradual replacement and eventual overrunning of white Europeans by non-European immigrants. Formulated in 2012 by Renaud Camus in his *Le Grand Remplacement*, it has found truck in certain right-wing groups and fringe cells, including Brenton Tarrant, the accused gunman behind the mass shootings in Christchurch, New Zealand on 25 March 2019 (Polakow-Suransky & Wildman 2019). The terminology has also been deemed by Austria's Deputy Chancellor and leader of the far-right Freedom Party 'a term of reality' (Olterman 2019), while its endorsement has not passed the attention of Orbán himself, who has given it a conspiratorial edge in arguing that it is a European Commission plot funded by the Jewish American billionaire financier, George Soros (Mens 2018).

In this, Abbott's border protection vision and cultural identity meets Orbán's fears of cultural and ethnic displacement, with non-Hungarian groups at risk of turning the dominant Magyar race into a struggling, oppressed minority. As Abbott observed, the demographic problems of various countries, with declining birth rates, had necessitated dramatic action on border policies and immigration. Hungary was to be praised for looking inward in encouraging larger families 'rather than rely on immigration to keep populations going' (Abbott 2019). According to Abbott, the true 'extinction rebellion' threat was not environmental (increased carbon emissions and climate change) but demographic: people, certainly the right people, were not breeding enough.

Conclusion

The structural and bureaucratic response to irregular arrivals by sea in both Europe and Australia share what refugee advocates have considered to be disconcerting parallels. The Tampa solution and Operation Sovereign Borders have become internationalised examples of harsh border controls, boat turn-backs and regimes of detention. The particularly parochial expression of territorial insecurity expressed by Australian governments since the Tampa incident found firm root in populist circles in the European Union, suggesting all elements of what Ghezelbash (2018) has described as efficiency, prestige and coercion. Figures like Abbott have become minor celebrities in nationalist circles. From an administrative and bureaucratic perspective, the policies of Frontex are strikingly close in nature to those of the Australian Border Force, though the former's approach has contentiously claimed to be less heavy-handed. Issues of secrecy, alleged human rights breaches, and broader lack of accountability are all common ingredients in approaching irregular arrivals.

What is being witnessed, on a global scale, is an attempt to abrogate, or at the very least negate the letter of the Refugee Convention and maritime protocols. Refugees and asylum seekers are treated more as creatures of social ill and unease. Fault has been shifted, inculpating the individuals themselves, assisted by their colluding agents, the people smugglers and traffickers who constitute a nefarious, blameable business model. Pioneered, in large part, by the United States in 1981, the approach has been refined and sharpened by Australian policy makers, and then exported with telling effect to other countries. 'If Europe,' warns Ghezelbash, 'goes down the same path… it will be inflicting a mortal wound on the universal principle of asylum (p. 186). Such a wound, it can be said with some conviction, has already been inflicted.

References

Abbott, Tony (2016), Address to the Alliance of European Conservatives and Reformists, Lobkowicz Palace, Prague, Czech Republic. 17 September. http://tonyabbott.com.au/2016/09/address-alliance-european-conservatives-reformists-lobkowicz-palace-prague-czech-republic/.

Abbott, Tony (2019). 5 September. Address to Budapest Demographic Summit. http://tonyabbott.com.au/2019/09/address-to-budapest-demographic-summit/.

Abbott, Tony (2019), Diary. *The Spectator.* 14 September, https://www.spectator.co.uk/2019/09/diary-712/.

Andersson, Ruben & David Keen (2019), 'Partners in Crime? The impacts of Europe's outsourced migration controls on peace, stability and rights', Saferworld, London. https://www.saferworld.org.uk/downloads/partners-in-crime.-the-impacts-of-europes-outsourced-migration-controls-on-peace-stability-and-rights.pdf.

Andrew & Renata Kaldor Centre for International Refugee Law. (2014), 7 July. Statement by Legal Scholars Regarding the Situation Concerning Sri Lankan Asylum Seekers. https://www.kaldorcentre.unsw.edu.au/news/statement-legal-scholars-regarding-situation-concerning-sri-lankan-asylum-seekers.

Associated Press Reporters (APR). (2019), 29 June, 'Aid ship captain arrested after migrants step on to Italian island.'

BBC (2018), 11 June, 'Italy's Matteo Salvini shuts ports to migrant rescue ship'. https://www.bbc.com/news/world-europe-44432056"44432056.

BBC (2014), 12 November, 'Mediterranean migrants: EU rescue policy criticised'. https://www.bbc.com/news/world-europe-30020496.

Correctiv. (2019), 15 August, 'Frontex: watching the watchers' https://correctiv.org/en/top-stories-en/2019/08/15/frontex-watching-the-watchers/.

Crisp, Jeff (2019), 'Refuge Lost: Asylum Law in an Interdependent World. Book Review', *Journal of Refugee Studies,* vol. 32 no. 1, 172-174.

Crock, M & B Saul (2002), *Future Seekers: Refugees and the Law in Australia,* The Federation Press, Leichhardt.

Crock, M (2003), 'In the Wake of the Tampa: Conflicting Visions of International Refugee Law in the Management of Refugee Flows', *Pacific Rim Law & Policy Journal*, vol. 12, no. 1, 49-95.

Deutsche Welle (2019), 6 October, 'Germany's Horst Seehofer warns of "refugee wave" bigger than in 2015', https://www.dw.com/en/germanys-horst-seehofer-warns-of-refugee-wave-bigger-than-in-2015/a-50713279.

Di Maio, Luigi & Matteo Salvini (2018), Contrato per Il Governo del Cambiamento. https://s3-eu-west-1.amazonaws.com/associazionerousseau/documenti/contratto_governo.pdf.

European Commission (2019), 17 April. European Border and Coast Guard: Stronger EU borders with a new standing corps of 10,000 border guards. Press Release. https://ec.europa.eu/commission/presscorner/detail/en/IP_19_2166.

European Council (2016), 18 March. EU-Turkey Statement, 18 March 2016. Press Statement. https://www.consilium.europa.eu/en/press/press-releases/2016/03/18/eu-turkey-statement/press/press-releases/2016/03/18/eu-turkey-statement/.

European Council (2002), 28 November. Council Directive 2002 defining the facilitation of unauthorised entry, transit and residence. https://eur-lex.europa.eu/legal-content/EN/ALL/?uri=celex%3A32002L0090.

European Court of Auditors (2020), 20 January. Audit Preview: Frontex. https://www.eca.europa.eu/Lists/ECADocuments/AP20_02/AP_Frontex_EN.pdf.

Farrell, Paul (2016), 23 August. Danish MP confirms visit to Nauru camp at heart of offshore detention outcry. *The Guardian* https://www.theguardian.com/australia-news/2016/aug/23/danish-politicians-seek-to-visit-nauru-site-at-heart-of-offshore-detention-outcry.

Frontex (2018), Main Operations: Section: Operation Themis (Italy). https://frontex.europa.eu/along-eu-borders/main-operations/operation-themis-italy-/.

Frontex (2016), 10 October. Focus: Joint Operation Triton (Italy). https://frontex.europa.eu/media-centre/focus/joint-operation-triton-italy--ekKaes.

Ghezelbash, Daniel (2018), *Refuge Lost: Asylum Law in an Interdependent World*, Cambridge University Press, Cambridge.

Hargrave, Karen & Sara Pantuliano (2016), September. 'Closing Borders: The ripple effects of Australian and European refugee policy', Humanitarian Policy Group, Overseas Development Institute. https://www.odi.org/sites/odi.org.uk/files/resource-documents/10868.pdf.

Hyndman, J and Mountz, A (2008), 'Another Brick in the Wall? Neo-Refoulement and the Externalization of Asylum by Australia and Europe', *Government and opposition*, vol. 42 no. 2, 249-269.

Lindsay, Robert (2016), 16 March, Answers to the EU External Affairs Subcommittee. House of Lords. Evidence Session 4. http://data.parliament.uk/writtenevidence/committeeevidence.svc/evidencedocument/eu-external-affairs-subcommittee/eu-naval-force-mediterranean-operation-sophia/oral/30963.html.

Lloyd, Peter (2014), 4 February, 'Asylum seekers on boats turned back to Indonesia say Australian Navy mistreated them' ABC News. https://www.abc.net.au/news/2014-01-08/asylum-seekers-on-boats-turned-back-to-indonesia-speak/5191024.

Loewenstein, Anthony (2018), 'Australia's Brutal Refugee Policy is inspiring the Far Right in the EU and Beyond', *The Nation*. 29 June.

March, Stephanie (2017), Donald Trump told Malcolm Turnbull 'you are worse than I am' on refugees during call, leaked transcript reveals. ABC News. 4 August. https://www.abc.net.au/news/2017-08-04/donald-trump-told-malcolm-turnbull-refugee-deal-was-stupid/8773368.

Marmouyet, Françoise (2018), 30 June, 'EU migration deal 'agrees that they don't agree on anything', France 24. https://www.france24.com/en/20180630-eu-migration-deal-france-italy-greece-visegrad-refugees-macron-conte-salvini.

McMaster, D (2001), *Asylum Seekers: Australia's Response to Refugees*, Melbourne University Press, Melbourne.

Marr, D. & M. Wilkinson (2003), *Dark Victory: The Military Campaign to Reelect the Prime Minister*, Allen & Unwin, Sydney.

Mével, Jean-Jacques (2019), 15 June. 'Un nouvel axe alpin se constitute en Europe contre les migrants.' *Le Figaro*. https://www.lefigaro.fr/international/2018/06/14/01003-20180614ARTFIG00377-ue-a-cote-du-quatuor-de-visegrad-le-nouvel-axe-alpin-contre-les-migrants.php.

Mens, Yann (2018), 5 March, 'Hongrie: le 'grand replacement', version Orbán', *Alternatives Economiques*, No. 378, https://www.alternatives-economiques.fr/hongrie-grand-remplacement-version-orban//00083862.

Minns, John, Bradley, Kieran, Chagas-Bastos, Fabricio H (2018), 'Australia's Refugee Policy: Not a Model for the World', *International Studies*, vol. 55, no 1, 1-21.

Morrison, Scott (2013), 23 September, Transcript of joint press conference, Sydney: Operation Sovereign Borders, https://parlinfo.aph.gov.au/parlInfo/search/display/display.w3p;query=Id:%22media/press-rel/3099126%22.

Nethery, A, Rafferty-Brown B & Taylor S (2013), 'Exporting Detention: Australia-Funded Immigration Detention in Indonesia', *Journal of Refugee Studies*, vol. 26, no. 1.

Odysseus Network (2017), Memorandum of understanding on cooperation in the fields of development, the fight against illegal immigration, human trafficking and fuel smuggling and on reinforcing the security of borders between the State of Libya and the Italian Republic. Trans. Sandra Uselli, revised by Marcello Di Fillip, Elena Maratai and Anja Palm. http://eumigrationlawblog.eu/wp-content/uploads/2017/10/MEMORANDUM_translation_finalversion.doc.pdf.

O'Grady, Desmond (2018), 13 June, 'Italy's Matteo Salvini 'stops the boats'. *Sydney Morning Herald*. https://www.smh.com.au/world/europe/italy-s-matteo-salvini-stops-the-boats-20180613-p4zl4s.html.

Olterman, Philip (2019), 29 April, 'Austrian deputy leader endorses far-right term 'population replacement', *The Guardian*. https://www.theguardian.com/world/2019/apr/29/austrian-deputy-leader-endorses-far-right-term-population-replacement.

Orbán, Viktor (2019), 5 September, Prime Minister Viktor Orbán's speech at the 3rd Budapest Demographic Summit. http://abouthungary.hu/speeches-and-remarks/prime-minister-viktor-orbans-speech-at-the-3rd-budapest-demographic-summit/.

Orbán, Viktor (2020), 21 September. Együtt újra sikerülni fog. Magyar Nemzet. https://magyarnemzet.hu/belfold/egyutt-ujra-sikerulni-fog-8692965/.

Pannonhírnök (2018), 5 June, Matteo Salvini – Orbán Viktorral az EU szabályok megváltoztatásán fogunk dolgozni. https://pannonhirnok.com/matteo-salvani/.

Polakow-Suransky, Sasha & Sarah Wildman (2019), 16 March, 'The Inspiration for Terrorism in New Zealand came from France', *Foreign Policy.* https://foreignpolicy.com/2019/03/16/the-inspiration-for-terrorism-in-new-zealand-came-from-france-christchurch-brenton-tarrant-renaud-camus-jean-raspail-identitarians-white-nationalism/.

Public Eye (2016), 29 February, 'Dark suit of the Force: why are posted immigration staff donning uniforms?' *Sydney Morning Herald.* https://www.smh.com.au/public-service/dark-suit-of-the-force-why-are-posted-immigration-staff-donning-uniforms-20160229-gn63tj.html.

Report München (2019), 6 June, Video: Frontex under Druck – Eine EU-Agentur und der Umgang mit den Menschenrechten, https://www.daserste.de/information/politik-weltgeschehen/report-muenchen/videos/frontex-unter-druck-schaut-die-eu-agentur-bei-menschenrechtsverletzungen-zu-report-muenchen-video-100.html.

Robertson, Aaron (2018), 13 June, 'Xenophobia Meets Reality in Italy', *Foreign Policy.* https://foreignpolicy.com/2018/06/13/xenophobia-meets-reality-in-italy/.

Spindler, William (2015), 8 December 2015, 'The year of Europe's refugee crisis. UNHCR', https://www.unhcr.org/en-au/news/stories/2015/12/56ec1ebde/2015-year-europes-refugee-crisis.html.

SOS Méditerranée (2018). June. Charter. https://onboard-aquarius.org/uploads/2018/07/Charter-EN.pdf.

Squire, Vicki (2019), 2 July, 'Sea-Watch 3 captain arrested: EU complicit in criminalising search and rescue in the Mediterranean' , *The Conversation.* https://theconversation.com/sea-watch-3-captain-arrested-eu-complicit-in-criminalising-search-and-rescue-in-the-mediterranean-119670.

Tavan, Gwenda (2019), 3 May, 'Issues that swung elections: Tampa and the national security election of 2001', *The Conversation*, https://theconversation.com/issues-that-swung-elections-tampa-and-the-national-security-election-of-2001-115143.

Ultsch, Christian (2016), 4 June, 'Kurz: Rettung aus Seenot ist kein Ticket nach Europa', *Die Presse*, https://www.diepresse.com/5003144/kurz-rettung-aus-seenot-ist-kein-ticket-nach-europa.

Umurbilir, Emre (2015), 1 January. Kurtarilan kaçak sayisi 24 kat artti. AA.com.tr. https://www.aa.com.tr/tr/turkiye/kurtarilan-kacak-sayisi-24-kat-artti/87831.

UNHCR (2014), 7 July, 'Returns to Sri Lanka of individuals intercepted at sea', https://www.unhcr.org/afr/news/press/2014/7/53baa6ff6/returns-sri-lanka-individuals-intercepted-sea.html.

4

Populism and Political Leadership in France and Australia – Emmanuel Macron and Malcolm Turnbull

Stephen Alomes

Keywords: Globalisation, Neo-liberalism, Populism, Leadership, Ambition, France, Australia

Abstract

The era of globalisation and neo-liberalism since the 1980s has seen different and interacting forces, including a new politics of leadership involving celebrity and style as Western developed nations fear relative decline. In France and Australia rising distrust with political leaders, governments, parties, and the media, has engendered the emergence of differing populisms. Strong Right populisms, from Jean-Marie and Marine Le Pen and the Front National (now 'National Rally') in France, and the marginal Pauline Hanson One Nation Party in Australia, have shaped conservative mainstream political discourses and behaviour. Other forces have arisen, especially since the Global Financial Crisis of 2007-8. The presidential victory of Emmanuel Macron's *En Marche!* Movement in May 2017 was a rare case of a centrist populist party securing power. How politically important are leadership and its attendants, often style and image? How important is sometimes good and sometimes overweening self-confidence, informed by a degree of narcissism (Walter 1980)? In Australia and France, the ascent of two wealthy former merchant bankers, the ambitious Malcolm Turnbull and Emmanuel Macron, to political leadership has been another contemporary development. This comparative and contrast study analyses the interactions of political leadership with globalising neo-liberalism and different populisms in the two countries, focusing on Macron and Turnbull.

Introduction

As a contemporary Australian Studies researcher and a student of populism and nationalism, with a comparative interest in France, I am fascinated by the emergence of Emmanuel Macron and the success of his centre or middle class reformist populism. Right populism has become a major force across the Anglophone world and in Western and Eastern Europe, sometimes leading to parties and populist leaders in government or sharing government. In contrast, Left populism has had limited political influence. However, the exceptional centrist populism that powered the successful 'Macron wave' raises questions of leadership.

A comparative approach to contemporary social-political research can be illuminating. While the different histories and political and ideological structures of France and Australia suggest contrast studies, difference also illuminates in a comparison and contrast study of the two polities, in popular metaphor, apples and oranges.

The two major progressive and conservative parties in Australia, the Australian Labor Party (ALP) and the Liberal/ National Party (LNP), have not lost their ascendancy, as, in 2017, did the Socialist Party and the conservative party (now 'Les Républicains') in France. However, a shared debate concerns leadership and declining trust in politicians, parties, governments and media. In France, the problems of the conservative president Nicolas Sarkozy, includ-

ing corruption allegations and the lacklustre presidency of the socialist François Hollande have left the two traditional parties in dis-
array. In Australia, numerous party leadership changes, a revolving
door of prime ministers and party leaders after party coups (ALP
- Kevin Rudd, Julia Gillard, Kevin Rudd, Bill Shorten; LNP – Malcolm Turnbull, Tony Abbott, Malcolm Turnbull, Scott Morrison)
and American-style negative campaigns have led to a similar disillusionment with politics. (Alomes and Jones 2009, Alomes 2012)
Researchers and pollsters demonstrate declining satisfaction with
democracy, in Australia at only 45 % by 2018 (Democracy 2025).
Paradoxically, in an era of declining trust in political elites, 2017
IPSOS opinion polls, covering 22 countries, showed popular support for the idea of a strong leader. In Australia and France, over
70 per cent believed the nation 'needs a strong leader to take the
country back from the rich and powerful' and in Australia nearly
half believed that 'to fix the country, we need a strong leader willing
to break the rules'. (*Sydney Morning Herald* 2017, Tingle 2018)

In most populist discourses, the ordinary people feel forgotten
or neglected and that their country has lost its way due to the vices
of different elites. A new leader, a populist saviour, can lead the
people, offering regeneration to the nation, often a return to past
glories, as in the Trump slogan, 'Make America Great Again', and
his emulators around the world.

Populism merges into the changes in election politics since the
successful 1960 marketing of John F. Kennedy, a young and good-
looking American presidential candidate. The politics of image,
style and youth have become important, perhaps more in France
and Australia than in the seemingly less ageist USA. (Rubinstein
1995). While strong leaders and the 'big man' were staples in the
earlier 1930s populist era, in this globalising and neo-liberal moment, further factors characterise the principal actors on the political stage, and its screen extensions, including celebrity and image.

In the new culture of politics an obsession with wealth has become important. In Gordon Gecko's saying in the 1987 film *Wall St*, 'Greed is good'. Wealth and politics go together, not only in Vladimir Putin's special relationship with the capitalist oligarchs in Russia. Dramatic examples include the celebrity populist Italian leader, the media magnate Silvio Berlusconi, and the television star and the casino/property development magnate, Donald Trump.

The other pattern is worsening inequality as neo-liberalism, the contract state and offshoring of industry make the rich richer and the poor poorer, particularly low-paid workers. In this social-political context, Macron, as president from 2017 and Turnbull, sometimes the progressive face of the increasingly conservative Liberal Party, becoming prime minister in a party coup from 2015, and at the helm until 2018, seemed different. They are. The specific similarity is that both were successful merchant/investment bankers who became millionaires. While not in the same wealth league as Berlusconi, or even Trump, the millionaire prime minister and president arguably constituted a new phenomenon. The new populism, with its visage of celebrity, even as it ranges across the political spectrum, offers different responses to the contemporary sense of crisis, sometimes embodied in different leaders. (Revelli 2019)

A significant comparison and contrast between France and Australia, and beyond, in contemporary society and politics concerns leadership. Some observers on both sides of the Atlantic saw Macron, the incoming 'new broom' president, as a French Barack Obama, a young president offering 'HOPE' as in the Obama posters, or as '*un president providentiel*', the embodiment of an enlarged future for the nation.

Consider the personal and political comparison between Emmanuel Macron and Liberal Prime Minister Malcolm Turnbull. (Manning 2015, Crabb 2016). Their very names said something.

Malcolm Bligh Turnbull carried the middle name of an early, and controversial, governor of the colony of New South Wales, William Bligh, who was sacked twice, once as governor and once as captain, in the mutiny on the Bounty. Macron's full name, Emmanuel Jean-Michel Frédéric Macron, suggested tradition or parental aspiration. Despite some difficulties in Turnbull's childhood and Macron's regional origins, these clever young men became top students at elite universities, Macron at the *Ecole National d'Administration*, Turnbull, like Bill Clinton, winning a Rhodes Scholarship. These two relatively young political leaders seemed a breath of fresh air. Stylish and good-looking with a high level of public charm and verbal skills, (Whitlam 2020) they also got on well. In Turnbull's 2020 autobiography (Turnbull 2020, 589) he painted a slightly exaggerated picture of shared worldviews:

> Macron and I got on well from the first time we met at the Hamburg G20 in 2017 and then dined in the garden of the Elysée Palace. We shared a similar outlook and values, just as we shared a concern about the rise in right-wing authoritarian populism around the world and the protectionism and xenophobia that has come with it.

Both had had significant careers outside politics, Turnbull in 1990s in the 'Spycatcher' MI5 legal-political case and as leader of the Australian Republican Movement and Macron in numerous fields in banking and on the edge of government. Paradoxically, the 1999 referendum was defeated by conservatives adopting populist themes (Alomes 2000). Both men, it is sometimes suggested, might have ended up on either side of the traditional Left-Right divide, although Turnbull chose the conservative side, the Liberal Party, and Macron, initially, the French Socialist Party.

French and Australian politics may seem fundamentally different. French political traditions include complex intellectual discourses, street protests, currently expressed by the 'gilets jaunes' (yellow vests) and the anti-pension reform protests, and a greater government role in economic life. Stylistically, the differences can be dramatic, especially in contrasting President Macron with current LNP Prime Minister, Scott Morrison. 'ScoMo', mocked as 'Scotty from marketing', a reference to his career as an often unsuccessful marketing manager, happily wearing the hats of a suburban Pentecostalist and a sports follower. However, both countries share socio-economic angsts and politicised fears over foreigners and recent arrivals; in Australia 'boat people' refugees, in France, the Calais refugee camps and fears regarding terrorism and France's Islamic population. Both phenomena have contributed to rising populism, a reflection of popular attitudes towards elites and outsiders, including greed and corruption in public and private sectors, especially in France, and recently in Australia.

The Rise of Populism

Populism has grown in France and across the Western world since the 1980s. Predominant has been Right populism, wearing nationalist, anti-immigration, sometimes anti-EU hats. The *Front National* of Jean-Marie Le Pen and then his daughter Marine Le Pen, now renamed the *Rassemblement National*, became influential from the 1990s. In Australia, from 1996, the Pauline Hanson One Nation Party, in two incarnations, has had a small parliamentary presence but significant influence. (Mondon 2013, Grant 2018) However, in Australia, as in France, populism permeates more widely and deeply. One is the rise of 'anti-party' or 'anti-politics' independents in several states and the centrist Nick Xenophon parties in South Australia. In a rhetorical expression, mainstream politicians habitually adopt populist gestures and phrases, especially three Liberal prime ministers, John Howard, Tony Abbott and Scott Morrison. Howard picked up and beat Pauline Hanson's anti-refugee drum, borrowing the phrase 'We decide who comes into this country'. In government, he became a 'permanent populist'. (Wear 2008, Alomes 2012) Scott Morrison, who followed Tony Abbot in beating the 'Law n'Order' and anti-refugee drums, handed over this torch of 'penal populism' to Home Affairs minister Peter Dutton; supported by the Murdoch media, they also beat the 'anti-elite' drums of assailing alleged Left 'political correctness' and an ersatz Left minority's game of 'identity politics'.

The success of the Liberals permanent populism - from echoing Pauline Hanson to public lies about boat people throwing children overboard to Tony Abbott turning back boats and, finally, offshore refugee camps - made it possible for Turnbull to play another role, as chairman of the board from 2015 to 2018, presenting himself as more gentlemanly and moderate. This was indeed a role and made his claims of sharing with Macron a distaste for authoritarian populism disingenuous.

In fact, in the apples and oranges metaphor, except for their style and public charm, the politics of Macron and Turnbull were fundamentally different. Turnbull had few major policy positions, knowing the Liberal National parties opposition to a republic. He followed Tony Abbott in another inefficient roll-out of the national NBN fibre telecommunications network. He was defeated by his Right colleagues on same sex marriage; they demanded, and enacted, a divisive and sometimes hateful plebiscite/referendum rather than a parliamentary conscience vote. Except for his Snowy Mountains hydro scheme, they also curtailed his environmental policy, as a condition of him becoming prime minister.

Turnbull and Policy Achievements

After Malcolm Turnbull's eviction from the Prime Ministership, both commentators' articles and books concluded that the record of achievements of Turnbull and his government was brief. Aside from his limited implementation of environmental policies he had little interest in Indigenous issues during debates about constitutional recognition and an Indigenous voice to Parliament, including his lukewarm response to the Uluru Statement from the Heart in 2017. Turnbull, as a would-be small liberal captain on the bridge of a conservative ship, contrasted with Macron.

Macron's aspirations were suggested in a book title as *Revolution Francaise: Emmanuel Macron and the Quest to Reinvent a Nation* (Pedder 2018). Despite the centrist populist election campaign through a movement, *En Marche!*, and its meetings with electors, and the erratic moments and gestures of the President, he has been a radical reformer. Reform proposals regarding railways and other state employees, pensions, petrol prices, school and tertiary education, businesses and work laws, taxation and more constituted a juggernaut of radical or disruptive reform. Macron sought to restructure traditional French institutions, arguably to his electoral cost.

Contemporary populism was once primarily associated with Right movements: One Nation in Australia, the Tea Party in the US and then Donald Trump, and several European parties and movements including Fidesz in Hungary, the Swiss People's Party, the Danish People's Party, Matteo Salvini's League (formerly Northern League) in Italy, the Dutch Freedom Party, the *Alternativ für Deutschland* (AfD) and Austria's Freedom Party. The new millennium has also seen emerging centrist and Left populism, including Podemos in Spain and Occupy and the 'democratic socialist', Bernie Sanders in the US.

In 2016, Left populism emerged through 'La France Insoumise', France Unbowed, led by the once Socialist Party deputy, Jean-Luc Mélenchon. The Le Pens on the far right had criticised outsiders and the European Union's bureaucratic elites. Now, the socialist radical Mélenchon also claimed to speak for the voiceless, for those who felt marginalised in 21st century France, those who felt dispossessed, the older, the suburban and the regional to workers, some small business people and the young unemployed. Even earlier 1990s Gaullist prime minister, Jean-Pierre Raffarin, had contrasted 'la France d'en bas', the traditional France of the regions, with the urban elites. According to the geographer Christophe Guilluy, the success of the old and new capitalists, and the 'Bobos', the bourgeois bohemians of the inner cities, working in finance, IT and cultural industries, left many ordinary people in the country and the urban peripheries feeling displaced, and pressured by rising prices and diminishing purchasing power. (Guilluy 2015) As the urbane Macron and Turnbull appealed to urban elites, Right populist voters proliferated according to distance from the cities.

A competing force was the 'radical centrist' populism of the banker Emmanuel Macron, organised as his *En Marche!* movement. Perhaps this was surprising, given Macron's elite credentials, even given his non-metropolitan childhood. His parents were professionals, a doctor and a professor. Growing up in Amiens, he then attended an elite Paris high school, and after studies at Nanterre University, joined the elite at *Sciences Po*, followed by the *Ecole National d'Administration*. The *énarque* (ENA graduate) Macron became an investment banker with Rothschild and La Cie Banque. Historically, Left and labour populism was critical of the banks. 1920s-1930s cartoons in Australia and Europe depicted bankers and other capitalists as the cigar smoking fat man, often Jewish, while criticism of banks and elite corruption has remained a consistent theme in public debate. (Love 1984) That subject made a dramatic return in Australia as the 2017-19 Royal Commission into Misconduct in the Banking, Superannuation and Financial Services Industry demonstrated a pattern of greed, deception and rip-offs from the four big banks and related companies. The horrific revelations of exploitation of customers were as dramatic as the omnipresent corruption tales in French business and politics. A banker becoming a populist leader of the people against the elite seemed a contradiction in terms.

Popular ambivalence about a populist politician who might deliver them from the desert, or might re-energise the French economy, does not sit easily with the reality of elite leaders distant from the people. Malcolm Turnbull, who was never a populist, had a public charm accompanied by a reportedly difficult temper in private. The less politically adept President Macron often found himself in hot water, after several remarks suggested contempt for lesser citizens.

Macron had progressive as well as elite credentials, becoming the Minister of the Economy, Industry and Digital Affairs from 2014 to 2016 in the Hollande Socialist government. His own declared political orientations seemed to vary especially in government. He also rejected the terms 'populist' and 'nationalist' which, referring to Italy, he associated with 'leprosy', leading to diplomatic tensions. Were there similarities between the two leaders? The critics disliked the wealth and personal ambition of Malcolm Turnbull, including former Tony Abbott Chief of Staff, Peta Credlin who dubbed him 'Mr Harbourside Mansion', intensifying after his 2018 defeat as party leader and his criticisms of the government. His personal aspirations were significant, perhaps suggesting in the vernacular that 'It is about me!' As I wrote in a poem about Malcolm Turnbull

> A reasonable man
> Republican in recess
>
> …
>
> [He] sold his soul
> to the Liberal God-squad
> A Faustian bargain
> 'Leader' sounds good

'PM' sounds even better

Fame wanted, desperately,

His $2 million helped

Or was it just $1.5

to buy a ticket to the Lodge.

(Alomes 2020, 27)

Was becoming Prime Minister Turnbull's primary political aim? Did Macron's shifting political positions suggest, aside from his reform agenda, his fundamental belief was in himself and his superior abilities? Ego has always been a prerequisite for political leadership, but may now be even more important.

Despite historical populist suspicions of bankers, in 2016 Macron formed *En Marche!*, sometimes written with that populist suggestion of action, a concluding exclamation mark. Later, becoming a de facto political party, it acquired the more formal title of *La République En Marche!* (LREM).

Appropriately, Macron promised a renovation of French institutions, reforming many of the continuing inefficiencies and inequities bedevilling France. A powerful country with successful multinationals, one of the world's biggest arms industries, a rich agricultural producer and the world's leading tourism destination was facing continuing problems in the global era: high levels of youth unemployment, limited wage growth and national economic growth and high levels of government expenditure and regulation. It contrasted with the Anglo-Saxon countries like Australia, which also faced worsening inequalities in the neo-liberal era, compounded by low wage growth. Their 21st century burden was excessive deregulation, whereby 'self-regulation' and privatisation had become synonyms for oligopoly, self-interest, and greed.

Could any president solve France's economic problems and maintain electoral support? This would be even more difficult, given climate change. Macron, the former Socialist Party minister, declared that he would favour neither side of politics, as Donald Trump, in campaign mode, was aiming to improve the economic conditions of steelworkers. In government, both cut taxes for the rich.

Was *En Marche!* a vehicle for 'the leader', for personality politics around Macron, as celebrity populism had enhanced the popular appeal of Silvio Berlusconi, with his sports-named and action-themed party, *Forza Italia*, and the television personality and casino owner Donald Trump? The 'movement's' initials, 'E M', were those of its young and vital leader. Has the rise of demagogic and media, and populist, politics, with the cult of the leader, the populist saviour or redeemer, supplanted parties, policies and principles in our global era? Aside from Trump's shifting positions and endless tweets and lies, Boris Johnson, now the Brexit-populist Tory prime minister of the UK, has been described as personifying rampant and empty 'Blond Ambition', 'a great actor, a great showman', the most ruthless man I have ever met', according to his biographer, Sonia Purnell. His belief was in his destiny to become Prime Minister. (*Guardian*, Boris Johnson 2011). A Politico article declared that often 'The man is the message.' (*Politico* 2019)

In August 2017, *En Marche!* swept the field, winning a majority of seats in the National Assembly, with the support of another middle grouping, the Modems. The two traditional major parties, the Socialists and the conservatives (currently called *Les Républicains*) fell into massive decline, especially after François Fillon, the Républicains candidate was defeated in the first round of the presidential elections due to personal corruption scandals. In May 2017, Macron won the Presidential election against Marine Le Pen, 61.1 % to 33.9%. The mainstream collapse contrasts with Australia; despite several independents and populist minority parties in Queensland, and a small Greens party, the progressive and conservative parties, Labor and Liberal/National, still dominate.

In France, Macron, whose campaign book *Révolution* (2016) sold 200,000 copies, did not quite take the people with him. His approval rating eventually plunged, from 62% to a low point of 23%. Despite his appeal, as the youngest president in history, and associations with France's previously youngest leader, Napoleon Bonaparte, and with Barack Obama, and the political positive of a stylish and intelligent, although older, wife, Brigitte Trogneux, the Macron ideal soon faded.

His style and attitude in government, the loss of staff and ministers encouraged a popular critique, of Macron as a president for the wealthy, a *président des riches*, and as the leader of a government facing crisis after crisis. Inaction over *'L'affaire Benalla'*, involving erratic behaviour by Macron's head of security, Alexandré Benalla, known in Anglophone parlance as 'Benallagate', did not help. Outside elite Paris one 'periphery' response was to ask 'does he think we are idiots?' regarding the president's unwillingness to take responsibility. (*Guardian*, Affaire Benalla 2018) In October 2018, departing interior minister Gerard Collomb, the third minister to leave within two months, declared that Macron was leading a government 'lacking in humility'. (*Guardian*, Collomb quits 2018) In a country in which cars with central Paris number plates had sometimes been damaged in the country, Collomb differentiated himself and his people from the President. 'This guy thinks he's a *seigneur* [French noble], that's the problem. …The provincials, and I'm one of them, already had a natural tendency to think Parisians have a big head and snub us, and [Macron's use of] expressions like 'the new grammar of politics' or 'the start-up nation', they don't relate to that.' (*Sydney Morning Herald*, Gloss coming off Macron 2018).

The Macron administration faced two problems. One concerned the suggestion that his 'reforms' favoured the rich, seemingly rhetorically reflected in Macron's views of those who had not made something of themselves. Other problems were those typical of populist administrations, as populist movements, rising quickly, lacked strong administrative structures and contained many members of government inexperienced in politics and administration. Macron, the technocratic leader, was not always good at choosing 'experts' with political savvy, ones able to implement policies effectively without provoking popular opposition. Populism's characteristics included the idea of the regenerative leader giving voice to the forgotten people and their populist critiques of elites and outsiders. Other populist movement characteristics included internecine strife, personality conflicts and emerging divisions, and, in government, sackings and resignations due to inefficiencies, gaffes and corruption. That was one story of the Macron government. Paradoxically, given his populist campaign and the populist characteristics of his government's stumbles, and his suggested tendency towards authoritarianism, he was a radical reformer rather than a populist.

The Macron government's busy and radical legislative program was hailed by some and condemned by others. Its early achievements were considerable despite the many missteps. The new President in a hurry implemented much legislation in 2017-18. He reformed SNCF working conditions, including retirement ages, after several presidents had failed. His significant parliamentary reforms included a smaller Senate and a new electoral system for the *Assemblée Nationale*, whereby a portion of MPs (about 15 to 20%) are elected by proportional vote, rather than first past the post. However, he deferred his progressive proposals to replace nuclear power with renewable energy and higher petrol prices to reduce fuel consumption.

Macron's labour laws, following the 2015 '*loi Macron*', which liberalised French shop opening hours, loosened restrictions in several industries and opened up coach routes, expressed the neo-liberal aspiration to deregulate French industry and work. It was officially described as a 'law on economic growth, activity and equal opportunities'.

The new labour laws, which revise parts of France's historic 3,300-page labour code, addressed high youth unemployment and offered practical programs including improved vocational training. However, Left critics saw many of the 'reforms' as 'deforms', as neo-liberal steps backwards. Even the *New York Times* headline read 'French Companies Have Newfound Freedom … to Fire'. (*New York Times* 2018) Enterprise level bargaining, specified damages provision after dismissal and relaxed contract employment laws for companies with over 50 employees, which may have 'freed up' business, were less warmly welcomed by progressives. The neo-liberal agenda seemed confirmed by one of his first measures in government, the repeal of the wealth tax. Critics saw the abolition of the ISF (*impôt sur la fortune*), a tax aimed at those with a wealth of over 1.3 million euros, as a clear breach of the Macron promise to govern for all.

Politically, it may have been a grand folly in his self-described 'Copernican revolution'. Had the young, energetic, 'doing' president over-reached himself, as wiser heads might observe? In politics, rapid-fire reform can produce a reaction, as revolutions produce a Thermidor. Macron's language suggested a President entering new territory. Most often demanding traditional formality and intoning grave Presidential authority in addresses to the nation, he also spoke as a vernacular advocate of disruption. Speaking to American students he adopted a playfully arrogant populist Twitterati persona, remarking '*Toujours suivre les règles, c'est du bullshit*' ['Always follow the rules, that's bullshit'.] (*Marianne* 2018)

French presidents have always assumed a larger role for post-imperial France as a powerful military nation, and France has a continuing role in Africa. Macron maintained a strong commitment to the European Union, in contrast to the Le Pen opposition. While Macron has made some interesting international performances, including the symbolic power play, the continuing handshake with Donald Trump, as in most Western democracies, domestic matters have greater electoral significance.

Despite the initial optimism, the young president, his movement and their 'new broom', the Macron presidency has been vexed and challenging regarding his policies, his personal style and his attitudes to those further down the social scale. A populist campaigner and technocratic reformer, the 'new' political leader often lacked political judgment.

The overarching reform of France's pension schemes, unifying them into one scheme and a later retirement age, was arguably a political miscalculation. His grand project led to new street protests and strikes from late 2019 across several industries, from the railways, the SNCF, to the Paris Opera. Had the 'revolutionary' overreached himself again?

Macron's lack of electoral experience makes an interesting contrast with Malcolm Turnbull, who had been in Parliament since 2004, Liberal Party opposition leader 2008-9, then, after being deposed once, becoming prime minister from 2015-2018, until another party spill ended his career. The LNP gambled on the suave presentable Turnbull as an election winner. (Errington and Van Onselen 2016) However, Turnbull lacked political judgment in dealing with the factional pressures within his government. His problems partly derived from his personality and his failings as a negotiator. They also emanated from the admixture of ambition and ideology. Numerous accounts depicted Turnbull as 'the man who would be PM', driven by overweening ambition. Others focused on his Faustian bargain with the hardline Right of the Liberal Party to put aside his progressive policies. That meant not fully addressing climate change, which, echoing the 'Murdochracy' media, they did not accept, and not simply passing gay marriage through Parliament – the LNP instead forced a divisive, even if affirmative, 2018 plebiscite (Crabb 2016).

That was their price for making him Prime Minister, and the price he paid to achieve his goal. Turnbull's failure to obtain party support for his National Energy Guarantee (NEG), the energy efficiency and reliability proposal, indicated a leader with his hands tied. Unlike Macron, who had made a party in his own image, in August 2018 Turnbull would eventually fall victim to his dirty deal, initially challenged by the hard Right ex-copper and 'Law'n'Order' Home Affairs minister, Peter Dutton. He was vanquished days later by his own 'ally', the moderate Right's Scott Morrison, a little while after 'ScoMo' had declared, with his arm around Turnbull's shoulder, although also across his back, that 'This is my leader and I'm ambitious for him!' The scene echoed with images of both *Macbeth* and the Ides of March. (Savva 2019)

In France, in November 2018, street protests emerged in Paris and the provinces, in a continuing French tradition of '*les manifs*' or, sometimes, the violent jacqueries of history. Upwards of 100,000 '*les gilets jaunes*' (the yellow vests) appeared, often with roadblocks, in Paris and other cities, initially protesting against increased fuel taxes, wearing the vests required in all cars. Soon during the next months of Saturday protests over 2018-19, posters demanded '*Démissioner*', calling for Macron to resign. Macron recognised his limitations, increasing the minimum wage and deferring, and then scrapping, the environmentally driven fuel tax increase. While popular support for the street protesters diminished as some seemed to be street fighting men intent on violence, the protests became one of several thorns in the new President's side. Was his centrist reform dream either flawed or simply not realisable?

Pride comes before a fall? Political arrogance and popular distrust

Despite the differences between the political traditions and modes of France and Australia, the shared reality is that of growing inequalities of wealth and the political disillusionment that flows from it. In the populist ideal, as personified by Macron, the populist leader will take the people out of the wilderness and revive the nation.

However, in both countries there was an attitude problem. Macron and some Liberal ministers in Australia talked a language of superiority and criticised the lower orders. Joe Hockey, the Liberal Treasurer from 2013-15, suggested that workers had lower petrol costs as they either did not have cars or drove less. He also criticised the sense of 'entitlement' of those on social welfare, a term which the critics later inverted to refer to the conservative political elite, including Joe Hockey, who double-dipped, receiving both his parliamentary superannuation and the Washington ambassador's salary. Nor did he win popular approbation when photographed with Mathias Cormann, the Minister for Finance, smoking celebratory cigars in a parliamentary courtyard. (*Sydney Morning Herald*, Hockey and Cormann cigars 2014)

While Macron sought to address France's problems, partly derived from over-regulation, he may have succumbed to another less egalitarian tradition. Macron's sense of superiority was expressed in several infamous gaffes, remarks about the lower orders, which I have captured in the poem '*Le roi Macron*' (Alomes 2020, Appendix One) The technocrat looked down on those who were 'nothing', lectured the young on respect, and suggested that some French people were 'lazy'.

In late 2018, responding to the yellow vests' criticisms, Macron acknowledged that he needed to listen more, setting up a series of 'town hall meetings' to hear from the people. Like a good populist, or a good politician, he 'rolled his sleeves up' and engaged at town halls around France. He later set up Citizens Councils to discuss how to approach climate change. His change of approach, and a popular reaction against the aggressiveness of some yellow vest street protests, saw a slight revival in his approval ratings, reaching over 30% by mid-February. However, Marine Le Pen's RN would just edge past LREM in the May 2019 European Union elections.

In a powerful and historically imperial nation such as France, the President personified the state and the nation. Perhaps, as in Macron's story, the office encouraged the inheritance of certain traditional attitudes, even predating the French Revolution of 1789. In those successive formulations 'The King is dead. Long live the Emperor. The Emperor is gone. Long live the President.' Was this inheritance Macron's problem? Or was the problem Macron's own self-association, with Jupiter, king of the Gods, and perhaps, emotionally, with royal sovereignty? Several demonstrators carried images of Macron as Louis XVI, the Bourbon king who met the guillotine during the French Revolution. Others appended play crowns to Macron's image, YouTube videos mocked the would-be King and God, while headlines, and book titles shouted 'Neo-liberal King', the 'Technocratic King' or the return of the 'Sun King'.

In other readings, France was difficult to govern, with rigid traditions and the contradictory popular desire for lower taxes and substantial social supports. Was this a question of leadership and contemporary politics? Were Nicholas Sarkozy's two pessimistic assessments correct, that leading France was impossible and that 'modern democracy destroys leadership'? (Traub 2018) In one observer's comparison of recent presidents, 'Sarkozy was denounced as too 'bling'; François Hollande was denounced as too ordinary; now Mr Macron is too haughty'. (Rachmann 2018) Sarkozy was a special case, fusing celebrity and populism, argued Patrick

Charaudeau in an account of his presidential victory, *Entre populisme et peopolisme* (Charaudeau, 2008). However, was the problem France, not a particular president? Would the revolutionary with royal aspirations meet his own political guillotine? He had apparently told his predecessor François Hollande that 'The French elect their president to be a monarch. Then they want to cut his head off.' (*Irish Times* 2017)

Did Australia, with five prime ministers in nine years after party coups and elections, confirm Sarkozy's assessment of the destructiveness of contemporary polities?

Despite Macron's political and economic aspirations, and enacted reforms, an unstable government, allegations regarding corruption and his public attitudes may not augur well for Emmanuel Macron. In a populist era, Hillary Clinton's unfortunate elitist remark about some Trump supporters as 'a basket of deplorables [who] were racist, sexist, homophobic, xenophobic, Islamophobic – you name it ' helped ensure her 2016 defeat.

Could Macron's suggested arrogance have serious political consequences? Might it ensure victory in a presidential contest by Marine Le Pen of the National Rally, the *Rassemblement National*, who also claimed to speak for the French people? While progressives and centrists believed that it was unthinkable that the French would elect Marine Le Pen, given the 2002 election when '*Votez Jacques Chirac!*' became the strange cry of the French Left when the conservative was opposed by Jean-Marie Le Pen, the opinion polls were worrying. Despite that poll bounce after the town hall meetings of early 2019, negative perceptions were common.

Neither leader was a true populist and only Macron was a great utiliser of 'politicians' populism', that is the rhetorical devices and gestures of populism. Wealthy and stylish, they were more upper middle class in their presentation of self than the different celebrity populists, the moneyed media men, Berlusconi and Trump, or per-former populists such as Trump. In Australia, Scott Morrison, af-ter his palace coup within the Liberal Party, successfully waved the politicians' populist flag during the 2019 federal election. Suddenly, the former Treasurer, after over a decade in Canberra, adopted a 'matey' people's persona, as the voice of the 'quiet Australians', the people in contrast to the elite, as he derided, and separated him-self from, 'the Canberra bubble' (following Trump's 'Draining the swamp' rhetoric regarding Washington). Like Trump and Macron, he won.

Critics described the two former merchant bankers as distant from ordinary people or as associated with favouring the rich. Un-doubtedly, responding to such criticisms, both made symbolic ges-tures - to forgo some of the benefits of office. Turnbull donated his prime ministerial salary to charity, along with a $1.5- $2M election campaign donation to the Liberal Party, in the 2016 federal election in which they just scraped in. Macron was under more pressure due to popular critiques of him as a ruler for the rich, which his defend-ers suggested was unfair. In December 2019, as widespread strikes against his pension reforms mirrored the yellow vests protests of a year before, he decided to forgo the president's lifetime monthly pension of 6,000 Euros.

Strangely, the emergence of the Covid-19 global pandemic saw a return to populism. Macron's persona as the 'strong national leader' in the fight against the 'invisible enemy' nurtured a momentary re-vival in his fortunes, while Scott Morrison's 'tough persona' sought the same role, although more tentatively due to continuing indeci-sion and lack of leadership.

Early 2020 opinion polls had suggested that a majority of French people were dissatisfied with their president, as they had been with his predecessors, and that they rejected his grand pension reform. The permutations of leadership and populism are variable. Neither

Macron nor Turnbull have worn the theatrical hats of exaggeration of several populist performers (Trump, Haider, Berlusconi, 5 Star Movement founder, comedian Beppe Grillo), although Macron's socio-economic policies are transgressive and disruptive. Now, Malcolm Turnbull's race has been run, although he throws darts at those who overthrew him. His fall came partly from his personal weaknesses in dealing with colleagues (Whitlam 2020) and the fact voters perceived him as arrogant, a paradox given the popular desire for strong leaders. His mainstream populist successor, the self-styled 'suburban man' or 'ScoMo', Scott Morrison won the unwinnable election in May 2019, partly because Opposition leader Bill Shorten was perceived as an out-of-touch professional politician, and now ever-smiling Morrison benefits from Australia's relative success in suppressing the Pandemic.

In France, the 2022 presidential elections will decide Macron's future. Marine Le Pen is only 5-10% behind according to polls. Further, while a crisis often benefits an incumbent, in the role of 'national leader', as France's failure to lessen the deadly impact of the Covid-19 pandemic, ensured that his popularity dropped further with a disapproval rating of over 60%, and several progressive environmentalist deputies defected from LREM in May 2020. Hasty reflex actions coming days after LREM's disastrous failure in the 2020 municipals included green policies, and, in contrast, a conservative new prime minister, Jean Castex, demonstrated Macron's poor political skills. Has the 'Great Disrupter' established the principle of disruption, of 'revolution'? As 1789 began a decade of dramatic permutations, has Macron opened the door to a now more moderate *Rassemblement National*? Could Marine Le Pen become President in 2022 after her *'relooking mariniste'*, the makeover of the Front National, now shorn of its anti-Semitism and moderating its Euroscepticism? More generally, will Macron be reviewed in retrospect as a man of ego and ambition, a neo-liberal reformer or a technocratic reformer riding an initial populist wave? Will the loss of *En Marche* centrist idealism in his move to the Right and his lack of leadership in responding to the pandemic, and the heavy economic consequences of that failure, doom his 2022 prospects? Anti-Islamic gestures, in face of terrorism, may strengthen Macron's support from the Right and the centre. Given a fissuring of the Left and the Greens opposition, and lack of Républicain leadership, he may survive the first round and then benefit from an anti-Le Pen coalition across Left and Right in the second round, rather than joining Malcolm Turnbull on the couches of history. Despite the similarities between French and Australian contemporary popular angsts, and between the two ambitious men, this may be an exercise in contrast studies rather than comparative studies. Finally, the contemporary historian must conclude regarding the success or failure of the Macron political moment in an uncertain France, and the future of different populisms, that only time will tell. In the recurring words of the similarly struggling Donald Trump, 'we'll see what happens'.

* * * * *

APPENDIX ONE

Le roi Macron

I had painted Emmanuel Macron,

In the week of his election,

The boy president,

captured in miniature,

With the coiffed older wife, stylish,

Contemporary, feminist, but seen as

today's Marie Antoinette *peut-être*?

Yet I did not quite understand Citizen Macron,

The banker who wrote a book called *Révolution*,

The minister in a socialist government,

Then I did,

As in the name of his movement,

No, not Berlusconi's *Forza Italia*

But *En Marche!*

The initials gave it away, 'E M'

Emmanuel Macron,

A cult of personality

and one of superiority,

The banker liked Versailles,

The technocrat looked down on those who were 'nothing',

lectured the young on respect, and

suggested that some French were 'lazy',

Bludgers on the system,

Perhaps 'deplorable' even.

'*Le roi est arrivé*',

The king has arrived,

le roi Macron?,

with more gaffes than a Bourbon,

the *énarque* prefers purple to yellow.

Is the young president not a man of the people

just a new leader of the elites?

APPENDIX TWO

Characteristics of 21st Century Populism

Populism is a response to the inequities and disruptive structural changes of the global, digital neo-liberal era.

It is expressive, not instrumental, expressing frustrations more than solutions.

Like its close relative, nationalism, it can be an empty vessel filled with liquids of different political colourings; often has nationalist and/or nativist themes – 'the people'.

Variations include Right, Centre, Left and mainstream party versions.

Involves a separation between the virtuous people and real or imagined elites and the people and 'outsiders'. The former seen as conspirators or thieves of the people's birthright.

While populism involves a new tabloid language and narrative it is more than a discourse.

While xenophobia is a recurring tabloid emotion, nativist and anti-refugee/foreigner sentiment and scapegoating/blaming are expressions of overall populist discontents rather than the primary cause, with some exceptions.

Involves a saviour or redeemer who will lead the people out of the wilderness. Sometimes, whether outsider or mainstream, with demagogic style and narcissistic elements.

Charismatic, celebrity, sometimes rich, leaders in the contemporary and visual New Populism era. An era of tabloid emotions, simplifications, memes and visuals often expressed in social media.

Elites are often defined inaccurately as 'experts', 'bourgeois bohemians' or 'latte sippers' - real economic elites are forgotten.

In times of crisis both outsider demagogues and mainstream politicians can wear the mantle of the populist leader who will save the people and regenerate the nation.

References

Alomes S (2020), *Selective Ironies*, Ginninderra Press, Port Adelaide.

Alomes, S (2014-15), 'Le mal napoléonien and the global malaise', *French Australian Review*, no. 57, 96-107.

Alomes, S (2012),' "Got so many bad habits": Federal politicians, the public, and media', in C. Elder and K. Moore (eds), *New Voices New Visions: Challenging Australian Identities and Legacies*, Cambridge Scholars Press, 187-202.

Alomes, S (2012), 'Margins to mainstream: Populism in Australia and Japan' in S.Alomes, P. Eckersall, R. Mouer and A.Tokita, (eds), *Outside Asia: Japanese and Australian Identities*, CBC, Melbourne, pp.155-168.

Alomes, S (2000), 'Populism, disillusionment and fantasy: Australia votes', *Overland*, no. 158, Autumn, 92-94.

Alomes, S & B Mascitelli, (2013), 'Celebrity meets populism in Europe: The political performances of Nicholas Sarkozy and Silvio Berlusconi', *Australian and New Zealand Journal of European Studies*, vol. 4, no. 2-vol.5, no.1, 2013, 30-43.

Alomes, S & K Jones (2009), 'Bad behaviour' in the House and beyond: Australian Representative assemblies', in A. Cowan, (ed), *Parliaments, Estates & Representation*, Ashgate, Farnham Surrey, 159-173.

Charaudeau, P (2008), *Entre populisme et peopolisme: Comment Sarkozy a gagné!*, Vuibert, Paris.

Crabb, A (2016), *Stop at nothing: the life and adventures of Malcolm Turnbull*, Black Inc., Melbourne.

Democracy 2025, www.democracy2025.gov.au/.

Errington, W and P van Onselen (2016), *The Turnbull gamble* Melbourne University Press, Melbourne.

Grant, B, Moore, T & Lynch, T (eds) (2018), *The rise of right-populism: Pauline Hanson's One Nation and Australian politics*, Springer, Singapore.

The Guardian (2018), Collomb quits https://www.theguardian.com/world/2018/oct/03/emmanuel-macron-nudged-nearer-crisis-after-ex-loyalist-gerard-collomb-quits.

The Guardian (2018), Affaire Benalla https://www.theguardian.com/world/2018/jul/27/benalla-scandal-france-peripherique-sours-macron.

The Guardian (2011), https://www.theguardian.com/politics/2011/oct/23/just-boris-johnson-sonia-purnell.

Guilluy, C (2015), *La France périphérique: Comment on a sacrifié les classes populaires*, Flammarion, Paris.

Irish Times (2017), 7 November, https://www.irishtimes.com/opinion/the-french-elect-a-president-to-be-a-king-then-they-want-to-cut-his-head-off-1.3281941.

Love, P (1984), *Labour and the Money Power: Australian labour populism 1890-1950*, Melbourne University Press, Melbourne.

Manning, P (2015), *Born to rule: The unauthorised biography of Malcolm Turnbull*, Melbourne University Press, Melbourne.

Marianne (2018), https://www.marianne.net/politique/video-suivre-les-regles-du-bullshit-le-message-de-macron-aux-jeunes-americains.

Mondon, A (2013), *The mainstreaming of the extreme right in France and Australia: A populist hegemony?*, Ashgate, Farnham Surrey.

New York Times (2018), 'French companies have newfound freedom … to fire', 23 January.

Pedder, S (2018), *Revolution Francaise: Emmanuel Macron and the quest to reinvent a nation*, Bloomsbury, London.

Pew Research (2019), https://www.pewresearch.org/topics/trust-facts-and-democracy/.

Politico (2019), https://www.politico.eu/article/europes-cult-of-political-personality-emmanuel-macron-boris-johnson-jeremy-corbyn/.

Rachmann, G (2018), 'Macron protests show that leading France seems like an impossible job', *Financial Times*, 1 December, https://www.ft.com/content/f0b113e0-fc5f-11e8-ac00-57a2a826423e.

Revelli, M (2019), *The new populism: democracy stares into the abyss*, Verso, London.

Rubinstein, RR (1995), *Dress codes*, Westview Press, Boulder Co.

Savva, N (2019), *Plots and prayers: Malcom Turnbull's demise and Scott Morrison's ascension*, Scribe, Melbourne.

Sydney Morning Herald (2014), https://www.smh.com.au/politics/federal/treasurer-joe-hockey-and-finance-minister-mathias-cormann-pictured-smoking-cigars-ahead-of-tough-budget-20140509-zr8i3.html.

Sydney Morning Herald (2017), https://www.smh.com.au/politics/federal/ipsos-survey-australians-want-a-strong-leader-to-take-country-back-from-rich-powerful-20170117-gtsu9v.html.

Sydney Morning Herald (2018), https://www.smh.com.au/world/europe/why-the-gloss-is-coming-off-emmanuel-macron-the-man-they-call-jupiter-20181012-p5098d.html.

Tingle, L (2018), *Follow the leader: Democracy and the rise of the strongman*, Quarterly Essay, Black Inc., Melbourne.

Traub, J (2018), 'Macron has changed France's political DNA', *Foreign Policy*, 5 June, https://foreignpolicy.com/2018/06/05/macron-is-french-for-obama/.

Turnbull, M (2020), *A bigger picture: An autobiography*, Hardie Grant, Melbourne.

Vice (2017), National Front, https://www.vice.com/en_au/article/9aebdp/a-history-of-the-national-front.

Walter J (1980), *The leader: a political biography of Gough Whitlam*, UQP, St Lucia.

Wear, R (2008), 'Permanent populism: The Howard government 1996–2007', *Australian Journal of Political Science*, vol. 43, no. 4, 617-634.

Whitlam, N (2020), review of Malcolm Turnbull, *A bigger picture*, in *Pearls and Irritations*, https://johnmenadue.com/nicolas-whitlam-malcolm-turnbull-a-bigger-picture-hardy-grant-books-2020/.

5

SMART SPECIALISATION: FROM CONCEPT TO IMPLEMENTATION IN HUNGARY

Sarah Howe

Keywords: European Union, Smart Specialisation, Hungary, Regional Innovation Systems, Governance

Abstract

The European Commission under the Junker administration introduced the Smart Specialisation policy agenda (2014-2020) in response to the Global Financial Crisis amidst concerns about the low levels of innovation found across diverse regions of Europe. The policy represents an ambitious attempt to combine industrial and regional programming to lift innovation performance across diverse regions in Europe. This chapter explores the extent to which the policy has faced implementation barriers in the case study of a Less Developed Region, Western Transdanubia, Hungary. The chapter presents the findings of research that reveals that there are significant barriers to effective policy implementation.

Introduction

The Global Financial Crisis (GFC) of 2007-8 exposed in Europe low levels of innovative activity occurring in the union, compared to the USA and Japan. In this context, in 2009, the European Union

(EU) launched the flagship Europe 2020 agenda, which set as the central aim of all its policies the aim to foster smart growth that was both sustainable and inclusive. In relation to regional policy, the new agenda would have a significant new focus on this policy agenda. Regional policy funds account for the single largest part of the EU budget for 2014–20 (351.8 billion euros out of a total 1082 billion euros) and therefore is the main investment arm of its programming. As part of the Europe 2020 agenda, the EU made it conditional that regions in receipt of regional grants devise Smart Specialisation strategies and also lift the innovation performance across both economic core and periphery regions of Europe.

Consequently, while EU regional policy has traditionally been developed as an expression of solidarity between countries with the bulk of funding dedicated to less developed regions (LDR), during the 1960s and 70s, regional projects concentrated on redistributing wealth from wealthier regions to poorer regions through traditional infrastructure-led economic and social projects to help these regions to fulfill their economic potential, despite regional disparities across Europe.

In contrast, the Smart Specialisation policy is based on a systems way of thinking about innovation and growth. The policy places emphasises on the economic potential of a region given its place within a complex regional system. The overall concept envisages the structural transformation of regional economies based on a 'sound analysis of the regional economy, society and innovation structure' which aims to assess both existing assets and prospects for future development (EC 2012q, 9). Regions are encouraged to identify development opportunities and induce suitable structural change. It targets the integration of existing specialisations with new developing specialisations, and thus diversification into areas related to regional strongholds. The policy aims to build capabilities in fields in which a region has the potential to develop a unique selling proposition and competitive advantage in the near future (Foray, 2015). For this reason, some theorists argue that 'smart diversification' would be a more appropriate expression for this approach (Asheim et al. as cited in Isaksen 2018).

Smart Specialisation is a policy concept that 'emphasises the principle of prioritisation in a vertical logic (to favour some technologies, fields, the population of firms) and defines a method to identify such desirable areas for innovation policy intervention'(Foray & Goenaga, 2013, 1). Under the policy, a region is required to specialise in a particular set of industries and identify sectors that can achieve critical mass. To achieve this, policy design should take into account the concepts of regional embeddedness, relatedness, and connectivity (EC 2012). Foray and Goenaga (2013, 1):

> ... robust and transparent means for nominating those new activities, at the regional level, that aim at exploring and discovering new domains for constructing regional competitive advantages. Thus, rather than offering a method for determining if a hypothetical region has a 'strength' in a particular set of activities, e.g., tourism and fisheries, the crucial question is whether that region would benefit from and should specialise in certain R&D and innovation projects in some lead activities such as tourism or fisheries

Economic priorities should be precise and focused, such as being limited to the involvement of a group of 10–20 firms and institutions only (Foray, 2015) and priority areas should not be presented in a 'too generic way....to be credible, effective and suitable for a concrete action plan, the priorities need to be expressed (...) precisely', such as ICT-based innovation for active aging, innovative solutions to reduce city congestion, wood-based solutions for eco-construction, etc.' (EC 2012, 51).

The Commission in drafting the new policy direction was particularly focused on the need to not repeat common approaches from the past, including 'spreading money across powerful lobbies with the frequent outcome that there were too many priorities aimed at preserving the status quo rather than looking at future opportunities' as well as repeating the past policy problem of regions 'imitating other regions' (EC 2012, 51). The policy implicitly builds on the relatedness concept and focuses on the concept of related diversification. The idea being that new activities do not start from scratch and are built on existing local capabilities (knowledge, skills, networks, institutions) that create the conditions in which new activities will be feasible to develop in a region.

Strategies for diversification fit into two different categories; related diversification and unrelated diversification. The concept of related diversification is about a strategy for strengthening existing specialisations. Boschma warns that this approach 'is not a good option for regions that are trapped in low complex activities' as it will create the risk of 'lock-in' and argues that instead, regions in this situation should go down the track of aspiring for 'unrelated diversification' where regions should aim for radical change based on building new capacities. He argues that in pursuing a strategy based on 'unrelated diversification' old industrial regions could potentially overcome the trap of achieving related diversification in low complex activities: this is the case when opportunities for related diversification are only in low complex activities: like in many Rustbelt states in the United States (Rigby and Balland cited by Boschma, 2019). Given that 'unrelated diversification' is complicated to achieve given the need for new capabilities (knowledge, skills, institutions) and may only give a 'small economic bonus' for countries, he argues that a combination of both strategies should be employed and that regions where possible should aim for a situation of both unrelated and related diversifications based on a higher economic impact upon diversification in complex activities (Boschma 2019).

In the context of how the European Commission understand the key concept of Smart Specialisation, the perspective used in this chapter is to gain an understanding of how the policy, underpinned by the concept, may face barriers in the implementation phase. The policy has the potential to either consolidate an existing economic model or assist regions, particularly less developed regions (LDR), to embark on visionary strategy and 'place-based' economic diversification founded in the knowledge economy, in other words on a foundation of more complex activities.

In analysing whether the potential of the policy can be as transformative in the manner that is envisaged by the policy architects at the European Commission (EC), this chapter draws heavily upon the findings of the author's Ph.D. research study that addressed the experience of the regional participation of Western Transdanubia, located in the south-west of Hungary and a LDR, within the policy framework (Howe, 2018, which will be referred to as the WT case study research herein).The region offers a good example of a less developed industrial region seeking to grapple with new economic strategies to enable improved economic performance in the context of being situated politically in an increasingly authoritarian political context, since the election of Fidesz, the party of Hungarian prime minister Viktor Orbán.

Western Transdanubia economically has a strong history of automotive industry-focused industrial development, given a history in the Communist era of heavy manufacturing production associated with the armaments industry. The subsequent dependency of the region on a single industrial giant – the foreign-owned Volkswagen subsidiary Audi – presents risks, as the performance of the region depends on the performance of the company. This risk became clear during the GFC when world car sales faltered and unemployment within the region rose to 11.8

percent (in 2008–09). Documentary and interview data from the WT case study will be referred to in this chapter; documentary data relating to the Smart Specialisation policy was sourced from the EC, the Hungarian Government, and the Western Transdanubia region. Interview data was gathered relating to the Smart Specialisation policy, from interviewees identified as key policy actors within the Western Transdanubia regional innovation system 'Quadruple Helix representative' groups (government, business, civil society, and university sectors).

A key element of the new policy direction deemed necessary for successful implementation of the policy is the need for strong institutional settings to enable the new policy direction to work. Theoretically, a devolved governance process would ideally align with strong institutional links between and assist with the capacity for strategic interactions would be needed between and strategic interaction between public and private actors in a regional innovation system, including researchers, policymakers and entrepreneurs would result in the building of strong regional actors and institutions capable of building the innovation system at the level of place (Isaksen 2018). Taking into account the importance of both the need for strong governance and institutional settings at the level of place to achieve the effective translation of the policy from the concept phase to practice, this chapter seeks to understand how the policy concept may face barriers in practice. It does so by addressing two key components of the policy; firstly, the governance arrangements required to establish an effective entrepreneurial discovery process, and secondly, the institutional arrangements at the level of place that would enable strong and effective institutional links between all of the actors within the quadruple helix innovation system (universities, business, civil society, and government) that make up the regional innovation system.

The challenge for implementation posed by regional governance arrangements and unfavourable regional innovation systems

The Smart Specialisation policy represents an ambitious attempt at devolved programming with respect to the scale of resources involved and the demands placed on public sector institutions such as the regional state, which is expected to orchestrate a collaborative economic search process, 'the entrepreneurial discovery process' (EDP) and craft more inclusive governance arrangements to enable the diversity of 'voice' at the level of place (Foray in Morgan 2016). Critical to the success of the policy is the need for a devolved policy governance process to enable an effective EDP that would enable regions to bring together key actors from a region to partner with the EC in the design and implementation of economic strategies and that regions be empowered to help themselves by 'encouraging key regional players to interact, share a vision and jointly commit efforts and resources, (which is seen as) of paramount importance for the development prospects of a region' (Landabaso as cited in Cooke et al. 2012, 21).

Thus, central to the policy is the need for a regionally driven development and implementation process, focused upon the strategic interaction between public and private actors in a regional innovation system, including researchers, policymakers, and entrepreneurs (Isaksen 2018). The policy process should follow a complex and iterative logic that cannot be described either as essentially 'top-down' or essentially 'bottom-up'. As Foray and Hall explain, 'this bi-directional dynamic process is one in which the principle of entrepreneurial discovery plays an essential role and yet so does public policy intervention, which may occur at several distinct stages in the identification, evaluation, and targeted support for new, emerging lines of regional specialisation' (Foray & Hall, 2011, 2).

In order for the policy to work effectively, it is suggested that inclusive economic institutions need to be supported by, and support,

inclusive political institutions that distribute political power in a plu-
ralist manner (Marques & Morgan, 2016). An implied requirement
by the policy is for the state to be able to devolve power to regions
to have their own autonomy, administrative capability, and financial
resources to design and implement their own regional innovation
strategies is a key determinant to the success of the policy. (Tripp et al
Healy, 2018; Pronesti 2019). The strength of sub-national governance
arrangements and the density of institutions found at a regional level,
therefore, becomes critical when considering the capacity for effective implementation of the policy (Morgan 2017; Rodrik, 2003).

A key measure of the strength of regional governance arrangements at the level of place is the quality of regional and local government, when considering the potential impact of the policy in European regions. For instance, in the case of European Cohesion Fund
investments prior to the introduction of the Smart Specialisation
policy, that returns on regional fund investments do not necessarily
come from the amount of investment itself but from the quality of
government in the region receiving it, and from how government
affects implementation (European Commission 2014; Rodriguez-
Pose & Garcilazo 2015).

Politics, and governance challenges in Less Developed Regions

There are particular challenges facing LDRs, in implementing regional innovation policies such as Smart Specialisation posed by
governance barriers. For instance, place-based region policy frameworks being implemented in Central Eastern European (CEE) regions have been found to face particular difficulties. This is due to
multiple reasons including that CEE states have been found to often have a regional administrative capacity that is weak, with often
centralised policy-making, a culture of mistrust, politicised decision making and clientelism (Gorzelak 1996; Bachtler & Mendez
2013, Bachtler & McMaster 2008; Paraskevopolous & Leonardi in
Dabrowski 2012; Morgan 2016). Dabrowski found that in situations

where a central government has control over the contents of a regional plan (e.g. in Hungary and the Czech Republic) it defied the purpose of strategic planning tailored to regional specificities due to national government-led policy processes that have resulted in regional specificities being overlooked (Dabrowski 2012). Further, in North-East Romania, Healy found that central government priorities dominated the regional agenda, with a nationally driven science-led approach that took precedence over priorities that were established by the regional authority Weak regional institutions led to a strong plan being developed that 'signalled the region's' economic strategy, but where implementation was ultimately determined by central government priorities (Healy 2016).

Similarly, Cooke in a study of policy implementation in regions in Portugal, found that a centrally driven policy process in the Portuguese state conspired against de-specialisation aspirations in Algarve. Regions were concerned that within the policy process, regional administrations were weak and disempowered in the national policy framework, meaning that they could not determine an alternative economic strategy that emphasised economic priorities quite different from the one being imposed upon them from above. Algarve perceived itself as regionally 'locked-in' to a future in 'tourism of the narrowest kind' despite the policy being about an agenda of empowerment of regions to try and diversify into broad new related and unrelated areas industrial development that would place the region on an upward economic trajectory. Cooke observes that 'Algarve reported an aspiration to develop its own Regional Innovation Agency for the design and delivery of Smart Specialisation policy outcomes in future policy development processes, so as to pursue a diversification strategy based on the aspirations of the region, rather than referencing specialisation as mandated by the EU or Member State'(Cooke 2016, 1509). Cooke demonstrates that regions often have quite different aspirations to the national governments that sometimes end up controlling the policy design processes. This situation then has the impact of regions being forced to very narrowly define what constitutes a new growth strategy based on new industries, the mix of related and unrelated diversification aspired to, and the degree to which regions can aim to significantly 'upgrade' industries rather than face a situation of lock-in to a low-technology developmental trajectory (Cooke 2016).

In relation to the Western Transdanubia case study research, the Hungarian government was also found to have centrally managed the process of consulting regional stakeholders' input into the policy's design. This reflects the increasing centralisation of political power in Hungary. In the elections held in April 2010, Hungary's centre-right Fidesz political party secured a two-thirds majority in the parliament making it possible for the government to change fundamental laws, including making crucial economic changes, without having to consult the opposition. Hungary became a unitary state and national regime change saw an increasingly centralised approach to government policy development processes with regard to major policy domains, including innovation policy (Dory & Havas 2014).

It has been observed that since the Fidesz regime have been elected, that there has been a gradual decline in standards of governance and political freedom in Hungary. Hungary has dropped 14 places since 2010 on Heritage Foundation's Index of Economic Freedom, scoring badly on measures of judicial effectiveness and government integrity. In addition, Hungary has been accused of political corruption, in part in relation to how EU funds are expended. In Hungary's case, EU investments accounted for 4.6% of GDP over 2006-15 – the most of any member state – and for 80% of all public investment. However, it is argued that due to Hungary having poor procurement rules and the concentration of decision-making authority over disbursement of funds in the prime minister's office, that there is lack of transparency in relation to the administration of projects and hence checks on the misuse of pollical power (Rohac 2019).

The impact of political developments in Hungary has had a major impact upon the capacity for policies such as Smart Specialisation to ferment local economic reform initiatives. In this system, local governments are not financially powerful enough to finance innovation activities; they can only 'influence these activities indirectly by operating local industrial parks (or cooperating with them) and by offering various advantages (like tax exemptions, favourable infrastructural conditions) to investments with a higher knowledge content' (Dory & Havas 2014). The political oversight of the administration of EU regional policy has increasingly been over time managed by the national government. Regional governance within the national policy framework became weaker after the dissolution of the Regional Development Councils (RDCs) in January 2012. The role of regional institutions, such as previously established intermediaries like Regional Innovation Agencies, also became uncertain. After the dissolution of RDCs, their role was performed by county-level authorities (Dory & Havas 2014). A new set of national institutions was created to oversee economic development at the local level and the previously democratically elected county government system was dismantled (PNNDRIN 2013).

A newly constituted national authority – the National Development Cabinet – was set up and chaired by the Prime Minister; this in turn established a National, Research, Innovation and Science Policy Council or NKITT (Dory & Havas 2014). NKITT was charged with coordinating the national innovation strategy and its power extended to the policy design governance connected with the development of the Western Transdanubia Smart Specialisation strategy (WT Strategy); the NKITT was given ultimate oversight of regional input. Subsequently, the Hungarian strategy was developed centrally with 'input and design work' from the Western Hungarian Regional Development Agency. The regional plan was managed by a process initiated by the National Regional Innovation Strategy

Council under their 'guidance and supervision'. The National Office for Research and Technology Innovation developed the WT Strategy centrally, with a process reportedly involving extensive consultation with regional actors who were given 'ample opportunity for feedback on the plan, based on principles of planning and public debate' (PNNDRIN 2013, 20).

Despite this centralisation of power, official Hungarian government documentary sources described the extensive involvement of regional stakeholders in Smart Specialisation policy processes. The regional strategy was coordinated centrally, with the Hungarian Ministry for National Economy overseeing the production of strategies and carrying out social consultation processes and also carriage of regional plans which were completed in April 2013 (Dory & Havas 2014, 19). According to the WT Strategy, careful procedural adherence was given to the European Commission 2012 document *Guide to Research and Innovation Strategies for Smart Specialisations* (RIS 3) in designing the regional plan, with the input of stakeholders drawn from all of the Quadruple Helix representative groups (PNNDRIN 2013). The regionally place-based entrepreneurial process of discovery consisted of consultation processes, such as two county workshops, and reviews of proposals by representatives from regional businesses, RDI (research, development, and innovation) actors, and economic development and public administration professionals (80 to 90 people). A further 100 people, such as specialists and innovation actors, indirectly worked on the strategy (PNNDRIN 2013).

However, interviewees located in Western Transdanubia argued that the dismantling of regional political institutions led to a downgrading of the importance of local voices in policy design processes, rendering involvement in these processes as symbolic and with local actors unable to leverage real power in determining economic priorities for regions. This has important implications when considering the extent to which the sector priorities determined by the WT Strategy actually reflect the regional concern about a strong emphasis upon a related diversification model built on the regions strength in the automotive industry, but given the fiscal constraint of the regional governance arrangements, may be one that consolidates a low developmental technology trajectory, given the emphasis on building supplier capacity rather than the capacity for highly specialised positioning in global markets. The following table details the areas of priority and main actions also contained within the strategy and illustrates the issue of the automotive industry as encouraging the growth of domestic suppliers as opposed to aspiring to create a unique and new field of scientific excellence, or a position of advocating for higher value-added capacity within the automotive industry (for instance to bring design and engineering departments to the region). The strategy appears to put the region at the risk of economic lock-in, which emerged as a key concern of interviewees in the Western Transdanubia case study research.

Table 1: Smart Specialisation policy thematic priority areas and industries and actions (PNNDRIN 2013).

Key sector/industry	Strategy	Actions to strengthen the Western Transdanubia RIS
The automotive industry will continue to develop and specialise in a wide range of domestic suppliers, system engineering, mechanical engineering and plastics industrial areas	Provide up-to-date electrical and mechatronics training in region Encourage growth of domestic suppliers	Renew related R&D infrastructure, knowledge production and use, and strengthen their relationship, as well as networking with SMEs Strengthen the social aspects of innovation and knowledge to raise awareness of sustainable growth and ensure integration
Forestry industry	Build renewable energy sources through wood industry-related activities	

Health and thermal tourism	Build a health tourism industry based on existing internally important spas in region	of cross-cutting tools to support growth in agriculture, forestry and animal husbandry
	Connect to an overall approach that also develops an organic food and health services	Pursue new innovations in biotechnology and biodiversity to ensure long-term economic security for the region's rural population and increasing quality of life improvement, sustainable conditions for development
		Promote products derived from the region's agricultural sector and on-site consumption and increase the competitiveness of services
		Improve the region's R&D efficiency, differentiated development of resources in terms of background, which includes the traditional, emerging and ancillary industries and improve the infrastructure of social activities
		Improve technology and knowledge transfer, knowledge production and use of support services development

Interviewees in the WT case study research confirmed that national political developments and the election of the Fidesz government in 2010 had indeed an impact upon regional governance processes and the way in which the WT Strategy was formulated between 2009 and 2012. The changed political context was seen by interviewees as a major factor in how regional governance processes operated in comparison with the policy design of the regional strategy. The centralisation of power in Hungary has led to a perception at a local level that any form of regional policy development – including the formulation of the WT Strategy – had actually been developed centrally on behalf of key regional decision-makers. For instance, an interviewee who worked at a local regional innovation centre emphasised the extent to which these political developments had affected regional planning and a growing feeling among regional policy stakeholders that they were not genuinely part of centrally managed regional economic planning processes. It was observed by the interviewee that there was a sense that 'regional development just happens around you' and that centralised political processes had reduced the capacity for local 'seeding points for new ideas to emerge', and has undermined the development of a 'politically active citizenship' engaged with regional development.

This perspective raises questions about the regional governance processes adopted with the centrally coordinated policy design of the WT Strategy. The Smart Specialisation policy aspires to a consultative approach to the process of determination of expert competencies developed by key stakeholders in the region during the EDP phase, to achieve a specialised, scientifically excellent strategy in the region. Yet a regional stakeholder warned of the danger of a 'business as usual' approach to regional economic development based on a traditional regional economic model underpinned by infrastructure projects. Another interviewee, an executive working within the automotive industry, noted that the governance process associated with the WT Strategy was developed and discussed with 'all of the research institutes and all the companies and interest groups' within the region. However, given the political developments in Hungary and the removal of regional-level representation, the process was based on small county-led discussions. This undermined the regional focus of the policy. It was observed by the interviewee that large companies still play a major role in lobbying to establish the political agenda with state and EU-funded research outcomes. For instance, the establishment of a new joint cooperative research centre afforded a major role to Audi. This was thought to be a driver for the growth of innovative development and new SMEs emerging in the region in the automotive sector, potentially privileging that sector over other growth areas of the economy, such as the forestry industry. Given that the Smart Specialisation policy envisages a strategy based on both related and unrelated diversification in regional economies, political power should be diffused so as to enable not only the EPD to work to empower local enterprises. This is in turn a situation that requires financial independence of regions from national governments and significant funds allocated to regions to enable significant innovation advances in a decentralised model of economic planning. The insights in the WT case study support the findings of other recent empirical work (Rodriguez-Pose & Garcilazo 2015; Morgan 2017; Rodrik 2003; European Commission 2014) that have also suggested that the quality of regional and local government is therefore a critical feature to enable the policy to have impact in European regions.

2.2 The challenge of building a regional innovation system in Less Developed Regions

It is also evident that the policy may also face challenges in the implementation phase for regions who have unfavourable research and innovation systems characterised by 'organisational thinness (weak institutions) lock-in to declining sectors and outdated technologies, fragmented systems that inhibit networking and knowledge exchange, and a weak capacity to drive transformative change'(Coenen et al. 2015; Healy 2016). Regions with unfavourable innovation systems have less potential to diversify into new industrial areas due to unfavourable economic structures and a weak endowment of knowledge organisations (Boschma cited in Trippl et al 2016). They may also have a low capability to use funds due to a weak capacity to absorb change; for instance, they often do not have an innovation ecosystem based on a regional innovation system that includes all of the key institutions that make up a quadruple helix model (Marques & Morgan 2018).

This problem for LDRs is also explained well by Capello and Kroll who maintain that in LDRs that lack local preconditions for innovation, the policy emphasis upon moving towards a 'practice-based innovation' (or DUI – learning by Doing, Using and Interacting – mode), will face difficulties in these regions as they typically have few or no research institutions and high-tech clusters. The authors found that this risk was most evident in LDRs as these areas have difficulty in identifying their areas of smart specialisation, simply because they do not have a relevant critical mass in any domain, they lack connectedness, entrepreneurial spirit, size in terms of market potential, industrial diversity, quality of local governance and a critical mass of capabilities to develop collective learning processes. They argue that this has made the identification of local technological domains a difficult process (Capello & Kroll, 2016).

McCann and Ortega-Argiles also assert that one of the greatest challenges facing the application of modern regional innovation policies across EU regions concerns regions with very limited innovation-related assets. They argue that 'some regions, for example, contain no research institutes; whole other regions, particularly in Eastern Europe, as yet exhibit only a very limited capacity for developing an innovation system, as they are constrained by institutional and governance issues, and by technological issues' (McCann and

Ortega-Argiles, 2016, 1410). In addition, Veugelers maintains that the tendency towards policy homogeneity 'will produce wrong policy priorities in particular places; for example, in weaker economies aiming to catch up with more advanced parts of Europe the main priorities should relate to the absorption and adaptation of existing frontier technologies rather than initiatives aimed at fostering features such as creativity' (Veugelers 2015 in McCann and Ortega-Argiles 2016, 1410).

In the case of path renewal (new industrial pathway) in old industrial regions, Coenen (2015) has maintained that the infusion of new technology alone is often not sufficient to diversify regional economies; changing industry characteristics such as firm routines and encouraging institutional adaptation are also important and overlooked means of advancing innovation. In relation to the low capacity of LDRs to absorb state funding of innovation programs, Oughton et al (2002) suggest that resolution of the paradox requires policies that: '(i) increase the innovation capacity of regions by working on both the demand and supply side of the system to increase both private and public sector investment in innovation activity; and (ii) integrate technology policy and industrial policy by encouraging expenditure on innovation activity within mainstream industrial policy programs' (Oughton et al 2002).

Finally, despite the wide view of innovation promoted by the policy, it is maintained by Marques and Morgan that the policy is still very science, technology, and innovation (STI)-centric and that this model of innovation is deemed to be inappropriate for highly fragmented innovation systems in which the dominant features are public R&D institutes and Foreign Direct Investment (FDI) production-oriented facilities (Marques & Morgan 2016). According to Radosevic and Stancova, the policy needs to be less STI-centric, and more attuned to the specific context of local conditions, and in the case of LDRs, more open to the incorporation of FDI into policy prescriptions is needed (Radosevic & Stancova in Marques & Morgan 2016).

LDRs are often rural, thus the orientation of regional development policy around knowledge spill-overs to local industry is difficult to achieve because smaller regional universities face a lack of scale and a need to specialise, which works against the policy objectives (Charles 2016). There are some exceptions to this situation. For example, in the old industrial regions in the northeast of England, long-term bottom-up initiatives have generated an innovation ecosystem despite the centralising tendencies of funding R&D found in the national innovation system (Coenen 2006). Although the Smart Specialisation policy has recognised the extent to which universities are a critical asset for regions in developing an innovation ecosystem (European Commission 2011), for most LDRs, the policy is said to make 'heroic assumptions' about the institutional capacity for LDRs to design and deliver such a sophisticated regional innovation policy (Marques & Morgan 2016).

Within this picture, a sub-stream of empirical research has emerged addressing the particular challenges facing regions located within the CEE. This focuses on particularities of the challenges associated with building regional innovation systems in post-socialist countries and regions, developing countries, and cross-border areas (Isaksen et al 2018). Regions located in CEE countries are, for the most part, considered to be economically lagging in Europe, with many socialist-industrialised regions being associated with economic, social, and environmental degradation (European Commission; Lux in Dyba et al. 2018). By the fall of socialism, CEE regions were more industrialised, but still said to be less developed as they lacked innovation in technology and processes (Berend; Chojnicki et al. in Dyba et al. 2018). In addition, high levels of specialisation between CEE countries led to over specialisation and investment in obsolete technologies, a hallmark of 'old industrial' regions, thus withering the competitiveness of CEE countries amidst globalisation (Berend in Dyba et al. 2018).

The WT case-study research has also revealed that there were many barriers impeding effective implantation of the Smart Specialisation policy in that region. Barriers included low levels of private and public R&D; cultural factors impeding networking based on a quadruple helix model of co-operation and a human resource supply problem, with young people relocating to Western Europe, and an education system heavily focused on technical studies.

As has already been argued, the policy encourages a broad view of innovation to be derived from many sources of knowledge, yet, as the WT case-study research has demonstrated, many regions located in CEE still perceive R&D as an integral feature of building a regional innovation system to enable a more transformative economic program. For instance, Western Transdanubia focused heavily on building R&D capacity in its Smart Specialisation strategy. An Interviewee from a university in the region observed that while Western Transdanubia is rich in formal knowledge assets such as major universities and research centres, the region had recorded low levels of basic R&D, given that most research in the country has tended to be developed in the regions of South Plains and Northern Plains of Hungary. The interviewee pointed out that most researchers in the region have been engaged with applied research due to a history of a long-term decline in state investment in R&D. This was seen as a problem by the interviewee as basic research is considered to be essential to fuelling developments in applied research outcomes.

The WT Strategy addressed this problem by outlining a plan to place 'more emphasis and investment into building university-industry collaborative partnerships in growth areas of the economy'.

Szechenyi Istvan University is identified as the most important regional asset, due to the university's strong focus on automotive research and educating engineers for automotive companies situated in Western Transdanubia. But, it is clear that there is a great need for applied research capacity to be extended to many more universities and research centres to enable more industrial and scientific research and to link some key industries together in the automotive industry, such as electronics, wood, and renewable energy sources. It was stated in the WT Strategy that there needed to be increased use of policy tools such as clusters to facilitate cooperation between universities and industry (for instance in the agricultural sector). However, previous experiences of clusters in the region were that cultural issues including a lack of trust between competing companies had meant that they had failed. This is an issue that will addressed in the next section of the chapter.

Finally, a further barrier to the Smart Specialisation concept as it relates to its vision for diversified economic growth based on the emergence of entrepreneurs has also been found to face problems in the Western Transdanubia economic context. Indeed, even the prospects of 'entrepreneurship' emerging – entrepreneurial creativity and innovation within large established organisations- would prove to be difficult in the region (Corbett 2018). Audi's specialised production of engines at their production site could work against Smart Specialisation leading to new 'spin-off' companies emerging. An interviewee from the automotive industry in Western Transdanubia observed that potential entrepreneurs who leave the company had 'no chance of taking away design knowledge or strategic thinking', which has created knowledge gaps about innovation and building up an independent company to produce commercial products. He argued that this problem is then compounded by a regional university system, that is also not providing these entrepreneurial skills.

2.3. The role of culture and human resource supply problems

The Western Transdanubia case has confirmed that in CEE countries, a history of Communism and a command economic structure has led to particular cultural factors presenting a barrier to building regional innovation systems based on a vision for entrepreneurial activity to emerge. Interviewees have argued that the task of encouraging collaboration between public and private actors is difficult to encourage due to a long state corporatist tradition; it was observed by an academic interviewee that 'you don't [yet] have the institutional architecture to build an innovation ecosystem' based on a system of trust and relationships being formed between companies and universities. Interviewees in Western Transdanubia also highlighted their concern that long-term state underfunding of R&D compounded an additional problem, that of foreign automotive companies conducting 'high-end research' in their home countries and only 'low end research' in CEE regions.

The role of culture in the CEE regions was also identified as a factor impeding the success of business innovation initiatives in the regions. An informant pointed to the role of culture in generating a suspicious attitude directed towards entrepreneurs, one 'deeply ingrained within the Western Transdanubia regional culture' and, 'without positive role models in society', a cultural problem that 'will be difficult to overcome'. Culture aside, insufficient funding for SME development, low venture-capital investment, little business angel activity, a lack of skill development, and a lack of focus towards entrepreneurialism in the education system, were further barriers. The Western Transdanubia strategy proposes measures to address this challenge, such as changes to tax incentives and a shift from a supply- to a demand-led funding model, which it is hoped will assist with driving private investment. Private sector R&D outcomes are to be encouraged through a reformed system of venture-capital financing. Internal R&D to develop advanced technologies will take precedence over the purchase of external 'finished' technology, and the use of public procurement as a new policy tool will be promoted.

Human resource supply problems were also found to be a barrier to policy implementation in the CEE regions. The case study of Western Transdanubia emphasised the extent to which business and government needed to play a greater role in generating a supply-led transition to a diversified economy by overcoming the shortage in existing university training courses in growth industry areas, including advanced manufacturing. A key weakness identified was the region's traditional focus on technical studies as attempts to diversify tertiary courses were said to be 'hampered by lack of State funds'. The region also faces a challenge with its young people, however, who are turning away from the study of engineering and leaving to work in Budapest or other European countries. Thus, a major focus of the WT Strategy is dedicated to ensuring ongoing investment into institutions formed to encourage educating the region's young people in engineering.

The case of Western Transdanubia corroborates the findings of many empirical studies that have sought to investigate the innovation paradox confronting LDRs posed by the characteristics of their regional innovation system. It was argued in the literature that regions with less-favoured research and innovation systems have a low potential to diversify into new industrial areas due to unfavourable economic structures and a weak endowment of knowledge organisations (Buchman in Tripp et al 2016) and have a low capacity to use funds due to a weak capacity to absorb change; for instance, by not having an innovation ecosystem based on the triple helix model (Marques & Morgan 2018). In addition, McCann and Ortega-Argyles have also argued that one of the greatest challenges facing the application of modern regional innovation policies across EU regions is in regions with very limited innovation-related assets.

They argue that 'some regions, for example, contain no research institutes; other regions, particularly in Eastern Europe, as yet exhibit only a very limited capacity for developing an innovation system, because they are constrained by institutional and governance, and technological issues' (McCann and Ortega-Argiles 2016, 1410).

Conclusion

The Smart Specialisation policy represents a major reinvention of EU Regional policy – an amalgamation of industrial and regional policy instruments, with an emphasis upon establishing regional innovation systems at the level of place. The policy envisages the structural transformation of regional economies based on regions identifying development opportunities of comparative advantage centred around analysis of their region's economic strengths. The policy is seen as having the capacity to provide a strong approach for regions to transcend economic 'path dependence' and generate opportunities for 'new path development' in, for instance, many old industrial regions facing economic stagnancy. After the collapse of Communism, for regions located in CEE, the traditional model of economic growth based on FDI was already seen as being exhausted. Many CEE countries were aspirational around trying to shift towards an innovation-based development model – based on building a functional local innovation base of R&D, improved education and training, well-functioning institutions and improved social capital based on trust, cooperation, and political stability – to enable rapid economic growth (Berend 2009). It would appear that in more recent times, that Smart Specialisation has enormous potential to assist LDRs located in CEE countries to transform their economies through the fundamental reform agenda outlined by the policy.

However, as outlined, there are significant implementation challenges. The task of translating Smart Specialisation policy strategies into effective reform on the ground has emerged as a complex task, particularly in LDRs. In relation to the quality of governance arrangements, the WT case study demonstrates that the policy faces policy design and implementation challenges in regions located in CEE, given the often centrally driven policy design processes and ultimately a fiscal imbalance, in the absence of regional government being empowered to determine the expenditure of EU regional funds. This has implications for a region like Western Transdanubia whose regional stakeholders clearly support a future where there is a more diversified regional economy, and in relation to their area of speciality – the automotive industry- the upgrading of their export capacity in that sector, but worry that their ideas will not translate in the implementation phase due to weak regional governance arrangements. In addition, there was found to be a range of barriers impacting on institutional capacity building within regional innovation systems that also would be aided by decentralisation of power within the country. These included factors such as the presence of corporatist state actors, historical factors impeding social capital between actors within networks, and low capacity in relation to R&D and knowledge assets.

It is also clear from the findings that LDRs require significant capacity building in the task of building functioning regional innovation systems that go beyond the scope and resources attached to the Smart Specialisation policy remit. The study found significant political will at the level of the region for Smart Specialisation and has highlighted many of the challenges that will hopefully be overcome in future policy phases.

Many recent studies have suggested that the problem of weak regional governance and institutional settings in LDRs located in CEE states might be resolved by introducing reforms such as increasing EU control mechanisms, including strengthening the European Union ex-ante conditionality criteria used to allocate regional funds to member states to further encourage national ministries to strengthen the regional dimension, ensure regional quality governance within the new policy direction in the future and encouraging the use of intermediary bodies in implementation processes (Potluka 2010, Molle 2015, Healy 2016; Bachtler & Ferry 2015; Rodriguez-Pose & Garcilazo 2015). Given the political currency of the policy concept, it is hoped by many regional stakeholders that such reforms may occur under the leadership of Ursula von der Leyen at the Commission to greatly improve the policy implementation of such a potentially transformative regional-industrial policy.

References

Bachtler, J & Ferry, M (2015), 'Conditionalities and the Performance of European Structural Funds: A Principal-Agent Analysis of Control Mechanisms in European Union Cohesion Policy', *Regional Studies*, vol. 49, no. 8, 1258-1273.

Bachtler, J, Mendez C & Polverari, L (2016), Ideas and Options for Cohesion Policy Post 2020, IQ-Net Thematic Paper 38 (2) European Policies Research Centre, Glasgow.

Bachtler, J, Martins, J, Wostner, P & Zuber, P (2017), Towards Cohesion Policy 4.0: Structural Transformation and Inclusive Growth, Regional Studies Association Europe, Brussels.

Balland, P, Boschma, R, Crespo, J & Rigby, D (2018), 'Smart Specialisation policy in the European Union: Relatedness, Knowledge complexity and Regional Diversification', *Regional Studies*, 1-17.

Benneworth, P, Coenen, L, Moodysson, J & Asheim, B (2009), 'Exploring the Multiple Roles of Lund University in Strengthening Scania's Regional Innovation System: Towards Institutional Learning?', *European Planning Studies*, vol. 17, no. 11, 1645-1664.

Berend, I (2009), *From the Soviet Bloc to the European Union: The Economic and Social Transformation of Central and Eastern Europe since 1973*, Cambridge University Press, New York.

Boschma, R (2019), Strategies for Diversification and Regional Resilience, workshop New Framework for Regional Innovation Policy, RMIT University, 28 August 2019.

Boschma, R (2013), 'Constructing Regional Advantage and Smart Specialisation: Comparison of Two European Policy Concept', *Papers in Evolutionary Geography*, Urban and Regional Research Centre, Utrecht, pp.13-22.

Capello, R and Kroll, H, 'From theory to practice in Smart Specialisation strategy: emerging limits and possible future trajectories', *European Planning Studies*, vol. 24 no. 8, 1393-1406, 2016.

Charles, D (2016), 'The Rural University Campus and Support for Rural Innovation', *Science and Public Policy*, vol. 43, no. 6, 763-773.

Coenen, L, Moodysson, J & Martin, H (2015), 'Path Renewal in Old Industrial Regions: Possibilities and Limitations for Regional Innovation Policy', *Regional Studies*, vol. 49, no. 5, 850-865.

Cooke, P and Picculuga (2009), *Regional Development in the Knowledge Economy*, Routledge, New York.

Cooke, P, Parilli, M and Curbelo J (Ed) (2012), *Innovation, Global Change and Territorial Resilience*, Edward Elgar, London.

Cooke, P (2012), 'Relatedness, Transversality and Public Policy in Innovative Regions', *European Planning Studies*, vol. 20, no.11.

Cooke, P (2016), 'Four minutes to four years: the advantage of recombinant over specialized innovation – RIS3 versus 'smartspec', *European Planning Studies*, vol. 24, no. 8, 1494-1510.

Corbett, A (2018), 'The Myth of the Intrapreneur', https://hbr.org/2018/06/the-myth-of-the-intrapreneur.

Dabrowski, M (2012), 'Towards Strategic Regional Development Planning in Central and Eastern Europe', *Regional Insights*, vol. 2, 6-8.

Dory & Havas (2014), *ERAWATCH Country Reports 2012: Hungary*, JRC Scientific and Policy Report, European Commission, Brussels.

Dyba, W & Loewen, B (2018), 'Regional Development in Central-Eastern European Countries at the Beginning of the 21st Century: Path Dependence and Effects of EU Cohesion Policy', *Quaestiones Geograhicae*, vol. 37, no. 2, 77-90.

European Commission (2011a), *Cohesion Policy: 2014-2020 Investing in Growth and Jobs*, Directorate-General for Regional Policy, European Commission, Brussels.

European Commission (2011b), *Connecting Universities to Regional Growth: A Practical Guide*, European Commission, Brussels.

European Commission (2012a), *Guide to Research and Innovation Strategies for Smart Specialization*, European Commission, Brussels.

European Commission (2012b), *Europe 2020: Europe's Growth Strategy*, European Commission, Brussels.

European Commission (2014a), *Competitiveness in Low-Income and Low- Growth Regions; the Lagging Regions Report*, European Commission, Brussels.

European Commission (2014b), *An Assessment of Multilevel Governance in Cohesion Policy 2007-2013*; Volume 1-Study, DGREGIO, European Commission, Brussels.

European Commission (2018), *Regional Policy, factsheet*, European Commission, Brussels.

European Commission (2014), *Investment for Jobs and Growth: Promoting Development and Good Governance in EU Regions and Cities: Sixth Report on Economic, Social and Territorial Cohesion, report*, European Commission, Brussels.

Foray, D & Goenaga, X (2013), 'The Goals of Smart Specialisation', report, S3 Policy Brief Series (1), JRC Scientific Report, European Commission, Brussels.

Foray, D (2015), *Smart Specialisation: Opportunities and Challenges for Regional Innovation Policy*, Routledge, New York.

Foray, D, Morgan, K & Radosevic, S (2018), *The Role of Smart Specialisation in the EU Research and Innovation Policy Landscape*, European Commission, Brussels.

Foray, D, David, P & Hall, B (2011), Smart Specialisation: From Academic Idea to Political Instrument, the surprising career of a concept and the difficulties involved in its implementation, Management of Technology & Entrepreneurship Institute, MTEI Working Paper, 2011.

Gorzelak, G (1996), *The Regional Dimension of Transformation in Central Europe, Regional Policy and Development*, Routledge, London.

Healy, A (2016), 'Smart Specialisation in a Centralised State: Strengthening the Regional Contribution in North East Romania', *European Planning Studies*, vol. 24, no. 8, 1527-1543.

Howe, S (2018) Ph.D. RMIT, 'The EU Smart Specialisation Policy: Exploring European Commission and Regional Stakeholder Perspectives 2014-20'.

Isaksen, A, Martin, R & Trippl, M (Ed) (2018), *New Avenues for Regional Innovation Systems – Theoretical Advances, Empirical Cases and Policy Lessons*, Springer, Cham.

Isaksen, A & Trippl, M (2016), 'Path Development in Different Regional Innovation Systems', in Parrilli, M Fitjar, R and Rodriguez-Pose, A (Eds), *Innovation Drivers and Regional Innovation Strategies*, Routledge, London.

Landabaso, M (1997), 'The Promotion of innovation in regional policy: proposals for a regional innovation strategy', *Entrepreneurship & Regional Development*, vol. 9, no. 1, 1-24.

Marques, P & Morgan, K (2018), 'The Heroic Assumptions of Smart Specialisation: A Sympathetic Critique of Regional Innovation Policy' in *New Avenues for Regional Innovation Systems – Theoretical Advances, Empirical Cases and Policy Lessons*, Springer, UK.

McCann, P & Ortega-Argiles, R (2013a), 'Smart Specialization, Regional Growth and Applications to European Union Cohesion Policy', *Regional Studies*, vol. 49, no. 8, 1291-1302.

McCann, P & Ortega-Argiles, R (2013b), 'Smart Specialisation, Regional Innovation Systems and EU Cohesion policy', in Thissen, M, Van Oort, F, Diodato, D & Ruijs, A (ed) *Regional Competitiveness and Smart Specialization in Europe: Place-based Development in International Economic Networks*, Edward Elgar, London.

McCann, P & Ortega-Argiles, R (2016), 'The early experience of smart specialisation implementation in EU Cohesion policy', *European Planning Studies*, vol. 24, no. 8, 1407-1427.

Molle, W (2015), *Cohesion and Growth: The Theory and Practice of European Policy Making*, Routledge, New York.

Morgan, K (2015), 'Smart Specialisation: Opportunities and Challenges for Regional Innovation Policy', *Regional Studies*, vol. 49, no. 3, 480-482.

Morgan, K (2017), 'Nurturing Novelty: Regional Innovation Policy in the Age of Smart Specialisation', *Environment and Planning C: Politics and Space*, vol. 35, no. 4, 569-583.

Oughton, C, Landabasco & M, Morgan, K, (2002), 'The Regional Innovation Paradox: Innovation Policy and Industrial Policy', *Journal of Technology Transfer*, vol. 27, no. 1, 97-110.

Pannon Novum Nyugat-Dunantuli Regionalis Innovacios Nonprofit Kft (2013),

Nyugat- Dunantul Intelligens Innovacios Szakosodasi Strategiaja, Pannon Novum Nyugat-Dunantuli Regionali Innovacios Nonprofit Kft, Hungary.

Potluka, O et al (2010), *The Impact of Cohesion Policy in Central Europe*, Leipziger University, Leipzig, Germany.

Rodriguez-Pose, A (2013), 'Do Institutions Matter for Regional Development?', *Regional Studies*, vol. 47, no. 7, 1034-1047.

Rodriguez-Pose, A & Garcilazo, E (2015), 'Quality of Government and the Returns of Investment: Examining the Impact of Cohesion Expenditure in European Regions', *Regional Studies*, vol. 49, no. 8, 1274-1290.

Rohac, D (2019), 'Viktor Orbán and the corruption of conservatism', https://capx.co/viktor-orban-and-the-corruption-of-conservatism/.

6

THE WESTERN BALKAN ANGST: 'GREATER ALBANIA'

Perparim Xhaferi

Keywords: Greater Albania, Nationalism, Kosovo, Euro-Atlantic, European Union.

Abstract

The Western Balkan region has experienced turmoil, wars and repeated violence since the middle ages. At the end of the nineteenth century, the Albanian nation-state did not exist, and Albanian-speaking people were considered Turks. The collapse of the Ottoman Empire created conditions for a re-alignment of the Balkan region, and thus, options for Albanians were simply to be assimilated by other existing nation-states, or to establish an Albanian entity, which would include all Albanian-speaking territories or what is often called by the Balkan nationalists 'Greater Albania'. The theme of 'Greater Albania', focusing on its causes and how it emerged as a concept and its continuous domain in the twenty-first century will be analysed in this chapter. Whilst exploring whether 'Greater Albania' is a myth or reality, the chapter will also scan some options to examine if the unification of Albanians is feasible in the twenty-first century. At the moment, the unification of Albanians can only happen once Albania and other Western Balkan countries join the EU, thus, under the EU banner.

Introduction

It is often claimed that Albania is a Western Balkan country that is surrounded by Albanians. The Western Balkans is a region that comprises Albania and the former Yugoslav republics of Bosnia-Herzegovina, Croatia, Macedonia, Montenegro, Serbia and, since 2008, the new Republic of Kosovo. Albanians still live in at least five different countries including North Macedonia, Kosovo, Serbia, Montenegro and Albania (Danaj 2012).

At the beginning of the twentieth century, the decision made by the Great Powers to divide the Ottoman occupied lands in the Western Balkans, has not been able to stop political instability, which is mainly caused by historical-ethnic-odium. This struggle has continued through to the twentieth century and it seems that Western Balkans are far from reaching a sustainable peace agreement in the twenty-first century. Nationalism is a common occurrence on the Balkan Peninsula; however, the projects of Greater Serbia (*Nacertanie*), Greater Croatia, and Greater Greece (*Megali-Idea*)—all older than 'Greater Albania'—have ceased, at least for the time being (Bogdani and Loughlin 2007). Why then, is 'Greater Albania' still alive?

The end of the Cold War marked the beginning of disintegration of the Yugoslavian federation. This period coincides with the end of the communist regime in Albania, a time that more students from Kosovo crossed Yugoslavian borders to study in Albanian Universities. Despite their low economic position, since the closure of borders from the Albanian communist regime in 1945, Albanians were meeting with other Albanians from North Macedonia, Kosovo and Montenegro that were more advanced economically. Some critics have analysed this issue in a simplistic way, to the point that the re-union of Albanians is equated with the 're-birth' of the Albanian nationalism. This is now seen as the beginning of a new project – 'The Greater Albania', with the aim to 'extend the boundaries of the current Albanian state' (Pettifer 2001).

The 'Greater Albania' obsession

The paranoia of a 'Greater Albania' (Kushi and Kushi 2015) seems to have not come to an end in the twenty first century. For Albania's neighbours, Serbia, Montenegro, Macedonia, and Greece, the anxiety over a 'Greater Albania' is mounting (Bogdani and Loughlin 2007). Since the independence of Kosovo in 2008, Slav Northern-Macedonians have always feared that, in the long-term, the 'ethnic Albanian goal is secession and union with a future independent Kosovo or even a Greater Albania' (Judah 2001). Serbs also fear the Albanian unification, as seen from the reaction of the First Deputy Prime Minister and Minister of Foreign Affairs Ivica Dačić, who contemplates the danger of Albanian expansionism to be everywhere – in the drone flying over the now infamous Albania-Serbia football match (*CNN* 2014), or at Albanian Prime Minister Edi Rama's residence, where a light display projected the map of 'Greater Albania' on New Year's Eve (*B92* 2015). Greeks are also concerned, and the Greek government has supported the Greek's defence minister's decision to condemn and punish seven Greek soldiers of Albanian origins, who formed the Albanian double eagle symbol with their hands (*SBS Australia* 2017).

Reaction from neighbours to censure the Albanian unification concept irritates Albanian nationalism. A scholar who has observed Balkan nationalism, Judah noted that many Western scholars believe that Greater Albanian nationalism is now replacing Greater Serbian nationalism as the biggest threat to stability in the Balkan Peninsula (Judah 2001). Nonetheless, Judah believes that in Kosovo, Macedonia and to some extent, in Southern Serbia and Montenegro, there is an active 'Albanian question' (Judah 2001).

Pettifer describes the 'Greater Albania' issue as a myth that has been created by the European Union to obscure an attempt to revive Serbian dominance in the region. However, according to Pettifer, the EU overall is losing any leverage they might have had, and in the Balkans, the EU is essentially seen as pro-Serb (Pettifer 2001). Judah argues that 'there is considerably less to Greater Albanian nationalism than meets the eye' (Judah 2001). Here, it is crucial to understand how the concept of 'Greater Albania' originated.

Disagreements between the Western Balkan populations of different ethnicities go back to the end of the nineteenth century. During the eventual collapse of the Ottoman Empire, at the end of the nineteenth century, the Great Powers partitioned Turkish domains and Albanian speaking territories to satisfy the appetite of the Albanian neighbouring countries that 'showed not the slightest hesitation or moral qualm in planning the partition of Albanian lands' (Jelavich and Jelavich 1977: 320).

The Ottoman-Albanian territories ready for the taking – Albanian nationalism in ascent

After a long bloody war with Russia, the declining Ottoman Empire was forced to sign The Treaty of San Stefano in March 1878. This Treaty ended the Russo-Turkish War and further weakened the Ottoman Empire by recognizing the Principality of Bulgaria, which ended 500 years of the Ottoman rule. In the same year, through The Treaty of Berlin, the Great Powers attempted to resolve the Balkan question by re-drawing the Balkan map. However, the Berlin Treaty completely ignored the Albanian question, as it did not exist for Bismarck (Hall 2000). The Porte, the government of the Ottoman Empire, known as Porte or Sublime Porte, was forced to cede its Balkan territory to the emerging Balkan states of Bulgaria, Serbia, Montenegro and Greece at the end of the nineteenth century. This shift directly affected the Albanian-speaking territories, at the time considered as Turkish domain. Albanian nationalism started to rise, whereas the Ottomans opposed the creation of the Albanian entity. At the end of the nineteenth century, Albanians well understood the danger of the disappearance and disadvantage they had compared to their neighbours, Serbia, Montenegro and Greece – states that were already recognised by the Great Powers (Charles and Barbara Jelavich 1977, in Peter F. Sugar ed., 224; Xhaferi 2019, 37).

It is argued that the project of a 'Greater Albania' originated at the Prizren League in 1878. The Prizren League initially had the Otto- man support, and was politically used to halt Serbian advancement in Albanian-speaking territories. However, once the Porte realised the ambition of the Albanian plan for secession from the Empire, the Porte crushed the League. Despite the political miscalculation of requesting autonomy or independence from the Ottomans, the fact remains that the Prizren League requested an Albanian entity through a petition, which included the four Albanian-speaking vilayets of Manastir, Kosova, Shkodra and Janina. Thus, the seed of a mutual Albanian entity was planted (Morgan 2010, 11).

At the beginning of the twentieth century, Albanian nationalism experienced a sharp rise that brought about social unrest to four Turkish *vilayets* inhabited mainly by Albanian speaking popula- tions. While the Ottoman Empire was declining, Albanians were mortified as their culture, language and their lands faced extinc- tion. The Albanian prominent writer, Kadare thinks 'European Albanians' feel humiliated by the European Great Powers' deci- sion to re-draw the Albanian map (Kadare 2004). Paraphrasing the Albanian linguist Arshi Pipa, Schwandner-Sievers points out the importance of the Albanian indigenous culture, the folklore and its unique language, which 'became the basis of constructing a dis- tinct national identity and pride, and a distinct territorial definition' (Schwandner-Sievers 2008).

Nevertheless, the Ottoman Empire was still strong enough to oppose the Albanian uprising at the beginning of the twentieth cen- tury, but powerless to protect the four vilayets of Albanian-speaking lands from their partition. As discussed by Psilos, the Ottomans' destructive military campaign in North and South Albania came to an end in October 1910, leaving Albania in total 'devastation and anarchy' (Psilos 2006), which further aggravated the situation through promises by the Young Turks (Misha 1999). The Turkish devastations and divide-and-rule policy implemented by the Sultan Abdülhamid II, while catalysing more reaction to the Albanian uprisings, brought about more complications in protecting the four vilayets. On the other hand, Albanian frustrations increased in December 1912 as they were not invited to join the Orthodox union of the Balkan League (created by Serbia, Montenegro, Bulgaria and Greece), – a union that aimed to oppose the Turks and extend their territory at the expense of Albanian-speaking territories. Thus, Albanian nationalism found itself in direct opposition to all forces in the region: Turks, Serbs, Montenegrins and Greeks. The only hope that remained was a declaration of independence and the hope of being recognised by the Great Powers.

The London Conference – the confirmation of a 'little' Albania

The first Balkan War that broke out on October 1912 forced the Great Powers to make another attempt in resolving the Western Balkan question. The London Conference (also known as the Ambassadors' meetings), chaired by the British foreign minister Edward Grey, officially started in December 1912, and continued for more than six months (Ferraro 2020). Although it was proposed for the conference to be held in Paris, because of the links between France and Russia, Austria argued for it to take place in a neutral location to avoid bias in decision making. While the London Conference aimed to resolve territorial disputes between the Turks and the Balkan League members, the Albanian state and its territorial boundaries became the main topic of the conference. On 30 May 1913, the Conference made the important decision to recognise the Albanian state as an individual entity. However, Albania's autonomy from the Ottomans was only officially recognised at the fifty-fourth meeting of the Conference of London on 29 July 1913 (Elsie 2016). Despite the decision to officially recognise Albania, the Conference decided that the 'boundaries of Albania were to be fixed by the great powers' (Ferraro 2020).

The aim of the Conference was to bring peace to Europe, regardless of the cost to any single state. The criteria of re-drawing the ex-Ottoman territories were based on rewarding winners at the expense of the Ottoman losers. However, the Conference struggled to provide solutions when military advancements overlapped territories of every single Balkan state. Although the other focus was on the ethno-linguistic elements, according to Grey, reaching a peace agreement was the main goal. Although Grey promised to keep the neutral position, in reality, he protected interests of Great Britain, especially when dealing with Greece. As he states, 'we could not destroy the achievements of the London Conference for some Albanian towns such as Gjakova...' (Grey 1927). Thus, Grey admits that the town of Gjakova was an 'Albanian town', and also shows unwise decisions to leave this and other Albanian-speaking towns out of the Albanian map, foreshadowing future dangers. The London Conference was characterised by disputes between Austro-Hungary and Italy on one side, and Russia and France on the other. Austro-Hungary and Italy were supporters of Albania, whereas Russia was known for their support of Orthodox countries in the Balkans, especially Serbia.

The Great Powers presented two proposals to Grey. The Russian proposal included cities with a majority of Albanian-speaking populations such as Plava, Ulqini, and Guzija as part of Montenegro. The Russian aim was to secure at least one access to Adriatic Sea for Serbia. The Russian proposal included within the Serbian territories the plains of Kosovo and North Albania, while leaving out from Albania territories the Western part of today's Northern Macedonia and did not oppose the Greek claim on North Epirus. Thus, the Russian proposal lobbied for Serbian, Montenegrin and Greek interests at the expense of Albanian-speaking territories.

Unlike the Russian proposal, Austro-Hungary and Italy spent the majority of their energy to secure Shkodër for Albania and to block Serbian access to the Adriatic Sea. Their proposal included Prizren, Gjakova and Pec; however, they compromised on leaving out some territories of today's Kosovo, such as its capital, Prishtina. They also excluded most of the Albanian speaking territories of Manastir, and other towns that are located within today's Northern Macedonia. Nevertheless, the Austro-Hungarian plan strongly opposed Greece's claims on South Albania.

To its disadvantage, Albania did not have a recognised government at the time. However, the Albanian head of the first provisional government, Ismail Qemali, decided to send an Albanian delegation, which was comprised of Mehmet Konica, Filip Noga, and Rasim Dino. The Albanian chair of delegates, Konica, claimed in 13 minutes that the Albanian map should include all territories shown in the Austro-Hungarian proposal, the entire Kosovo region, Ulqini, Plava and Guzije in Montenegro, and the Chameria region, including most of the Epirus region down to Preveza (Hoxha 2000:16). In order to claim Albanian-speaking territories, Konica argued on an ethno-linguistic approach, claiming that the majority of the Albanian population in all four *vilayets* were comprised of people who speak a unique Albanian language, which had no similarity to Serbian, Montenegrin or Greek languages.

The Great Powers analysed these three proposals but did not agree with any of them. Focusing on their own interests, and not having clear criteria, they decided to re-design the Albanian borders, which since then, has been of what we know of today's Albania. Reflecting on Albania's current borders, it became clear that the decision made by the Great Powers was to 'compromise' between the two proposals satisfying neither of the contending parties and, most of all, angering Albania. Hence, the Chameria region was given to Greece, but not what Greece considers as the North Epirus. Kosovo was attached to Serbia; Plava, Guzia and Ulqini to Montenegro, and the Eastern part to Macedonia (today's North Macedonia), which, in the aftermath of World War I, became part of the Kingdom of Yugoslavia. Thus, the Albanian speaking territories were used to satisfy the demands of Albania's neighbours (Danaj 2012). As a result of this, the Conference was responsible for redrawing the Balkan map, a map which, for Albanians, remained largely unchanged, and still not conceding full territorial integrity.

The unification into a 'Natural Albania'

The struggle of unifying Albanian speaking territories continues in the twenty-first century. Kosovo is not connected to Albania, however, the project of unification with the 'mother-land' is supported by the Kosovar political Party *Lëvizja Vetëvendosje* (LVV) [Self-determination Movement], which was founded in 2004 (*Vetëvendosje* 2020). This party fundamentally supports the idea of people's self-determination; opposing foreign involvement in the internal affairs of Kosovo. The LVV statute declares that the people of Kosovo must have 'the right to unite with Albania' (Vetëvendosje 2020). Although this mission unleashes the Albanian aspiration for a 'Greater Albania', its implementation seems impossible without involvement of the current major international actors, as Kosovo is not yet recognised by five EU members: Greece, Spain, Romania, Slovakia and Cyprus. This also means that Kosovo is unable to realise its aspiration of becoming a member of the UN, and thus gain the ability for self-determination. The Kosovar elections on 11 June 2017 revealed that the LVV started to become the first preference for Kosovars, achieving more votes than any other party, the leading Democratic Party of Kosovo (PDK) and the Democratic League of

Kosovo (LDK) (Bytyci 2017). The LVV was crowned by winning the last elections in 2019 with Albin Kurti being the Prime Minister of Kosovo in 2020. The new government responded to several immediate challenges with the unification issue to be secondary. The US representative appointed in charge of the dialogue Serbia-Kosovo, Richard Grenell, has asked the new PM Albin Kurti to immediately abandon the 100% tax policy for all goods imported from Serbia and Bosnia Hercegovina, in force since November 2019. Kurti has claimed that the LVV has agreed to replace this tax with a 'reciprocating policy' between Serbia and Kosovo, which he did. However, Kurti lost the majority in Parliament and stepped down in March 2020, accused by the opposition as an authoritarian who had jeopardised relations with the US administration.

The unification sentiment with Kosovo also exists in Albania. In March 2011, the *Aleanca Kuq e Zi* [Red and Black Alliance] Party was founded in Albania. Supporting 'Greater Albania', this party claims protection of Albanian rights in 'Albania, Kosovo, Macedonia, Montenegro Chameria and the Presevo Valley' (*Aleanca Kuq e Zi* 2015). However, the party was resoundingly defeated in the 2013 Albanian elections, receiving only 0.59 percent (10196) of votes (*Panorama on line* 2013). Since then, the party has kept a low profile. It can be argued that the defeat of *Aleanca Kuq e Zi*, the only political party to promote 'Greater Albania' in Albania, shows the hesitancy of Albanians who live in Albania to unite in a Greater Albanian nation-state. However, the reluctance of Albanians to unite in a 'Greater Albania' remains a contentious question. The issue became more complicated when questioning whether the Albanian diaspora is more committed than those who live in Albania and Kosovo to the ideal of a 'Greater Albania'?

In 2010, Koço Danaj, an Albanian University professor founded in Albania the first movement, 'The Platform of the Natural Albania'. According to Danaj, the Platform has only one goal: the creation of the Albanian nation-state, or what he calls 'The Natural Albania' (Danaj 2012). Danaj claims the Platform is nothing more than what was declared at the Vlorë Parliament on 28 November 1912: an appeal for a 'Natural Albania', a request to implement a judicial act. Danaj argues that this act was ignored by the London Conference, which instead made a 'colonialist' and 'criminal' decision by dividing the Albanian-speaking territories between five different nation states (Danaj 2012).

For Danaj, unification in a 'Greater Albania' is the only option as this is supported by the Albanian people. It seems that the polls conducted by Gallup in 2010 have inspired Danaj who thinks that supporters of 'The Natural Albania' are firstly Albanians: '82 percent in Kosovo, 64 percent in Albania and 89 percent in Macedonia' (Damjanovic and Chapman 2010). Not only is this data contentious, the quantitative analysis seems to be presented in a simplistic and superficial way. An example is the defeat of *Aleanca Kuq e Zi* in 2015. Nevertheless, Danaj argues that Albanian politicians accept the importance of unification, but are divided between those representing their own vilayet, and others who are still scared to speak out (Danaj 2012).

According to the Platform, history needs to be revisited, the injustice needs to be addressed and the London Conference decision needs to be reversed in such a way that the Albanian territories from Preshevo Valley to Preveza, from Durrës to Skopje again join 'The Natural Albania' (Danaj 2012). Danaj argues that the London Conference decision can be reversed, and Albanians can be united under the same nation-state umbrella in a similar way that the Germans reunified. Furthermore, Danaj claims that the decision to dissolve the Yugoslavian federation revoked the previous decision (Danaj 2012). However, the case of Albanian unification is more complicated as it affects not one, but five Western Balkan nation-states.

Although it can be argued that the decision to divide Albanian-speaking territories may be used as a legal argument, realistically, it is difficult for Albania to challenge the decision made by the Great Powers and unite all Albanian-speaking territories claimed by the Albanian delegation at the London Conference in 1913. Firstly, the composition of today's Great Powers and the political environment are different. Of the Great Powers of 1913, only Russia can be still considered a global power. Others, such as Germany, the United Kingdom and France, are economically better placed than Austria, Hungary and Italy, and thus, might be defined as 'Great Powers' in the twenty-first century. However, along with the transformed landscapes of Europe, governments of these countries may be reluctant to change political decisions made in 1913, and subsequent geopolitical arrangements. In addition, challenging the London Conference decision in a court of law seems impossible as appropriate courts do not exist.

The unification of Kosovo and Albania is also a challenging project. Martii Ahtisaari's 2007 binding proposal to resolve the status of Kosovo still makes it impossible for Kosovo to seek a union with 'any State or part of any State' (*United Nations Security Council 2007*). According to Marcus Tanner, even the removal of Kosovo from Serbia cannot undo the damage done in 1913, and the only way to resolve 'Greater Albania' is the integration of the whole region into Europe, which will render their borders semi-redundant. 'Then, not before, the ghost of Greater Albania will be laid to rest' (Tanner 2015). Are there other opportunities for Albanians to unite in a 'Greater Albania'?

A 'Greater Albania' under Turkish leadership?

Turkey has been Albania's strongest supporter in the region since the creation of the Turkish Republic in 1923 (Xhaferi, 2017b: 45). One might merely mention the strong historical-cultural bridge that links Albanians in the twenty-first century with five million Turks, who, according to Genci Muçaj, the Albanian former Ambassador in Turkey, are conscious of and proud to mention their Albanian heritage (*Telegrafi* 2015). The political statements in the direction of the West may well be reversed. A more aggressive Turkish foreign policy to come closer to Albania is already using historical-cultural links between Albania and Turkey to bring about Albania's alignment with the East (Xhaferi 2019). Turkey may also use Albania's economic, geo-political and security concerns, which remain high for Albanians in the twenty-first century.

Due to these links with Turkey, the opportunity for Albanians to unite under Turkey is also contemplated by another scholar, Cuneyt Yenigun, who thinks that unification of Albanians under the same nation-state umbrella cannot happen for another two decades (Yenigun 2010). In order to surpass this, Yenigun offers his solution for immediate unification of Albania with Kosovo and Macedonia. He proposes a type of cooperation called 'Albkomac' (183); similar to that of Belgium, Holland and Luxembourg (Benelux) or the Gulf Cooperation Council (GCC), which is composed of Saudi Arabia, Kuwait, Qatar, United Arab Emirates, Bahrain and Oman. According to Yenigun, the GCC model of cooperation in fields such as economy, trade, customs, legislation, agriculture, and joint military forces is better for 'Albkomac' as collaborating with each other due to 'cultural, religion and historical background' (Yenigun 2010: 184) is more sustainable. Although the Albanian model compared to the GCC is lacking in capital, Yenigun argues that 'Albkomac' could be established under the leadership of Turkey. He reasons that Turkey, as the second fastest growing country in the world, would be able to nurture this unification based on the historical, cultural and religious links with Albania.

Unlike Yenigun, Kadare thinks 'European Albanians' are Christians, and thus, should not join Turkey (Kadare in Xhaferi, 2017a:

123). It is a fact that, being under the Ottoman rule for more than five centuries, Albania's religious orientation has changed; having a 70 percent Muslim (both Sunni and Bektashi) population. It is also known that Albanians were forced (but also converted on a voluntary basis) in large numbers to Islam (Xhaferi 2019). At a time when Albania has clearly identified the 'Euro-Atlantic' path as its priority, uniting under Turkish leadership may give mixed messages to its strategic allies, the US and the EU, and thus endanger the continued alliance. The large Albanian community in Turkey, which has been estimated to be of a similar size to both Albania and Kosovo, will always act as an established bridge that is built on historical, cultural and traditional links, and as a result, may always have ambitions to influence the Turkish government and side with Albania, regardless of the Albanian foreign policy swings. However, unifying under Turkey while naïve, may also have repercussions for the entire Western Balkan region.

A peaceful unification into a 'Greater Europe'?

The Western Balkans continue to be trapped between the East and West, with Russia supporting Serbian-orthodox-brotherhood, and the United States protecting Kosovo's independence and statehood. Others such as the European Union, but also China and Turkey, are all present in the region. While Kosovo and Serbia are preparing their final chapter of recognising each other, which might be crucial for the fate of both states to proceed with their membership of the EU, the Western Balkan nationalists are terrified that Kosovo may decide to unite with Albania (Tanner 2015).

During his Kosovo visit in February 2020, the Albanian foreign Minister, Gentian Cakaj, confirmed the plan to have joint embassies between Albania and Kosovo and removal of borders between Albania and Kosovo, which according to him are only 'imaginary' (*European Western Balkans* 2020). This agreement was reached during the unified Albanian and Kosovar government meetings in 2018. The Serbian Prime Minister, Ana Brnabic, had an immediate reaction, stating that the agreement is 'scandalous that there was no reaction from the United States of America' (*RTK Live* (2019).

Albania and Kosovo have both chosen the Euro-Atlantic way as their main priority. Albania joined NATO in 2014, and Albania's application for EU membership was submitted on 24 April 2009. It was only in March 2020 when formal negotiations for Albanian membership opened (*European Commission website* 2020). Despite this lateness, according to Gallup polls in 2017, Albania and Kosovo are more optimistic than any other country in Europe, with four out of five Albanian people in favour of joining the EU (Independent Balkan News Agency 2017). Albanian and Kosovar politicians cannot afford to disappoint the Euro-Atlantic partners. Therefore, the argument remains the same: the Albanian unification will only happen under the EU banner. In fact, the elite of the capital city, Tirana, does not seem to be interested in redesigning Albania's national borders to create the so-called 'Greater Albania'. In December 2011, former Albanian Prime Minister, Sali Berisha, stated that 'the best interest of Albanians is to protect the existing borders; hence Albania and Kosovo will be united inside the EU, as we cannot risk our territories' (24 Ore 2011). The current Albanian Prime Minister, Edi Rama, holds a similar opinion about 'Greater Albania'. His statement in April 2015 that Albania and Kosovo will unite in 'a classical way' sparked much criticism from European leaders and Albania's neighbours, Serbia and Greece. Immediately, the Serbian Prime Minister, Aleksandar Vučić, and Macedonian and Greek leaders contested Rama's statement. The statement was then corrected by Rama – reassuring the critics that the unification of Albania and Kosovo would only happen once both Albania and Kosovo have become European Union members. Hence, Judah thinks that 'no mainstream Albanian political party, whether in Kosovo, Albania or Macedonia, publicly espouses the idea' (Judah 2001) of a 'Greater Albania'.

The discussion about 'Greater Albania' is conducted differently in Kosovo, North Macedonia, Montenegro and Albania. While in Albania, a form of humiliation is expressed in a form of victimi-sation, which perhaps is based on the fact that Serbia, Montene-gro, Macedonia and Greece are still in charge of those Albanian-speaking territories given to them by the London Conference, the Kosovar government has its recognition as a first priority. On the other hand, Serbs, Macedonians, Bulgarians and Greeks are over-reacting to the misleading concept of 'Greater Albania', possibly indicating their fears of an Albanian rise in power in the region (*Telegrafi* 2015). Nevertheless, while it seems difficult to determine whether 'Greater Albania' is a myth or a possible future reality, it is also dangerous to disseminate such an idea at a time when Balkan countries need to unite and leave behind centuries of hate and wars. This can only happen under the EU umbrella and, at the beginning of the twenty-first century, a plan B is not evident.

References

24 Ore (2011), 'Berisha kunder bashkimit Shqiperi – Kosove' [Berisha against the unification of Albania with Kosovo], http://24-ore.com/index.php/kronika/qeveritare/8475-berisha-kunder-bashkimit-shqiperi-kosove.html

Aleanca Kuq e Zi [Red and Black alliance] (2015), 'Rreth nesh [About us]', http://www.aleancakuqezi.al/rreth-nesh/.

B92 (2015), 'Protest sent to Albania over display of expansionist map', https://www.b92.net/eng/news/politics.php?yyyy=2015&mm=01&dd=12&nav_id=92828.

Bogdani, Mirela and John Loughlin (2007), *Albania and the European Union: The Tumultuous Journey Towards Integration and Accession*, I.B. Tauris , Palgrave Macmillan, London, New York.

Bytyci, Fatos (2017), 'Kosovo centre-right coalition on course to win parliamentary vote', *Reuters*, https://www.reuters.com/article/us-kosovo-elections/kosovo-centre-right-coalition-on-course-to-win-parliamentary-vote-idUSKBN1910ZO.

CNN (2014), 'Serbia and Albania game abandoned after drone invasion sparks brawl', http://edition.cnn.com//2014/10/14/sport/football/serbia-albania-game-abandoned/.

Damjanovic, Viktor and John Chapman (2010), 'Two Years In, Kosovo Albanians More Sober on Independence', *Gallup*, http://www.gallup.com/poll/125978/two-years-kosovo-albanianssober-independence.aspx.

Danaj, Koço (2012), an interview of Bashkim Metalia, published on *The Albanian*, London, 'Shqipëria natyrale do të bëhet' [The natural Albania will be done] *Shqiperianatyrale.com*, http://shqiperianatyrale.com/index.php?option=com_contentcontent&view=article&id=177:koco-danaj-shqiperia-natyrale-do-te-behet&catid=34:analiza&Itemid=29.

Elsie, Robert (2016), 'The London Conference and the Albanian Question (1912-1914). The Dispatches of Sir Edward Grey', *Albanian Studies*, 27.

European Western Balkans (2020), 'Albania and Kosovo consider founding shared embassies and common economic space', https://europeanwesternbalkans.com/2020/02/19/albania-and-kosovo-consider-founding-shared-embassies-and-common-economic-space/.

Ferraro, Vincent (2020), *The Treaty of London 1913*, http://www.mtholyoke.edu/acad/intrel/boshtml/bos145.htm".htm.

France-Presse, Agence (2020), 'New Kosovo Leader Ready to Revoke Tariffs for Serbian Goods', *Voice of America*, https://www.voanews.com/europe/new-kosovo-leader-ready-revoke-tariffs-serbian-goods.

Grey, Edward (1927), *Memoires*, Payot, Paris.

Hall, Richard. C (2000), *The Balkan Wars 1912–1913: Prelude to the First World War*, Routledge, London & New York.

Hoxha, Ibrahim D (2000), *Viset kombëtare shqiptare në shtetin grek* [Albanian lands in Greece], author's translation, Tiranë: Dituria.

Independent Balkan News Agency (2017), 'Albanians are the most optimistic in the Balkans on EU integration', https://balkaneu.com/albanians-are-the-most-optimistic-in-the-balkans-on-eu-integration/.

Jelavich, Charles and Barbara (1977), 'The Establishment of the Balkan National States, 1804-1920', in *A History of East Central Europe*, ed. Peter F. Sugar and Donald W. Treadgold, University of Washington Press, Seattle and London .

Judah, Tim (2001), 'Greater Albania?' *Survival: Global Politics and Strategy*, 43, 7-18.

Kadare, Ismail (2004), *Poshtërimi në Ballkan* [Humiliation in the Balkans], Tirana, Onufri.

Kushi, Odeta and Sidita Kushi (2015), 'The Paranoia over "Greater Albania" Returns', *New Eastern Europe*, http://www.neweasterneurope.eu/articles-and-commentary/1459-the-paranoia-over-greater-albania-returns.

Misha, Glenny (1999), *The Balkans 1804-1999: Nationalism, War, and the Great Powers*, Granta Books, London.

Morgan, Peter (2010), *Ismail Kadare: The Writer and the Dictatorship 1957-1990*. Modern Humanities Research Association and Routledge, Oxford.

Panorama on line (2013), 'Rezultatet zyrtare, votat per cdo parti' [Official results, votes for each party], http://www.panorama.com.al/rezultatet-zyrtare-votat-per-cdo-parti/.

Pettifer, James (2001), 'Greater Albania', *The World Today*, no. 57, 18-20.

Psilos, Christophoros (2006), 'Albanian Nationalism and Unionist Ottomanization 1908 to 1912', *Mediterranean Quarterly*, vol. 17, 26-42.

RTK Live (2019) 'Cakaj and Pacolli 'shock' Serbia with diplomatic agreement', https://www.rtklive.com/en/news-single.php?ID=14366"14366.

SBS Australia, Greek language podcast (2017), 'Two years of SYRIZA ruling Greece – The Albanian eagle in the Greek army!', http://www.sbs.com.au/yourlanguage/greek/en/content/two-years-syriza-ruling-greece-albanian-eagle-greek-army.

Schwandner-Sievers, Stephanie (2008), 'Albanians, Albanianism and the strategic subversion of stereotypes', *Slovene Anthropological Society*, vol. 14, 47-64.

Tanner, Marcus (2015), 'The Ghost of Greater Albania Won't go Away'. *BalkanInsight*, https://balkaninsight.com/2015/03/27/the-ghost-of-greater-albania-won-t-go-away/.

Telegraf (2015), 'Third Balkan War in the making: Serbs, Greeks, Bulgarians

and Macedonians to unite against the 'Greater Albania'?', http://www.
telegraf.rs/english/1566600-third-balkan-war-in-the-making-serbs-
greeks-bulgarians-and-macedonians-to-unite-against-the-greater-alba-
nia.

Telegrafi (2015), 'Ambasadori i Shqipërisë në Turqi: Feja e shqiptarit është shq-
iptaria, në Turqi janë pesë milionë shqiptarë' [The Albanian Ambassador
in Turkey: The Albanian religion is Albanianism, in Turkey live five million Albanians], http://m.telegrafi.com/lajme/ambasadori-i-shqiperise-
ne-turqi-feja-e-shqiptarit-eshte-shqiptaria-ne-turqi-jane-pese-milione-
shqiptare-2-67961.html.

Today's Zaman (2015), 'Albanians in Turkey celebrate their cultural heritage',
http://mobile.todayszaman.com/national_albanians-in-turkey-celebrate-
their-cultural-heritage_254383.html".html.

United Nations Security Council (2007), 'Comprehensive Proposal for the
Kosovo Status Settlement', document number: S/2007/168/Add.1.

Vetëvendosje (2020), 'Statuti i Lëvizjes Vetëvendosje' [Statute of the self-determination movement], https://www.vetevendosje.org/statuti/].Xhaferi,
Perparim (2017a), 'The Political Contribution of Albanian Writers in Defining Albanian Identity: the Debate between Ismail Kadare and Rexhep
Qosja', *European Journal of Language and Literature*, 7, 121-128.

Xhaferi, Perparim (2017b), 'The Post-Ottoman Era: A Fresh Start for Bilateral Relations between Albania and Turkey?', *Australian and New Zealand
Journal of European Studies*, vol. 9, 42-62.

Xhaferi, Perparim (2019), 'Albanian National Identity in the twenty-first century: Escaping from the Ottoman heritage?' PhD, University of Sydney.

Yenigun, Cuneyt (2010), 'GCC Model: Conflict Management for the 'Greater
Albania', *SDU Faculty of Arts and Sciences Journal of Social Sciences: Special Issue on Balkans*, 175-186.

7

EUROPEAN UNION AND THE CASE
OF A ROGUE MEMBER STATE

Robert Mężyk

Keywords: Rule of Law, European Law, Autonomy, Countermeasures, Vienna Convention

Abstract

The spectre of authoritarianism is haunting Europe. The law of the EU does not offer an effective solution for dealing with a rogue Member State which does not wish to leave the Union and, at the same time, disrespects its laws and procedures. Additionally, the principle of autonomy of EU law *prima facie* prohibits recourse to the measures of international law. I contend that this principle should be read functionally, and thus, the use of international law is allowed as long as it serves the purpose of safeguarding the European project. Consequently, the analysis offers an overview of possible mechanisms of applying retortions, countermeasures and the Vienna Convention of the Law of Treaties to counteract the situation of a rogue Member State.

Introduction

This chapter considers the case of a rogue Member State which intends to stay in the EU and, at the same time, openly disrespects the principles of the European legal system. The discussion is inspired by the rule of law backsliding in Poland and Hungary, both of which continue their illiberal journey towards authoritarianism. At the same time, these countries openly reject the EU's involvement with their domestic policies. I ask if the European system can legally tolerate the use of legal measures which, although not directly foreseen by the system itself, could prove effective at stopping the illiberal change in the member states of the EU.

The cases of Hungary and Poland exposed the inherent weakness of the Union: The 'nuclear option' from Art. 7 of the Treaty on European Union (TEU), specially created to target violations of the principles of the Union, could not be used because the two governments supported each other and potentially blocked the procedure which requires unanimity of the European Council. At the same time, the resistance of the Polish authorities to the case-law of the Court of Justice of the European Union ('ECJ') indicates the possibility that a Member State may refuse to obey the Court's judgements. The success of such resistance seems probable. The Polish government demonstrates a constantly Eurosceptic stance, having captured the top institutions of the domestic judiciary (Sadurski 2019). Following the path indicated by the German Federal Constitutional Court (Bundesverfassungsgericht 2020), Polish authorities can use the country's judiciary to declare the rule-of-law-case-law of the ECJ as exceeding the Court's competencies.

The following discussion assumes that a rogue Member State is willing to remain in the EU. At the same time, the country breaches the principles of the Union and disrespects the ECJ-judgements, which target such violations, by declaring these judgments to be ultra vires (beyond competencies). The European Treaties lack a regulation dedicated to such a situation and assume sincere cooperation of the Member States irrespective of the circumstances (Art 4 (3) TEU). The Treaties presume that a rogue Member State would either be unanimously held in contempt by all other Member States and subject to the procedure from Art. 7 TEU; or that the country will voluntarily leave the Union according to the procedure from Art. 50 TEU. Hence, there is a legal and political gap in the European legal regime. This text focuses on the legal aspects of the described situation, considering both European and international law.

I first examine the concept of the autonomy of EU law which isolates the legal system of the Union from international law. Although the principle of autonomy limits legal instruments available to the Member States, its overarching function consists of safeguarding the European project. I propose that, in the case of a rogue Member State, the purpose of the principle of autonomy implies opening the European legal system to the mechanisms of international law. Consequently, I discuss the possibility of applying retortions, countermeasures and tools foreseen by the *Vienna Convention on the Law of Treaties* (1969, 'VCLT') to react to the breach of the Treaties. I conclude the chapter by considering the possible inclusion of the discussed measures into the system of EU law by the ECJ.

The way there: from reciprocity to the autonomy of EU law

The principle of autonomy of EU law proclaims the sovereignty of the EU (Van Rossem 2012). It does so, among others, by separating the legal system of the EU from other legal systems: only European law should apply to the matters of the EU. Not written down in the primary law, it was derived by the ECJ from the nature of the treaties and used to safeguard European law from legal systems which would endanger its legal unity, both from the outside (international law) and from within (domestic law of the Member States). On the international level, the autonomy protects the European legal order from international arrangements with effects such as actually or potentially undermining the competencies of the Court (*Opinion 1/09* 2009) or infringing the system of judicial protection established by European law. This approach means that the EU, for example, rejected an automatic system of applying the resolutions by the UN Security Council, if they infringe the Court's institutional role and the protection of rights warranted by the EU (*Yassin Abdullah Kadi* 2005).

In the second aspect (EU-Member States), the principle of autonomy protects European law from being undermined by national laws or judgements (*van Gend & Loos* 1963). In other words, national courts cannot make decisions which would infringe European law. The judgement in the case van Gend presented the foundation on which the principle was established. According to the Court, the Treaties are 'more than an agreement which merely creates mutual obligations between the contracting states' (*Van Gend & Loos* 1963). Hence, the EU law constitutes a new legal order directly applicable to its citizens. The *Flaminio Costa v E.N.E.L.* (1964) judgement elaborated this perspective by prohibiting external measures from being applied within the community:

The integration into the laws of each Member State of provisions which derive from the community, and more generally the terms and the spirit of the Treaty, make it impossible for the States, as a corollary, to accord precedence to a unilateral and subsequent measure over a legal system accepted by them on a basis of reciprocity. Such a measure cannot therefore be inconsistent with that legal system. The executive force of Community law cannot vary from one State to another in deference to subsequent domestic laws, without jeopardising the attainment of the objectives of the Treaty.

However, we shall take a logical step back to understand the significance of the quoted judgement. The statements that the Treaties created an independent source of law and that they gave rights directly to citizens of the Member States are merely the consequences of the conclusion of the Treaties as an act of entering a mutual legal relationship by the Member States. To create the EU, all Member States agreed to limit their sovereign rights mutually and accepted the obligations stemming from the Treaties. Accordingly, to create the EU, France, Germany, Italy, Belgium, Luxemburg and the Netherlands established 15 reciprocal relations, pooled by and vested in the institutions of the community. Only then was the EU established. The initial act of trust and vesting of sovereignty is what, in the second step of the process of integration, has taken away the instrument of reciprocity (explained below) from the Member States.

Reciprocity is the classical instrument of international law which can be used to safeguard international obligations. In using reciprocity as a tool, one country fulfils its duties only if its partner-countries do; it withholds fulfilling its responsibilities if the other countries do not fulfil their obligations. Embodying the principle of reciprocity, Art. 60 VCLT allows a party to a treaty to terminate or suspend the treaty if the other party committed a material breach of the treaty. International humanitarian law exemplifies the principle of reciprocity using the general participation clause. Accordingly, Art. 2 of the 1907 Hague Convention IV states: 'The provisions contained (…) in the present Convention, do not apply except between Contracting Powers, and then only if all the belligerents are parties to the Convention'. In layman's terms, a country obeys its obligations as long, as its partners do.

In the EU, the Member States have given up reciprocity as a tool of international law and put it in the hands of the Commission and the Court. Were there no European institutions, the Member States would have remained the primary 'guardians of the treaties' and reciprocity would have remained the tool for safeguarding the European Treaties. However, because the institutions exist, the principle of autonomy detaches the European system from other systems of law, including the mechanism of reciprocity. This detachment, in turn, creates effects directly for the citizens of the Member States. If one Member State breaches European Treaties, other Member States do not need to violate the Treaties to punish the wrongdoer (as reciprocity would require). Instead, they can have the Commission and the ECJ do their job.

Since the conclusion of the European Treaties, the restraint on using reciprocity has become binding and shapes the principle of the autonomy of the EU law. The Member States can no longer apply reciprocity because the EU applies its autonomous measures of law enforcement. The 1979 *Mutton and lamb* case (*Commission of the European Communities v French Republic* 1979) illustrates this mechanism. In this case, France infringed European law by subsidising its lamb industry. France justified these measures by pointing out that the UK breaches the same rules on its side. The Court stated that in case of a breach of European law by one of the Member States, another Member State could not take recourse to measures not foreseen by EU law. This means that France could not take the case in its own hands. According to the Court, 'although it is still necessary to take special measures, a decision to adopt them can no longer be made unilaterally by the Member States concerned; they must be adopted within the Community system which is designed to guarantee that the general public interest of the Community is protected' (ibid, para. 7). Therefore, if France claims that the UK is in breach of the European law, 'it has the opportunity to take action, either within the Council, or through the Commission, or finally by recourse to judicial remedies with a view to achieving the elimination of such incompatible features' (ibid., para. 9). This and a similar judgement in the case *European Communities v Federal Republic of Germany* (1984) expressly excluded the possibility of justifying breaches of the Treaties by reference to reciprocity.

The autonomy of European law leads to the primacy of European law. If legal relations within the EU are vested in the European institutions, then the European regulations must enjoy primacy over domestic measures of the Member States. To make autonomy of the EU law work, the Member States cannot unilaterally decide about the legality of the actions of the other Member States or the EU. The ECJ confirmed this conclusion in the judgement *Internationale Handelsgesellschaft* (1970). The Court stated that the validity of European law could be only assessed (decided) in the light of European law itself, and by the institutions of the community. Otherwise, the *'legal basis of the Community itself [is] being called in question'* (ibid., para. 3).

The Court delivered further judgements advancing the principle of autonomy (Van Rossem 2013). The relevant cases covered limiting the possibility of using a dispute resolution mechanism external to the EU (*Commission of the European Communities v Ireland* 2006) or protecting the Union from direct legal effects of a UN Security Council resolution (*Yassin Abdullah Kadi* 2005). All of these cases follow the same logic: The mutual bond constituting the EU precludes challenging the validity of European law by domestic measures of the Member States, and the only means of law enforcement are those foreseen by EU law. The negative aspect of autonomy (exclusion of challenging the validity of EU law by the Member States) and the positive one (limitation to law enforcement measures consistent with the Treaties) are the Yin and Yang of the consistency of the European project, which is the end-goal of the described mechanism. In this respect, autonomy is a means to an end and not an end in itself.

Way back: from autonomy to mistrust

Prima facie, the principle of autonomy of EU law cripples the EU when dealing with a rogue member state (Phelan 2012). As the case of Poland or Hungary shows, the EU lacks effectiveness in coping with authoritarianism. Both countries introduced multiple 'reforms', such as capturing the system of the judiciary, which infringe the principle of the rule of law. Thus Hungary and Poland advance towards illiberalism, trumping values anchored in the European treaties. The EU measures foreseen by the Treaties, which should counteract such a change, are either paralysed by political alliances of the rogue State (Art. 7 TEU and blocking the 'nuclear option') or lack effectiveness (ignoring the ECJ judgements). These show that the EU cannot adequately protect its principles through its legal mechanisms. Thus, the principle of autonomy, with its limiting consequences, no longer serves the purpose of safeguarding the European legal system. To the contrary, it limits the possibility of effectively counteracting the rogue State and its corrupting effects on the Union. Because the EU, and the other Member States, are limited by the principle of autonomy, they cannot take effective action against the rogue State but are to use the system of the European Union. When this system does not work, the principle blocks any other effective actions and is counterproductive.

The paradoxical paralysing effect of the principle of autonomy calls for its purposive interpretation and asking the question: Why is the principle of autonomy there in the first place? This process has to begin by recalling the reciprocal trust between the Member States, which underlies the Treaties. Trusting each other, the countries vested the institutional power in the EU and blocked their own actions. This trust, which allowed for the abolition of reciprocity in the EU, is no longer given. The Member States do not mutually cooperate to further the European project, but one (or more) of them consciously breach its principles and the underlying trust. Therefore, mutual trust can no longer serve as a basis for such a system. This breach, in turn, hollows out the foundations of the principle of autonomy.

The lack of trust leads to the revival of the principle of reciprocity. The Member States cannot count on the Commission or the ECJ to fulfil their law-enforcement function, because the Treaties limit these institutions. This limitation, which resulted from the original trust between the Member States, is no longer reasonable:

The principle of autonomy now safeguards the perpetrators of the breach of European law, not the European project. Consequently, the principle of autonomy needs to give way to its predecessor, the reciprocity.

Because the rogue Member State acts beyond the scope of the original trust underlying the EU, it cannot invoke the principle of autonomy to its defence. In the case *European Communities v Federal Republic of Germany* (1984, para 11) concerning the failed execution of European law by Germany, the Court stated:

> A Member State cannot, in any circumstances, plead the principle of reciprocity and rely on a possible infringement of the treaty by another Member State in order to justify its own default. Nor, therefore, can a Member State rely on the principle of reciprocity to contest the admissibility of an action brought against it for failure to fulfil its obligations.

The above quote can be interpreted teleologically: The principle of reciprocity could be used as long as it does not serve the purpose of justifying a default of the Member State but serves the purpose of defending the European legal order. In other words, as long as a country upholds European law, it could plead the principle of reciprocity.

The described reasoning follows a logical syllogism. Mutual trust between the Member States led to the abolition of reciprocity. Abolition of reciprocity led to the autonomy of the EU. Yet, the rogue Member State challenges mutual trust and abuses the system by ignoring its mechanisms. Consequently, the lack of mutual trust questions the abolition of reciprocity and cancels the principle of autonomy of the EU. Reciprocity revives in the extent which is necessary to safeguard the system.

THE ECJ's case-law relating to the Eurozone crisis and the financial support mechanisms confirms the preceding reasoning from the purposive perspective. One of the essential tools securing the stability of the Economic and Monetary Union was the no-bailout rule which forced the Member States to maintain budgetary discipline by prohibiting fiscal transfers (Mezyk 2018). However, as the system failed in 2009, in the *Pringle case* (2012) the Court has functionally interpreted the no-bailout rule and allowed extraordinary financial mechanisms. These mechanisms were to operate as long as they were consistent with the overarching goal of fostering the stability of the Eurozone. Thus, the Court functionally interpreted a mean (no-bailout rule) to an end (stability of the Eurozone) and allowed measures which contradicted the prohibitions of financial transfers. *Mutatis mutandis*, the principle of autonomy (mean) should not prevent the Member States from implementing measures aiming at protecting the legal order of the EU (end).

The competence from Article 7 TEU

Before discussing the specific measures which can be undertaken in reaction to the rogue state, we need to consider the role of Art. 7 TEU as a procedural norm. Read in the light of the principle of autonomy of EU law, Art. 7 appears to be the only way in which the EU can react to the rogue Member State, apart from the judgements of the ECJ issued when the rogue Member State breaches a specific norm of the EU law. However, this assumption is too hasty if we take into account the fact that Art. 7 TEU is a specialised procedure foreseeing cooperation within the EU, and not a competence of the EU in the understanding of Art. 3 or 4 TFEU. Accordingly, the provision does not exclude different ways of reacting on a breach of the principles of the EU by one of its Member States.

Art. 7 does not create competence to regulate any area of EU law but provides a procedure to counteract the violations of the general principles of the Union. The procedure is similar to actions in which the EU supports, coordinates or supplements the Member

States 'without thereby superseding their competence in these areas' (Art. 2 (5) TFEU). To illustrate it with an example, if one of the Member States conducts ethnic cleansing of its minorities and thus violates the human rights and the rule of law, obviously the other Member States can – and should – act against it irrespectively of the procedure from Art. 7 TEU. In its actions against the rogue State, the other Member State can either follow the way of retortions (the Austrian model) or countermeasures.

Retortions and the Austrian model

In the year 2000, Jörg Haider's rightist Freedom Party formed the Austrian government with the conservatives and caused angst among the EU Member States (Cramer, Wrange 2001). Already in the phase of negotiating the coalition, the other 14 Member States issued a statement threatening Austria with a set of three sanctions: not promoting or accepting any bilateral official contacts at the political level with an Austrian Government integrating the Austrian Freedom Party; not supporting Austrian candidates seeking positions in international organisations; and receiving Austrian Ambassadors in EU capitals only at a technical level (Portuguese Presidency 2000). These actions by the 14 took place in a space between the European Union and international law. On one side, no European institution participated in the steps, and the Commission was not informed about the sanctions before announcing them (Cramer, Wrange 2001). On the other side, the sanctions were announced by the presidency of the EU with reference to the European project and its values The content of the sanctions did not breach European law because the European Treaties do not contain obligations regarding the policies of international political contacts, nor regarding supporting candidates of a specific nationality (Merlingen, Mudde, Sedelmeier 2001). Consequently, the pressure exercised on Austria did not constitute a countermeasure (a *prima facie* illegal act) but merely a legal retortion (unfriendly but legal measure), both from the perspective of European and international law (Cramer, Wrange 2001).

Although it seems that the retortions from the Austrian model offer the least problematic reaction to the actions of the rogue state, their efficiency is doubtful. Because they necessarily fall outside the scope of the EU law, their impact is limited to issues not covered by the four freedoms and the regulations establishing the common market which forms the core of the Union. Consequently, no measures such as affecting trade or travels can be imposed on a rogue Member State, and the allowed actions would most likely be insufficient.

Countermeasures

Countermeasures are measures undertaken by states as a response to an internationally wrongful act. *Prima facie* unlawful, the acts constituting countermeasures are justified because of their relation to the wrong which they seek to rectify (Paddeu, 2015). Countermeasures are regulated in the Draft Articles on Responsibility of States for Internationally Wrongful Acts (2001, 'ASR') which reflect the customary international law. The ASR regulate the use of countermeasures in bilateral relations only. However, the use of countermeasures in multilateral relations and their status of customary international law remains an open question, with convincing voices acknowledging the legality of such measures (Dawidowicz, 2006).

Art. 50 (2) (a) and Art. 55 ASR indicate the subsidiary character of the ASR, which excludes the regulation from direct application in the context of the EU. Whereas Art. 55 ASR generally stipulates that ASR do not apply where special rules of international law are present, Art. 50 (2) ASR gives precedence to the rules of dispute settlement agreed by the parties of a particular Treaty. In this light, the European Treaties foresee a procedure to be applied when a

Member State breaches European law, and the case-law of the ECJ prohibits a unilateral application of countermeasures consisting in a breach of the EU law. Thus, the EU is a self-contained legal regime (Dörr, Schmalenbach 2012, 70) and contains rules applicable to breach of its law.

On the other hand, the Treaties do not foresee a situation in which a Member State effectively repudiates the Treaties and does not acknowledge the outcome of the agreed dispute settlement procedure. Thus, the system has a regulatory gap. Art. 7 TEU is politically paralysed in practice; the Treaty infringement procedures do not cover a case in which a Member State challenges the binding force of the ECJ judgements. This challenge leads to an absurd situation which the European Treaties do not offer a solution for. Remaining on the level of the Treaties only, the Court could only multiply its sanctioning judgements and fines against the rogue State. However, such a multiplication will not bring much should the rogue Member State declare the decisions to be *ultra vires*.

Consequently, in a case of a rogue Member State, the mentioned instruments from the Treaties (Art. 7 TEU, infringement procedures) should preclude any other measures and maintain the principle of autonomy only to a limited extent. This limit stops working when a Member State no longer retains its commitment to European law and respects the mechanisms sanctioning it. The principle of autonomy blocks reciprocity only as long, as the mutual trust between the Member States exists and justifies the abolishment of reciprocity. Consequently, when the rogue Member State disrespects the mutual trust, the other Member States can no longer be limited to using Art 7 TEU and the infringement procedures only.

Seen from another angle, if a Member State rejects the judgements of the ECJ and openly violates the principles of the Union, it rejects the legal system created by the Treaties as a whole. Because the principle of autonomy is built on the Treaties and safeguards them, when the rogue member state repudiates the Treaties, it also repudiates the principle of autonomy of EU law and the reciprocal waiver of countermeasures based on mutual trust of the Member States. Hence, the general mechanisms of international law may be used. These could include suspending the application of parts of the European treaties in relation to Poland or Hungary.

Vienna Convention on the Law of Treaties

Because Romania and France are not signatories to the Vienna Convention on the Law of Treaties (1969, VCLT), the Convention cannot directly apply to the Treaties (Aust 2019). However, as the VCLT reflects customary international law, its provisions can be used as such. Although the ECJ is cautious in referring to the VCLT and has not expressly confirmed its status concerning the Treaties, the Court has on numerous occasions used the Convention to strengthen its argumentation in the area of international law and confirmed its status as customary international law (Sanchez-Bordona 2018, *Racke* 2018). Recently, the Court has referred to the VCLT in its judgement in the case *Wightman* (2018) , concerning Brexit regulations, where it confirmed its interpretation of Art. 50 TEU, according to which a Member State may revoke its notification of withdrawal from the EU. The Court did this by pointing out that the VCLT 'was taken into account in the preparatory work for the Treaty establishing a Constitution for Europe' from which Art. 50 TEU is derived. In this light, the VCLT may be used, among others, to fill the gaps left by the EU law (Ziegler 2016, 44-45).

The VCLT constitutes a subsidiary legal regime, whose norms are applicable if the parties to a treaty do not regulate specific issues differently or leave some questions unaddressed (Art. 5 VCLT). Art. 60 VCLT regulates the legal regime surrounding the breach of an international agreement and is recognised as a reflection of customary international law (Dörr, Schmalenbach 2012, 87). However,

Art. 60 (4) VCLT states that the regulation of the consequences of the breach of an international agreement is 'without prejudice to any provision in the treaty applicable in the event of a breach.' In the case of the EU, such provisions could be Art. 7 TEU and Art. 258 – 260 TFEU. However, the same argumentation as in the case of countermeasures applies and weakens this subsidiarity (see above point 5).

Not recognising the judgements of the ECJ amounts to a repudiation of European Treaties according to Art. 60 (3) a VCLT and constitutes a material breach of the Treaties. This is because the ECJ is empowered by the Treaties to declare the content of the European law and the Member States have no competence to challenge the decisions of the Court. At the same time, disrespecting the principles of the Union is a 'violation of a provision essential to the accomplishment of the object or purpose of the treaty' (Art. 60 (3) b VCLT) because of the fundamental role these principles play in the legal system of the EU as the values on which the Union is 'founded' (Art. 2 TEU). Consequently, the situation from Art. 60 para 2 VCLT is realised, according to which a material breach of a multilateral treaty by one of the parties entitles the other parties to undertake one of the three possible actions linked to this circumstance. The first option (Art. 60 para. 2 c VCLT) – unanimous agreement of other parties to a treaty to suspend or terminate the treaty in relation to the party in breach – is not viable because the rogue Member State receives political support from at least one other member of the EU. The second, and the most viable, option authorises 'a party specially affected by the breach to invoke it as a ground for suspending the operation of the treaty in whole or in part in the relations between itself and the defaulting State' (Art. 60 para. 2 b VCLT). In this respect, all Member States could be seen as 'specially affected' because the actions of the rogue State affect the very core of the community's legal system and the rogue State exposes the citizens of other State to lawless treatment. Consequently, all Member States would be authorised to suspend or terminate the Treaties in relation to the rogue Member State. The third option (Art. 60 para. 2 c VCLT) influences the legal relationship between the invoking State and the multilateral treaty regime (non-performance) and is not suitable for targeting the breach of the Treaties by a different Member State.

Procedural aspects of the extension of autonomy

The independence of the European legal order and the principle of autonomy imply that the described use of the means of international law should be incorporated into the European system as much as possible and that their use should be allowed only to the strictly necessary extent. This means that the Member States should make a proportional use of the competencies stemming from international law and shape their measures in such a way, that they remain a mean to safeguard the European legal system and do not threaten it.

The use of the ECJ would uphold the procedural autonomy of the EU and protect it from an anarchical use of the means of international law. A judgement of the ECJ would thus authorise the use of retortions, countermeasures or the mechanisms from the VCLT by the other Member states. The functioning of the Court in this context would be consistent with the regulation from Art. 344 TFEU, according to which the Member States should not submit a dispute concerning the interpretation or application of the Treaties to any method of settlement other than those provided for therein.

The ECJ could be involved in legitimising the countermeasures or the use of VCLT on multiple ways. As indicated in the introduction, in the case of the rogue Member State, the ECJ would have issued a judgement which would have been ignored or openly challenged by the Member State. This would lead to the use of the sanctioning procedure from Art. 260 (2) TFEU in which the Court decides about the means to be taken in relation to a Member State which fails to implement the judgements of the ECJ. This procedure may be repeated, 'stacking up' the judgements in which the Commission would seek the Court to issue a judgment sanctioning the failure to obey a judgement which sanctioned the failure to obey a judgement etc. The content of one of the consecutive judgments could authorise the EU or the Member States to implement measures from the area of international law.

Conclusion

The recourse to international law to react to the actions of a rogue Member State exceeds the 'comfort-zone' of the European legal system. The creators of the Union have assumed that the Member States would sincerely cooperate for the benefit of the European project. Consequently, they have not equipped the Treaties with a mechanism to be applied when the laws and procedures of the EU are openly disrespected. In such circumstances, the principle of autonomy of EU law needs to be interpreted functionally, thus permitting the recourse to measures which could be effective in counteracting the decomposition of the EU. If applied proportionally, and possibly close to the Treaties, such measures could offer a viable option of saving the Union from failure.

References

A. K. and Others v Sąd Najwyższy (2019), Joined Cases C-585/18, C-624/18 and C-625/18, EU:C:2019:982.

A. Racke GmbH & Co. v Hauptzollamt Mainz (1998), Case no. C-162/96, EU:C:1998:293.

Aust, A (2006), 'Vienna Convention on the Law of Treaties (1969)' in Rudiger Wolfrum (ed) *The Max Planck Encyclopedia of public international law*, Oxford University Press, Oxford, 709-714.

Bundesverfassungsgericht, 2 Senat. (2020), Judgment of the Second Senate of 05 May 2020.

Commission of the European Communities v French Republic (1978), Case no. 232/78, EU:C:1979:215 ('Mutton and lamb case').

Commission of the European Communities v Ireland (2006), Case no. C-459/03, EU:C:2006:345 ('Mox Plant').

Cramér, P & Wrange, P (2001), 'The Haider affair, law and European integration', *Faculty of Law, Stockholm University Research Paper*, no. 19.

Dawidowicz, M (2017), *Third-Party Countermeasures in International Law* (vol. 131). Cambridge University Press, Cambridge.

Dörr O & K Schmalenbach (2012), Article 60. Termination or suspension of the operation of a treaty as a consequence of its breach, in: Dörr O., Schmalenbach K. (eds) *Vienna Convention on the Law of Treaties*. Springer, Berlin, Heidelberg.

European Communities v Federal Republic of Germany (1984), Case no. 325/82, EU:C:1984:60.

Flaminio Costa v E.N.E.L. (1964), Case no. 6-64, EU:C:1964:66.

International Law Commission, Draft Articles on Responsibility of States for Internationally Wrongful Acts, November 2001, Supplement No. 10 (A/56/10).

Internationale Handelsgesellschaft mbH v Einfuhr – und Vorratsstelle für Getreide und Futtermittel (1970), Case no. 11-70, EU:C:1970:114.

Merlingen, M, Mudde, C & Sedelmeier, U (2001), 'The right and the righteous? European norms, domestic politics and the sanctions against Austria'. *JCMS: Journal of Common Market Studies*, vol. 39, no. 1, 59-77.

Mężyk R (2018) *Die EU und die Finanzkrise*, Springer, Wiesbaden.

NV Algemene Transport-en Expeditie Onderneming van Gend & Loos v Netherlands Inland Revenue Administration (1963), Case no. 26-62, EU:C:1963:1.

Opinion 1/09 (2011), European Court Reports 2011 I-01137, EU:C:2011:123.

Opinion of Advocate General Campos Sanchez-Bordona (2018), Case no. C-621/18, EU:C:2018:978.

Paddeu F (2015), Countermeasures, in: Wolfrum, R. & Max-Planck-Institut für Ausländisches Öffentliches Recht und Völkerrecht, 2008. *Max Planck encyclopedia of public international law.*

Phelan, W (2012), 'What is sui generis about the European Union? Costly international cooperation in a self-contained regime', *International Studies Review*, vol. 14, no. 3, 367-385.

Portuguese Presidency (2000), Statement from the Portuguese presidency of the EU on behalf of XIV member states, Lisbon, 31 January 2000, http:// ec.europa.eu/dorie/fileDownload.do;jsessionid=Ng8KStTVk5CvsXhnJG cm4q8Rry89P6cT8bs35h08fhpvFPssDYGc!1615003456?docId=84237& cardId=84237.

Sadurski, W (2019), *Poland's Constitutional Breakdown*. Oxford University Press, Oxford.

Thomas Pringle v Government of Ireland and Others (2012), Case no. C370/12, EU:C:2012:756.

Van Rossem, JWW (2013), 'The autonomy of EU law: More is less? in 'Between Autonomy and Dependence: The EU Legal Order under the Influence of International Organisations', Sense Publishers, 13-46.

Vidmar, J (2019), Unilateral Revocability in Wightman: Fixing Article 50 with Constitutional Tools, ECJ 10 December 2018, Case C-621/18, Andy Wightman and Others v Secretary of State for Exiting the European Union. *European Constitutional Law Review*, pp.1-17.

Vienna Convention on the Law of Treaties (1969), United Nations Treaty Series, vol. 1155, 331, opened for signature 23 May 1969, entered into force 27 January 1980.

Yassin Abdullah Kadi and Al Barakaat International Foundation v Council of the European Union and Commission of the European Communities (2005), Case no. C-402/05 P and C-415/05 P, European Court Reports 2008 I-06351, EU:C:2008:461.

Ziegler, KS (2016), 'The relationship between EU law and international law' in Patterson D. and Sodersten A (eds), *A Companion to European Union Law and International Law*, Wiley Blackwell, New Jersey.

8

THE CHANGING FACE OF EUROPEAN SECURITY

Rita Parker

Keywords: Europe Project, Security, Liberal Democracy, Climate, Refugees, Populism, Political Extremism

Abstract

Europe has experienced conflict, war, and the rise and fall of regimes over centuries and each of these events has influenced security in subsequent times. Following the devastation of two World Wars, an initiative emerged that has subsequently shaped Europe, liberal democratic values and its history today. The Europe project was the foundation for the future of European peace and stability and the project has faced challenges as the nature of security risks and threats have changed.

This chapter examines ways in which the changing face of security in Europe has enabled or inhibited the Europe project and it analyses ways in which the existential crises within and beyond the Union affect its future security. Set within its historic context of security risks and threats, contemporary security issues are considered from three perspectives. First, in terms of Europe's strategic security relationships, secondly, internal challenges of political extremism and racism, and thirdly risks and threats that do not recognise sovereign borders that are referred to as 'problems without passports'.

Introduction

Examination of the changing face of European security is set within its historic context of European contemporary security challenges. Against the introductory background, three perspectives of Europe's security are examined with the goal of determining whether the Europe project has been enabled or inhibited. The first area considers Europe's external strategic security relationships. This is followed by examination of the drivers and forms of political extremism within Europe. The third area examined relates to risks and threats that do not recognise sovereign borders and are referred to as 'problems without passports'. Analysis of these existential risks and threats includes identification of ways in which Europe has sought to counter those challenges. This methodological approach provides insights into the development of the Europe project and the resilience of the liberal democratic model.

Europe's twenty-first century contemporary security challenges are set within their historic context, and the pivotal aspirations of political visionary Robert Schuman regarding the Europe project. Against this background it is possible to analyse whether liberal democracy has been enabled or inhibited by changing security challenges. Europe's understanding of, and approach to, security in the twenty-first century has been shaped over the centuries by an evolving geostrategic environment marked by different existential risks and threats including past conflicts, wars, and the rise and fall of political leaders, regimes and empires. After the destruction and devastation of two world wars, European leaders sought a way forward that would enable future peace and security. Among the most significant outcome of these experiences was the Europe project. Like a phoenix arising from the ashes, the Europe project emerged from the devastation of the Second World War. Since its inception, the Europe project as proposed by Robert Schuman meant that 'Europe will not be made all at once, or according to a single plan. It will be built through concrete achievements which first create a de facto solidarity' (Schuman, 1950). With the aim of a more united and peaceful Europe to achieve a 'de facto solidarity', the Europe project sought to build security and, initially, it developed democracy and the rules-based order within Europe's borders. But the emergence of new challenges has required constant review and innovation in security policies and strategies that reflect these changes and the role of the European Union as a global actor in the twenty-first century.

The Europe Project

Following the end of the Second World War, the nations of Europe were struggling to overcome the devastation of the war and five years after it ended European leaders were determined to prevent another such destructive war. This determination resulted in the Declaration by French statesman Robert Schuman in 1950 which stated in part that 'the pooling of coal and steel production should immediately provide for the setting up of common foundations for economic development as a first step in the federation of Europe, and will change the destinies of those regions which have long been devoted to the manufacture of munitions of war, of which they have been the most constant victims' (Schuman, 1950). The underlying rationale was that combining economic interests would help improve living standards and be a positive step towards a more united and peaceful Europe. As a result, the European Coal and Steel Community (ECSC) was formally established in 1951 by the Treaty of Paris, which was signed by six nations – Belgium, France, Italy, Luxembourg, the Netherlands and West Germany, with membership of the ECSC open to other European countries.

The post 1945 arrangement that established the Europe project has operated in various guises since that time and effectively made Europe dependent on US protection for its security. This was coupled with US financial, political and economic support for Western

Europe that upheld democratic values and the rules based international order and provided the architecture for multilateral institutions. In the post-war period, Western Europe, together with other nations such as the US and Australia, led the creation of the United Nations. Further collaborative efforts resulted in the establishment of the World Bank, the International Monetary Fund and the General Agreement on Tariffs and Trade, the forerunner of the World Trade Organisation. The European project for greater unity was encouraged and aided by the US as were the creation of the European Coal and Steel Community, the Treaty of Rome in 1957, the Treaty on European Union (or Maastricht Treaty) in 1992, the entry into force of the European single market in 1993, and the adoption of the euro (Wickett, 2018).

1.2 The Cold War

While the 1951 Paris Agreement helped the process to stabilise Europe, the Cold War meant that European allies continued to experience uncertainty and insecurity. Instead of focusing primarily on building peace, security and prosperity, they were required to focus on the strategic threat posed by the Soviet Union. The Cold War period was one of tense nuclear standoffs, proxy wars, and internal repression which were ideologically grounded – basically communism versus democracy. It was a time when the key concept of security was 'the security dilemma' which was defined as the situation in which 'the means by which a state tries to increase its security decreases the security of others' (Jervis, 1978). The Cold War was a period of several conflicts, the most notable were the Berlin Blockade in the late 1940s (1948-49), the Korean War in the 1950s (1950-53), and in the 1960s there was the Berlin Crisis (1961) and the Cuban Missile Crisis (1962). The Vietnam or 'American' War, as it is known in Vietnam, which lasted sixteen years to 1975, was followed in 1979 by the Soviet War in Afghanistan which lasted a decade.

1.3 The European Union

The end of the twentieth century was marked by the collapse of the Soviet Union and, in effect, the end of the Cold War. It also marked a new stage of the Europe project namely, the establishment of the European Union in 1993. Since that time the EU has grown through its program of integration, expanding to fifteen member states in 1995. At that time, Austria, Finland and Sweden joined Germany, France, Italy, the Netherlands, Belgium, Luxembourg, Denmark, Ireland, UK, Greece, Spain and Portugal as member states. That expansion meant the EU covered almost the whole of Western Europe. In 2004, the Union was further expanded to include Cyprus, Czech Republic, Estonia, Hungary, Latvia, Lithuania, Malta, Poland, Slovakia, and Slovenia. Three years later in 2007, Bulgaria and Romania joined the EU and Croatia joined in 2013 bringing the total membership to twenty-eight. The UK subsequently left the EU in 2020 after a referendum in 2016 which ended its forty-seven year formal membership association with Europe.

The above brief exposition of Europe's past security issues provides an historic context for examination of contemporary security challenges in the following sections. As will be shown, the issues examined below strained the 'de facto solidarity' aspiration first mooted in 1950 by Robert Schuman. Indeed, the very concept of solidarity and integration brought challenges to Europe and, in many cases, led to forms of political extremism that have tested the fundamental principles and values of the liberal democratic model that underpin the Europe project.

The remaining sections of this chapter address contemporary existential crises within and beyond the European Union within an increasingly complex geostrategic environment. Following a exposition of contemporary security challenges, specific issues are examined. First, Europe's critical relationships, namely with NATO, UK, US, Russia and China. In doing so the section sets out that those relationships are necessary for the future of European security, peace and well-being. The second section addresses internal security issues with a focus on forms of political extremism. The final section examines critical risks and threats that can be regarded as 'problems without passports'.

Contemporary security challenges

The beginning of the twenty-first century was marked by acts of extreme terrorism that caused nations across the globe to reassess their approach to security. It meant a significant shift in thinking and approach whereby there was no single 'threat', instead the threat became multidimensional. The strategic order and the nature of conflict changed, the world became a place of enhanced geostrategic complexity and dynamic change. Globalisation underscores that such changes occur in an interlinked way where security risks and threats can no longer be considered in isolation. The situation in the twenty-first century is further compounded by complex trade relationships and dependencies, energy supplies and vulnerabilities, technologies, complex nongeographic threats, as well as changing population mix due to regular and irregular migration flows, infectious diseases, and the fragility of nation states. Large numbers of displaced people are driven by conflict, climate change and natural disasters that affect food and water supplies as well as by seeking secure and safe places to live (Parker, 2018). Europe today is a microcosm of these global security issues where the EU and its member states face several complex security threats that are often compounded by the actions of external actors. Security risks and threats are becoming more varied and more international as well as increasingly cross-border and crosssectorial in nature. The EU integration process has also brought its own challenges. As such, many security risks are linked and these need to be considered as part of a complex interrelated system, not in isolation from each other. A confluence of risks and threats undermines the democratic values and principles and the rules based international order that reflect the EU.

As a result, today, perhaps more than any other previous decade, there is a pressing imperative for a shared strategic vision for the future security of Europe as a whole and for individual nations where their sovereignty is respected, and where the EU can be an effective geopolitical actor. The challenges of security in Europe today are multidimensional and complex in a more contested world where contestation is playing out in the global and regional strategic, economic and political spheres. Europe faces existential threats within and beyond its borders including strengthened extreme left- and right-wing actors, increasing authoritarian regimes, new hybrid warfare security threats, non-geographic threats, and risks and threats arising from non-state actors including rising anti-Semitism, violent Islamist terrorism and cyber attacks. The decision by the UK to leave the EU, and Europe's relations with some non-European nations are additional potential existential threats.

These more complex and inter-related security challenges have also required a change in security thinking which has led to a broader and more comprehensive approach to security which the EU has attempted to reflect in its various foreign and security policies over time. Yet, it was not until 2003 that the leaders of the EU approved the first ever European Security Strategy (ESS), proclaiming an intention to 'share in the responsibility for global security and in building a better world' (General Secretariat of the Council, 2003). This occurred amidst tensions in the lead-up to the Iraq war. The decision by the US to go to war in Iraq resulted in the US at odds with key European allies and NATO. The ESS was reviewed in 2008 with the intention of updating it but Britain and Germany opposed any new strategy and there were concerns that a new ESS would complicate implementation of the Lisbon Treaty that was finally passed in 2009 (Toje, 2010).

Although under challenge from several external and internal sources, the EU has a strong history of democratic politics, support for the rules based international order, market economy, and social welfare orientation that support peace and security. Its achievements were recognised in 2012 when the EU was awarded the Nobel Peace Prize for advancing the causes of peace, reconciliation, democracy and human rights in Europe. Nonetheless, the challenges remain, and new ones continue to emerge which challenge the democratic model and put at risk ongoing peace, stability and security in the EU and, implicitly, globally.

Under the Common Security and Defence Policy (CSDP) the EU relies on ad hoc forces contributed by member states for joint disarmament operations, humanitarian and rescue tasks, military advice and assistance, conflict prevention and peacekeeping, and crisis management. The European Security Agenda adopted in 2015 set out the Union's strategy to address security threats in the EU for the period 2015-2020. Recognising that member states have the front-line responsibility for security, the Agenda was an attempt to support the member states in ensuring security noting that they can no longer succeed fully on their own (European Commission, 2015). This was followed by the European Union's Global Strategy (EUGS) released in 2016 which argued that the world needs 'a strong European Union like never before. It is what our citizens deserve and what the wider world expects' (European Union, 2016).

In the spirit of the Europe project, the EU joint foreign and security policy is aspirational as it seeks to preserve peace, strengthen international security, promote international cooperation, and to develop and consolidate democracy, the rule of law and respect for human rights and fundamental freedoms. This joint policy is designed to resolve conflicts and foster international understanding based on diplomacy and respect for international rules (European Union, 2019). It was carefully structured and developed over several years with the unanimous agreement of all its member states at the time. The 2016 EU Global Strategy noted earlier called for such unity in the face of 'existential crisis within and beyond the Union'. It was the same year that the UK voted to leave the European Union and Donald Trump was elected President of the US. 2016 was a year of other notable events that would have far reaching consequences for European and global security, such as: the failed attempt by a faction of Turkish troops to overthrow the increasingly authoritarian President Recep Tayyip Erdogan; the humanitarian crisis deepened in Syria with the fall of Aleppo; Russia allegedly interfered in the US Presidential election; Rodrigo Duterte was elected President of the Philippines with just thirty-nine percent of the vote; North Korea conducted its fourth nuclear test; Iran severed international relations with Saudi Arabia; and major terrorist attacks occurred in Nice, Brussels, Lahore and Orlando (Lindsay, 2016).

While the Global Strategy may represent an aspirational expression of the EU standing united in facing the challenges and opportunities presented by the wider world (EEAS, 2016), it also reflects the reality of those existential crises within and beyond the EU.

Europe and Strategic Relations

As Europe heads towards the middle of the twenty-first century there is greater recognition that its security relies on maintaining stable strategic relationships. In this section, five such critical relationships associated with the future security of the EU - namely with NATO, UK, US, Russia, and China - are examined regarding how they enable or inhibit the Europe project and implicitly liberal democratic values.

3.1 Europe and NATO

The relationship between the EU and NATO has never been straightforward but there is a growing recognition that enhanced cooperation is a necessity in light of growing security challenges. NATO Secretary General Jens Sternberg (Stoltenberg, 2020) in his speech in January 2020 noted three key challenges to be faced by NATO and the EU. First, terrorism; secondly, Russia; and thirdly, emerging challenges such as technology, artificial intelligence, autonomous weapon platforms, and big data. With such priority areas in mind, NATO with at least fifteen NATO member countries and two partner nations scheduled exercise 'Europe Defender 2020', a joint, multinational training exercise from April to May 2020 with personnel and equipment movements occurring from February through July 2020. It was the third-largest military exercise in Europe since the Cold War with the exercise involving wide-spanning manoeuvres focused on the Baltic States, Poland and Georgia (Judson, 2019). Each of these areas has had a strained and complex relationship with Russia over many years and are examined below.

3.1.1. Poland

Poland was occupied by Soviet Russia at the beginning of the Second World War, and the Baltic States were under Soviet rule until 1991. All subsequently became EU member states in 2004. At the time of the Soviet occupation of Poland, it also annexed parts of Eastern Poland that remained part of the Soviet Union after the war and are still part of modern Belarus and Ukraine today. In 2008 during a meeting in Tbilisi, Polish President Lech Kaczyński delivered what can be regarded as a 'geopolitical prophecy' regarding the aggressive foreign policy of Putin's Russia. The President argued that Georgia was the first of the victims but later the Russian tanks could appear, in an order of succession, in Ukraine, the Baltic States and finally in Poland. The Polish President later died together with his wife, eighteen parliamentarians, ten generals and admirals representing Poland's top military leadership, and many other political notables, in the Smolensk air disaster on Russian territory in April 2010 at Katyn (Bielanski, 2017). The Polish President and his delegation had been *en route* to Katyn, a site near Smolensk, to commemorate the 22,000 Polish officers who were executed seventy years earlier, between 3 April and 11 May 1940. Poland joined NATO in 1999 and took part in exercise Europe Defender 2020.

3.1.2. Baltic countries

Throughout modern history, the Baltic countries have been under Russian rule, first as provinces of the Russian empire and then, after independence in the interwar period as Soviet republics – rather than simply as countries of the 'Eastern Bloc', like most other countries in Central and Eastern Europe. Until the early 1990s all three Baltic republics hosted former Red Army troops, together with various Soviet-era military installations ranging from a nuclear submarine training facility in Estonia to a large anti-ballistic missile radar in Latvia. It was not until 1995 that the Russian army left the Baltic States. Although all three Baltic States declared their independence from the Soviet Union the situation in those countries was unstable and unpredictable with Russia implementing both direct and indirect military, political, and economic pressure. In that environment, the Baltic States were striving to establish a national defence system in order to exercise full sovereignty over their territories. Initially they adopted a policy of neutrality, which subsequently changed to become more clearly oriented towards integration into Western security structures and the implementation of common European principles (Urbelis, 2003). In 2002 the Baltic nations applied for membership of NATO and the EU. All three became NATO members and joined the EU in 2004. The Baltic States are currently the only former Soviet states to have joined either organisation. The Russian annexation of the Crimea in 2014 increased disquiet in the Baltic States which resulted in NATO stationed battalions in Estonia, Latvia and Lithuania (Chemla, 2019).

3.1.3. Georgia

The third area of focus in Exercise Europe Defender 2020 is Georgia, which has experienced a strained relationship since it gained independence after the collapse of the Soviet Union. Following the election of Vladimir Putin in Russia in 2000 and a pro-Western change of power in Georgia in 2003, relations between Russia and Georgia began to deteriorate, reaching a full diplomatic crisis by April 2008. At that time, Russian forces crossed into Georgia and occupied several cities and held those areas beyond the ceasefire. This was the first war in history in which cyber warfare coincided with military action. An information war was also waged during and after the conflict. The EU played a significant role in negotiating a ceasefire agreement in August of that year when Nicolas Sarkozy, the President of France, held the presidency of the EU. But since the war, Russia has occupied Abkhazia and South Ossetia in violation of the ceasefire agreement of August 2008 (North, 2015). A 2015 report by the Committee on Foreign Affairs of the European Parliament stated that 'the reaction of the EU to Russia's aggression towards, and violation of the territorial integrity of, Georgia in 2008 may have encouraged Russia to act in a similar way in Ukraine' (Committee on Foreign Affairs, 2015).

3.2. Europe and the UK

Maintenance of the EU relationship with allies such as the UK is imperative. After forty-seven years of formal association with Europe, the UK is no longer a member of the European Union or a full partner in all European security operations, but it remains a member of NATO and took part in exercise Europe Defender 2020 noted above. The UK's withdrawal from the EU occurred at a time of geopolitical change in the global environment, and so it is even more important to consider the impact of the UK's withdrawal for the future of European geopolitics and security. The importance of the relationship has been recognised from the UK side. Former director general of the Security Service from 2007 to 2013, Lord Jonathan Evans, said in October 2019 that it was 'absolutely vital' to retain ties with Europol and the EU countries. He noted, 'I find it very hard to see any security upside from Brexit. It seems to me that our task is to minimise the downside,' adding that Britain's 'security interests remain international and globalised, because that's where the threats come from' (Dearden, 2019). The UK departure means it leaves the EU's common foreign and defence policies (CFSP and CSDP). But both sides recognise that they face a series of common security challenges and threats, that close links are vital and that cooperation in these areas does not, and should not, end completely.

But the UK departure meant it automatically lost access to EU databases such as the Schengen Information System (SIS) which is a governmental database maintained by the European Commission. The SIS is used by thirty European countries to find information about individuals and entities for the purposes of national security, border control and law enforcement. The significance of this loss of access was recognised in a 2018 UK House of Commons Report, 'Without UK access to SIS II, individuals who pose a genuine threat will be able to enter the UK or the EU without important intelligence being flagged to border officials. Losing access to it would be a calamitous outcome for the UK, which would pose a severe threat to the Government's ability to prevent serious crime and secure the border effectively, but it is an increasingly likely prospect' (House of Commons Home Affairs Committee, 2018). Such systems rely on collaboration and effective sharing of information and they are vital for ongoing security, as such, a sustained relationship between the UK and Europe is mutually beneficial.

3.3. Europe and USA

The third critical relationship for the future of European security is with the US. The US and European economies are deeply entwined. The EU accounts for approximately one-fifth of total US trade in goods and services, and the US and the EU are each other's largest source and destination for foreign direct investment. The US-European economy generates US$5 trillion a year in foreign affiliate sales and directly employs over 9 million workers on both sides of the Atlantic. As noted earlier, Europe has a longstanding relationship with the US but since the 2016 election of Donald Trump as US President, the US has recalibrated its relations with traditional allies, including the EU, under its 'America First' foreign policy.

But as often happens, politicians deliver different messages to their domestic political support base and to those elsewhere. For example, while public statements by US President Trump were critical of Europe and NATO, the US deployed 20,000 troops directly from the US to Europe as part of exercise Europe Defender 2020 referred to earlier. This is significant because it is the largest deployment of US forces since the end of the Cold War (Judson, 2019). As noted in the Trump Administration's 2017 *National Security Strategy* 'the United States is safer when Europe is prosperous and stable, and can help defend our shared interests and ideals' (Congressional Research Service, 2019). But tensions remain, such as the US withdrawal from the Intermediate-Range Nuclear Forces (INF) Treaty, its decision to withdraw from the 2015 multilateral nuclear deal with Iran as well as from the Paris Agreement on climate change. At the very least, the relationship between the EU and US is complicated but it has a sound historic basis of cooperation, partnership and alliance. These areas of mutual interest and shared values may help it endure as a necessary element for the future of European security and the Europe project.

3.4. Europe and Russia

Russia continues to be a critical strategic relationship for the EU, although that relationship is strained at times given the EU has expanded its membership to include former Russian states, and the NATO policy towards Russia. Russia's newfound foreign policy assertiveness seen through the 2008 war with Georgia and annexation of its territories, its annexation of Crimea and invasion of eastern Ukraine in 2014, and cyber-attacks on neighbours, have tested that relationship. Russia's increasing collaboration with China on mutual projects has also raised concerns within Europe (Parker, 2020). The delicate situation of the Baltic States with its Russian neighbour was highlighted in 2007 when Estonia was subjected to a wave of cyber attacks because the government relocated the Bronze Soldier monument dedicated to the Red Army, provoking the anger of the Russian minority and a diplomatic crisis with Moscow.

Exercise Europe Defender 2020 noted above has reportedly caused Russia's leadership to react warily (McDermott, 2020). Russia's political-military leadership frequently criticise NATO for its enlargement and for staging military exercises close to Russian borders. This pattern has intensified since Russia's intervention in Ukraine and the subsequent downturn in its relations with the US, the EU and their allies. While Russia may not want a full confrontation with Europe, if it continues to pursue its antagonistic foreign policy and to modernise its military, the future peace and security of the EU may be jeopardised.

3.5. Europe and China

The final strategic relationship in this category is China which has become an increasing security concern for the EU. China's aggressive moves to gain a strategic foothold in several European states through its One Belt One Road Initiative (BRI), and its increasing technological prowess mean the EU needs to take a long term strategic approach to its relationship with China. The BRI was initially seen as an opportunity for European economic recovery after the Eurozone crises, but the BRI has prompted new concerns. A wider understanding has developed within Europe that while the BRI promises global development, it also implicitly includes challenges, including security challenges. Since 2012 with the '16+1' platform, China has garnered eleven new EU member states and five candidate countries. Since then, three other EU countries, Greece (August 2018), Portugal (January 2019), and Italy (April 2019) have signed as members of the BRI.

China's Maritime Silk road is integral to its BRI, and Greece and Italy have become part of the strategic network. While China has made significant calculated developments with individual European nations, the EU has not achieved increased access to Chinese markets, despite many years of insistence. Of concern is Chinese influence that has extended to EU governance and implicitly the principles of democracy and the rule of law. The EU attempt in April 2019 to implement a new mechanism to screen Chinese investments in strategic areas across Europe, resulted in Italy abstaining from a vote on such a mechanism (Zeneli, 2019). An additional existential threat to the EU is the relationship between China and Russia who are increasingly acting collaboratively. Their relationship is based on the shared mutual interest of seeking to advance against the democratic model and rules based international order, values that are the foundation of the EU and the Europe project.

The five relationships discussed above are just some of the strategic security issues that are a cause of concern in the twenty-first century that emphasise the imperative for a shared EU strategic vision for future security if Schuman's aspirations for the Europe project are to be fulfilled. Europe needs to defend its technological sovereignty, while investing in new industries. Defence research, industry cooperation, the development of high-end capabilities are all aspects of those relationships that are necessary for the future of European security, peace and well-being.

Internal Security Issues

Under the Europe project, states moved towards and embraced the liberal democratic model with its shared common characteristics of free and open elections, universal suffrage, political freedom, the rule of law, separation of powers, and the protection of the rights and freedoms of individuals. Yet, in the twenty-first century liberal democracies across Europe are being challenged politically, economically and socially and this potentially weakens the resilience of this governance model and, ultimately, the Europe project. There is increasing evidence that people in many European states have become disenchanted with the political class and are feeling disenfranchised. This is reflected in the way the political class, populist leaders, and some sectors of the community have sought to frame some social and security issues. Political extremism and racism are examples of such disenchantment and disillusionment.

Political Extremism and Racism

Populism rejects pluralism as a tool of elites that champions the people as morally superior and populist leaders claim that they and they alone represent the people and their true interests (Müller, 2016). This approach suggests a vision of democracy that is majoritarian rather than pluralistic. That majority, namely, 'the people' are often defined by race or religion or class and by their compulsion to 'protect' the nation from what are seen as undesirable alien influences. Such populist movements are defined by their need for enemies, and multitudes of asylum seekers and refugees from conflicts around the globe readily fit this requirement and have become an easy target for populist leaders who often refer to them as 'illegals'. European and other democracies have struggled to cope with the Syrian civil war and other unresolved regional conflicts in the Middle East, South Asia and Africa. In addition to the increasing death toll of civilians in the affected territories, the conflicts are generating unprecedented numbers of refugees and asylum seekers.

Nationalism is often mistakenly thought to be an old concept because people have traditionally been attached to geographic places through family connections. Speaking the same language, sharing common interests, religion or politics all act to make people feel connected within a civil-society or community and, when threatened, hostile towards others. Nationalism is based on the premise that an individual's loyalty and devotion to the nation-state surpasses other individual or group interests. In times of perceived or actual uncertainty, nationalism is often associated with patriotism and used to rally people who readily or immediately identify in the same cultural, social, racial, religious or linguistic ways, or share political goals against a perceived threat from others (Parker, 2017). Changes in migration polices in European liberal democratic states have, in part, reflected populist sentiments against refugees and asylum seekers and challenged the principles of liberal democracy and the future of the Europe project based on Schuman's vision of 'de facto solidarity' and integration referred to earlier.

Some populist and political leaders have used heated and emotive arguments about the number of asylum seekers and refugees in European countries. They have sought to demonise asylum seekers and refugees who often cross borders in vulnerable circumstances. Anti-immigrant rhetoric presenting asylum seekers and refugees in a criminalised way mirrors the narrative of migrant as 'the other'. Instead of acknowledging the increasing diversity of source countries and recognising how this diversity could enrich host countries and civil-societies, alarmist narratives of populist far-right politicians describe migrants as 'others' and as threats to the existing social order. Such narratives have led to changes in public policy relating to migration generally, and to specific security policies and human rights when overlayed with terrorism and security concerns. These types of situations challenge the resilience of the Europe project and implicitly the liberal democratic model, particularly in relation to the principle of the protection of the rights and freedoms of individuals and the rule of law.

Of critical consideration is the extent to which populist and political rhetoric has influenced and changed migration and refugee policies in Europe. The impact of political extremism puts at risk aspects of liberal democracy and there is the risk that some of its characteristics will be overshadowed, or even diminished, to achieve short-term goals to the detriment of fundamental principles of the Europe project.

Problems without Passports

Another category of critical issues in the security environment include notable risks and threats that can be regarded, as 'problems without passports', that is, they do not recognise sovereign borders but affect the stability and security of the EU and individual member states. Climate change, the use of social media and deliberate electronic interference in elections, cyber attacks on European companies, systems, and political machinery cyber security, infectious diseases, and unregulated population migration caused by conflicts and poverty outside Europe, are increasingly challenging Europe's security. These are examples of such 'problems' that are the result of events and activities outside its geographic borders.

Threats by non-state actors and risks posed by non-human sources are among the range of problems without passports that challenge European and global peace, security, and well-being in the twenty-first century. Many of these challenges have come to prominence this century and they require critical consideration for the future of security and well-being. These types of contemporary security challenges can take several different forms and are transnational in effect; often occur with short lead-times; and their effects are not always immediate. Consequently, they are 'more intimidating than the traditional ones' (Chaudhuri, 2011) and generally negate the use of a traditional military response. Many such issues can move along a continuum from one requiring priority attention to a tipping point where they become a matter of security concern and subsequent drivers of instability. This stretches the options available to deal with these forms of risks and threats, and it challenges the effectiveness of traditional decision-making. Transnational risks and threats are novel in the way they are perceived and therefore framed and treated as issues requiring security attention by nation-states and international institutions (Caldwell and Williams, 2006).

These types of issues are risks and threats not just in and of themselves, but as multipliers that exacerbate the extent of the risk and threat posed and undermine resilience rather than enable it. The effects of many of these issues have been experienced by EU member states and contribute to a sense of unease and insecurity in civil societies resulting in rising nationalism and populist leaders as well as authoritarian regimes that seek to undermine democracy. These security challenges threaten the democratic model and the rules-based order which are the foundation principles and values of the European Union that ensure its security continues.

Hybrid threats

Within this category, hybrid threats are a reality of the twenty-first century security environment and hybrid activities by state and non-state groups continue to pose a serious and acute threat to the EU and its member states. Hybrid threats are diverse and ever-changing, and the tools used range from fake social media profiles to sophisticated cyber attacks and extend to overt use of military force and everything in between.

National vulnerabilities can have effects that reach beyond borders. These can include global positioning systems, transport systems or interconnected electric grids, where an attack against a vulnerable node in one country would inevitably have consequences on other countries where such vulnerabilities did not exist. A hybrid attack exploiting a national vulnerability may therefore require not only sovereign action but also common planning and a common response (NATO, 2018). These twenty-first century challenges reflect the ever changing face of security.

Climate change

A second example within this category is climate change. The links between climate change and security have gradually been recognised whereby changing climatic conditions are understood to be additional stressors which contribute to conflict and risks in several ways. Severe and long-term droughts in Syria have contributed to food shortages and water scarcity, instability, violence, conflict and mass unregulated migration. European and other democracies have struggled to cope with the Syrian civil war and other unresolved regional conflicts in the Middle East, South Asia and Africa. In addition to the increasing death toll of civilians in the affected territories, the conflicts are generating unprecedented numbers of refugees and asylum seekers. In 2019, approximately 6.7 million Syrians were refugees, and another 6.2 million people were displaced within

Syria since 2011. Globally, more than two thirds (sixty-seven percent) of all refugees come from just five countries: Syria (6.7 million), Afghanistan (2.7 million), South Sudan (2.3 million), Myanmar (1.1 million), and Somalia (0.9 million) (UNHCR, 2019). As noted in the previous section, throughout Europe factors such as the plight of these and other refugees seeking shelter from conflict and the lack of economic opportunities have given rise to populism and right-wing parties. In effect, these are a new form of authoritarian nationalism (Ulansky and Witenberg, 2016). Most European nations acknowledge the potential risks and threats posed by climate change although its impact is not always integrated into their strategic planning.

Conclusion

Europe has demonstrated its resilience thought the centuries and decades of changing risks and threats to its security. As noted in this chapter, the strategic order and the nature of conflict have changed over time where Europe has witnessed enhanced geostrategic complexity and dynamic change. Recognising that a united Europe would assist the process of achieving long term peace and security, the Europe project was conceived and implemented. While the Europe project in its various guises has faced its own challenges and crises, it has endured and expanded while continuing to maintain its core values.

Great power competition has changed, and these changes are increasingly shaping the European security environment as reflected in the need for the EU to develop critical strategic relationships with NATO, the US, UK, Russia and China to ensure the future security and peace across Europe. An added complication is the range of other risks and threats to peace and security: terrorism, hybrid threats, cyber attacks, climate change, infectious diseases, unregulated migration, and food and water scarcity. Sovereign borders are not barriers to many of these risk and threats, particularly when they arise from non-human sources. In turn, these contemporary risks and threats are exacerbated by political extremism that act to undermine security across Europe, liberal democratic values and the Europe project.

While there may be strength in numbers, the enlargement process of the Europe project of twenty-seven members of the EU has brought with it some additional challenges to Europe's security. This has been demonstrated by election results in some member states where nationalistic authoritarian regimes have been successful. To address the increased range of security risks and threats over the decades there is a pressing imperative for a shared strategic vision for the future security of Europe as a whole and for individual nations where their sovereignty is respected. It is only with such a vision that the EU can be prepared to face current and future security challenges and the aspirations of the Europe project may continue.

References

Banks, M (2019), 'European Union tees up new military-cooperation proposals', *Defense News*, 6 May 2019.

Bielanski, S (2017), 'Polish-Russian Relations and the Burden of History: A Neighbour's View', *ISPI*, 7 November 2017.

Caldwell D & Williams, RE (2006), *Seeking Security in an Insecure World*, Rowman & Littlefield Publishers, Lanham Maryland.

Chaudhuri, S (2011), *Defining Non-Traditional Security Threats*, Global India Foundation, New Delhi.

Chemla, N (2019), 'Baltic States' Russian Disquiet', *Courrier d'Europe – Made in Sorbonne*, 26 March 2019.

Committee on Foreign Affairs (2015), Report on the strategic military situation in the Black Sea Basin following the illegal annexation of Crimea by Russia (2015/2036(INI), Brussels, European Parliament, 21 May.

Congressional Research Service (2019), *U.S.-European Relations in the 116th Congress*, Congressional Research Service, Washington DC.

Dearden, L (2019), 'There is no upside' for UK's national security after Brexit, former head of MI5 says', *The Independent*, 30 October 2019.

EEAS (2016), 'Shared Vision, Common Action: A Stronger Europe: A Global Strategy for the European Union's Foreign and Security Policy', European External Action Service, Brussels.

EEAS (2020), United Kingdom of Great Britain and Northern Ireland: Josep Borrell announces first head of EU delegation in London, Press Release, Brussels: European External Action Service, 24 January 2020.

European Commission (2015), *European Agenda on Security*, Communication from The Commission to The European Parliament, The Council, The European Economic and Social Committee and the Committee of the Regions, COM (2015) 185 final, Strasbourg, 28 April 2015.

European Commission (2018), 'EU Missions and Operations Fact sheet', https://eeas.europa.eu/sites/eeas/files/csdp_missions_and_operations_factsheet.pdf.

European Parliament (2018), 'State of EU-US relations', At a Glance, Plenary, Brussels, September 2018.

European Union (2016), *Shared Vision, Common Action: Strong Europe*, European Union Global Strategy, Council of the European Union, Brussels, June 2016.

European Union (2019), Foreign and Security Policy, Europa. General Secretariat of the Council, (2003), *Secure Europe in a Better World – European Security Strategy*, 15895/03, PESC787, Council of the European Union, Brussels,12 December 2003.

Grey, A (2016), *The world's 10 biggest economies in 2017*, the World Economic Forum, 9 March 2017.

House of Commons Home Affairs Committee (2018), UK-EU security cooperation after Brexit: Follow-up report: Government Response to the Committee's Seventh Report of Session 2017-19, HC 1632, House of Commons, London.

Jervis, R (1978), 'Cooperation Under the Security Dilemma', *World Politics*, vol. 30, no. 2, 167-214, Cambridge University Press, Cambridge.

Johnson, B (2016), 'Beyond Brexit: a Global Britain', 2 December 2016 https://www.gov.uk/government/speeches/beyond-brexit-a-global-britain.

Judson, J (2019), 'Fighting the bureaucracy: For NATO, the Defender 2020 exercise in Europe will test interoperability', *Defense News*, 14 October 2019.

Lindsay, JM (2016), 'The 10 Most Significant World Events in 2016 and how they'll reverberate in the coming year', *The Atlantic*, 28 December 2016.

May, T (2016), *Britain after Brexit: a Vision of a Global Britain*, CCHQ Press, 2 October 2016, http://press.conservatives.com/post/151239411635/prime-minister-britain-after-brexit-a-vision-of.

McDermott, R (2020), 'Moscow Reacts Warily to NATO's Largest Military Exercise in 25 Years', *Eurasia Daily Monitor*, vol. 17, no. 11, 29 January 2020.

Müller, J-W (2016), *What is Populism?*, University of Pennsylvania Press, Philadelphia.

NATO (2018), 'Cooperating to counter hybrid threats', *NATO Review*, 23 November 2018.

North, A (2015), 'Georgia accuses Russia of violating international law over South Ossetia', *The Guardian*, 14 July 2015.

Parker, R (2020), 'Russia and China: A Seventy-Year relationship', *Asia Pacific Journal of European Studies*, vol. 18, no. 1, March-April 2020, 19-36.

Parker, R (2018), 'Unregulated Population Migration and Other Future Drivers of Instability in the Pacific', *The Interpreter*, Lowy Institute, July 2018.

Parker, R (2017), 'The European Liberal Democratic Model: Does it have a future in the Asia Pacific?', *Asia Pacific Journal of European Studies*, Vol. 15, Issue 1, Summer 2017, 113.

Schuman, R (1950), 'Declaration of 9th May 1950 delivered by Robert Schuman', Robert Schuman Foundation, European Issue, no. 204, 10 May 2011.

Seely, B & Rogers, J (2019), *Global Britain: A Twenty-First Century Vision*, Henry Jackson Society, London, 11 February 2019.

Stoltenberg, J (2020), Remarks by NATO Secretary General Jens Stoltenberg at the European Parliament Committee on Foreign Affairs (AFET) and Sub-Committee on Security and Defence (SEDE), 21 January 2020, European Parliament, Brussels.

Toje, A. (2010), 'The EU Security Strategy Revised: Europe Hedging Its Bets', *European Foreign Affairs Review*, Vol. 15, 171–190.

UNHCR (2019), *Global Trends: Forced Displacement in 2018*, UNHCR, Geneva.

Ulansky, E. and Witenberg, W. (2016), 'Is Nationalism on the Rise Globally?', *Huffington Post*, 31 May 2016.

Urbelis, V. (2003), 'Defence Policies of the Baltic States: from the Concept of Neutrality towards NATO membership', *NATO-EAPC Individual Fellowship Report*, 2001-2003, Vilnius.

Wickett, X. (2018), 'Transatlantic Relations Converging or Diverging?', *Chatham House Report*, The Royal Institute of International Affairs, London, 18 January 2018.

Zeneli, V. (2019), Are EU-China Relations at a Crossroads?, *Partner Perspectives*, 8 April 2019.

9

TRADE CONFLICTS OF THE TWO ECONOMIC SUPER POWERS: WHAT ARE THE IMPACTS ON THE EU ECONOMY?

Sang-Chul Park

Keywords: Trade Protectionism, Economic Growth, Trade Conflict, Economic Impacts, EU Economy

Abstract

Global trade has played one of the most important roles in creating global economic growth since the GATT system. However, trade growth has slowed down in the global economy since the global financial crisis in 2008. It seemed to recover in 2017, but declined again owing to the Trump Administration in the USA imposing trade protectionism in 2018 that led to trade conflicts with its global trade partners. The U.S. government took a hardline approach to China in terms of trade that is based on setting high tariffs on Chinese import goods. China also responded with corresponding measures. As a result, the trade conflict started by criticising each other, while the US represents its national interest first and China advocates the global free trade system. In reality, the trade conflict has influenced not only the U.S. and Chinese economy, but also the whole global economy negatively because the two economies, or G2, accounted for nearly 40 percent of the global outcome. Therefore, it is one of the most sensitive issues regarding global economic growth and how it will affect the global economy in general and to the EU economy in particular. This chapter explores why the trade conflict has emerged and ways to solve it. It also focuses on the economic impacts of the trade conflict on the EU economy as one of the three major economic blocs. Furthermore, it analyses how the EU deals with the negative impacts of the trade war between the G2 strategically.

Introduction

The economic super power of the U.S. has been facing strong Chinese challenges since China became the second largest economy in 2010. After the economic reform in 1978 named as the open policy, China's economic scale and foreign trade have been growing rapidly. It was rather dramatic and very fast. As a result, China's role in the global economy has grown to be even more significant particularly since the global financial crisis (GFC) in 2008. It is widely recognised that the bilateral relationship between the U.S. and China will be a crucial determinant of the world's direction in the 21st century because China has tried to build a new form of cooperative platform in world politics and the global economy by creating G2 in 2013. (Hsieh, 2009; Kirton, 2013; Park, 2017)

In order to play its global roles properly in the global economy, China requested additional voting rights in the International Monetary Fund (IMF) in the G20 Summit in 2009 that could increase its political and decision making power within the IMF. In 2016, the Chinese currency, Yuan, officially joined the Special Drawing Rights (SDR) basket and became one of the foreign exchange reserve currencies of the IMF along with U.S. Dollar, British Pound, Euro, and Japanese Yen. Furthermore, the quota of China in the IMF increased to 30.5 billion SDRs in 2017, rising from 1.8 billion SDRs in 1980. As a result, its total vote share increased to 6.09 percent. The currency composition of the SDR basket is reviewed every five years, and the current weights for the component currencies are U.S. dollar (41.73 percent), Euro (30.93 percent), Chinese Yuan (10.92 percent), Japanese Yen (8.33 percent), and British Pound (8.09 percent). (Momani, 2016; IMF, 2015)

Although the Chinese voting rights in the IMF are still weaker than those of the U.S. and the EU, its economic power is real as the second largest economy in the world since 2010. With the high economic growth of 6.6 percent and 6.1 percent in 2018 and 2019 respectively, not only the U.S., but also the EU officially announced China as an economic competitor in the pursuit of technological leadership and a systemic rival promoting an alternative model of governance. The EU urged that China is no longer regarded as a developing country, but a key global actor and leading technological power. Therefore, China should take more responsibilities for upholding the rules based international order and display greater reciprocity, non-discrimination, and openness in its system. For it, China's publicly stated reforms such as market opening, fair competition etc. must be carried out into policies, and actions commensurate with its role and responsibility. (European Commission, 2019)

With the rise of China, it is significant to understand the bilateral trade relations between the U.S. and China and the impacts of the two nations' increasing interdependence on the global economy. Several negative perspectives on the trade conflicts between the U.S. and China had been already expressed in the early 2000s. The major reason for the proliferation of trade conflicts between the two nations was based on the U.S.'s large trade deficit with China that may lead to a trade war between the two parties. The terms of trade war refer to an economic conflict caused by the fact that one nation imposes trade restrictions against the other nation prompting it to retaliate by imposing higher tariffs or non-tariff barriers. As a result, it leads to a deterioration of bilateral trade relations. (Stewart, 2006; Bezlova, 2007; Hsieh, 2009)

Such a trend has continued through all recent U.S. presidencies and led to protectionism since the Trump Administration that realised the trade conflicts as trade war although both parties are negotiating to solve the trade conflicts. China has noticed fundamental changes of the U.S. government on Chinese political and economic power. The U.S. considers China as a serious threat to U.S. global interests. It also ruled out the possibility of China reforming gradually towards the Western system that resulted in a comprehensive review of past decades' of US policy towards China. Accordingly, the core reason of the trade conflicts between the two nations is not only because of the economy, but also due to the politics in order to gain global hegemony. It means that escalation of conflicts and confrontation is inevitable for the two nations. (Chin et al., 2018)

This chapter analyses when and why the trade conflict between the U.S. and China started. It also analyses what may be impacts of the trade conflict between the two nations on the global economy as a whole and on the EU economy in particular. It also focuses on how to solve the trade friction wisely. Furthermore, it suggests how to prevent the possible trade conflicts based on protectionism in the future. In order to find answers of these questions, critical analysis of literature, inference and cross sectional analysis based on statistical data are employed.

Theoretical debates

Most economists in the world would agree with recent rebuttals to scepticism about the liberal trading order because of widely and rapidly spreading protectionism around the world. However, it is the fact that the intellectual and political support for free trade in the U.S. and elsewhere seems to have been weakened since the

GFC in 2008, and protectionism has started since then although G20 member nations agreed to prevent it at the G20 Summit in Washington D.C. Therefore, free trade based on multilateralism is regarded as wishful thinking for many countries particularly the U.S. since the Trump Administration. (Hufbauer & Schott, 2008)

Traditional economic theory suggested comparative advantage and economies of scale would create economic gains through economic efficiency. Therefore, tariffs led to competitive tariff retaliation, which result in a massive shrinkage in foreign trade and low global economic growth. Economic theory never urged that free trade is good for all industries and all people. However, the winners from free trade can afford to compensate the losers and every one could be made better off because the aggregate gains are positive. (O'Rourke and Williamson, 2001; Rosen, 2008)

Economic theory also says that resources will flow to more efficient uses. However, it does not apply when governments and markets do not work well. Therefore, Samuelson already urged in 1972 that the aggregate gains from trade are not necessarily positive for all nations. He expanded his idea further to claim that growth in the rest of the world can damage a country if it takes place in sectors that compete with its native exports having comparative disadvantage. As a result, a nation's relative and even absolute GDP per capita can fall in such a condition. Gomory and Baumol extended Samuelson's theory and urged that there is much possible equilibrium with vastly different outcomes for the countries involved in a modern free trade world. They stated further that it is perfectly possible or rather common for a nation's equilibrium trade outcome to be less than the self-sufficiency outcome so that good equilibriums are often created rather than bestowed by nature. Accordingly, countries can do much to affect their trading outcomes. Therefore, they urged protectionism in US trade policy. (Samuelson, 2004; Gomory and Baumol, 2009)

However, Bhagwati argues that Samuelson's explanation cannot be used as a justification for US protectionism. He also denies Gomory and Baumol's argument because the U.S. could not carry out effective industrial policies to remedy it although their argument is true. Krugman and Obsfeld support Bhagwati's criticism that it is an empirical question rather than a fact whether the growth of emerging economies has actually hurt advanced countries although the theoretical possibility still exists. (Bhagwati, 2009; Krugman and Obsfeld, 2009)

Economists have developed theoretical models for free trade and estimated welfare gains from reducing or eliminating trade barriers. In line with these models, Krugman, and Broda and Weinstein suggested that trade benefits society through gains in overall quality and variety. However, this standard static growth from free trade has left trade promoters quite vulnerable because the static growth models consider only the short run partial equilibrium efficiency gains. At the same time, the static models generate the gains from trade range as very marginal. (Krugman, 1997; Broda and Weinstein, 2006)

In order to deepen theoretical models finding long term efficiency gains and contribution of free trade to economic growth, economists have developed dynamic models estimating impacts of trade liberalisation used by cross country regressions. By using these models, Bradford et al. urged that the US economy in 2005 could generate higher economic growth than without post war trade liberalisation. However, Acemoglu left the issue of trade and growth undecided because there are models that highlight both positive and negative effects of trade on economic growth so that empirical work must be conducted. Accordingly, Lewer and Van den Berg pointed out that further development of dynamic models and additional empirical research are required. Additionally, linkages between trade and technology as well as trade and institutional quality must be further developed. (Bradford, et al., 2006; Acemoglu, 2009; Lewer and Van den Berg, 2007; Feenstra et al., 2009)

In this discussion, the dynamic models rather than static models can be adopted because the former can explain the long term benefits of free trade more precisely than the latter. Accordingly, the conservative dualism of trade theory explains why U.S. protectionism has emerged since the global financial crisis and it represents the Trump government's trade policy than any other theoretical background. However, it has limitations to generate the global economic growth sustainable. Therefore, it is possible that the dynamic models based on the long term efficiency gains and economic growth can correct the direction of protectionism towards free trade. It is the reason why the U.S. and China have started the trade negotiations since 2018 and its outcome may be visible in the near future.

Trade conflicts between the U.S. and China

Background

The large size of the trade deficit between the U.S. and China has been a significant issue in bilateral trade relations. The Trump Administration regards the trade deficit with China as a sign of unfair economic policies in China. Therefore, it has reportedly requested China develop a plan to reduce the bilateral trade deficit by $ 100 billion. However, there is a large difference between the two nations' views on their official trade statistics. According to the U.S. trade statistics in 2017, the merchandise trade deficit with China accounted for $375.3 billion, while Chinese trade surplus with the U.S. in the same year was $275.8 billion. Nearly $100 billion difference exists between the two nations that could cause a serious dispute between the two parties. However, a statistical working group established by the U.S. – China Joint Commission on Commerce and Trade (JCCT) in 2004 identified the causes of the statistical discrepancies that do not mean any error in the official statistics of either country. (Martin, 2018)

In fact, the U.S. has had the largest trade deficit in the world over three decades since the 1970s. Exceptionally, the U.S. briefly had a trade surplus in the mid 1970s, but has experienced continuous deficits since then. The U.S. deficit increased to over 5 percent of the national GDP in 2005 and fell to 2.9 percent of the national GDP in 2017. Owing to the rapid increase of the U.S.'s aggregate trade deficit, the Trump government criticised major U.S. trade partners generally and China in particular. The U.S. argues that China must correct its unfair trade policies generating huge trade surpluses with the U.S. that creates the trade imbalances between the two nations. (Genereux, 2017; WTO, 2018; Park, 2018)

Paths of trade conflicts between the U.S. and China

After a long free trade movement since the GATT system, the U.S. has recently shaken the foundations of the global trading system by imposing steep tariffs on imports from China and other major trading partners since President Trump took power in 2017. The trade conflicts between the U.S. and other trading partners in general and China in particular started as the US International Trade Commission (USITC) found that imports of solar panels and washing machines caused injury to the US solar panel and washing machine industries in October and November 2017 respectively. The two U.S. industries filed separate requests for the investigations in early 2017 under Section 201 of the *Trade Act* of 1974, the first industry petitions since 2001.

As a result, President Trump approved global safeguard tariffs on $8.5 billion in imports on solar cells and modules and $1.8 billion of large residential washing machines in January 2018 that were imposed beginning on 7 February 2018. As a counter measure, the Chinese government requested consultations with the U.S. under the WTO dispute settlement framework concerning these imports. Moreover, the Chinese government announced preliminary anti-dumping duties of 179.6 percent on imports of U.S. agricultural products, sorghum and imposed preliminary tariffs in April 2018. Chinese tariffs on US sorghum ended during negotiation in May 2018, and China also filed a WTO dispute against U.S. solar panel tariffs in August 2018. This signalled the significant trade conflict between the U.S. and China which had a negative macroeconomic impact on the global economy. (Bown& Kolb, 2018; NG & Chung, 2018; Bolt et al., 2019)

Moreover, the Trump Administration imposed tariffs on imports of steel of 25 percent and aluminum 10 percent in February 2018 because it regarded as threatening of the U.S. national security based on Section 232 of the *Trade Expansion Act* of 1962. Chinese portions covered only 6 percent of imports due to prior US imposition of anti-dumping and countervailing duties. Therefore, the Chinese retaliatory tariffs on this issue only accounted for $3 billion. China also imposed tariffs on various imports from the U.S. that included 128 tariff lines.

In addition to steel and aluminum, President Trump imposed 25 percent tariffs on 1,333 Chinese products in two phases starting July 2018 that accounted for $50 billion targeted intermediate inputs and capital products because the U.S. Trade Representative (USTR) found that China conducted unfair trade practices related to technology transfer, intellectual property, and innovation that were investigated under Section 301 of the *Trade Act* of 1974. China also issued an updated $50 billion retaliation list of 25 percent tariffs, including agricultural and food products, crude oil, automobiles, airplanes, chemical products, medical equipment and energy products etc. in two phases that accounted for 659 tariff lines. Since then, trade conflicts between China and the U.S. have continued, and President Trump directed the USTR to identify an additional

$200 billion of Chinese imports for additional tariffs of 10 percent in response to Chinese retaliatory tariffs in June 2018. The USTR finalised the tariff list containing 5,745 full or partial lines of the original 6,031 tariff lines that were on a proposed list of Chinese imports. The additional tariff was effective starting in September 2018. (Bown& Kolb, 2018; McLarty Associates, 2018; NG & Chung, 2018; USTR, 2018).

Since the additional tariff of 10 percent on $200 billion of Chinese imports, the ongoing trade conflict between the two nations has continued. Amid the trade conflict, the U.S. government threatened to impose tariffs as high as 25 percent on all U.S imports from China if China implements its further retaliation measures. President Trump decided on increasing the tariffs to 25 percent on $200 billion of Chinese imports in May 2018 as the trade negotiation between the two nations was not met. As a result, China also responded its retaliation measure to set the high tariff up to 25 percent on $ 60 billion of U.S. imports. Due to the ongoing trade conflict, the neighbouring countries of China such as Japan, South Korea, Thailand, and Vietnam suffered from a stiff decline of their exports to China although their exports to the U.S. increased at the same time. Additionally, China started to consider all options to strike back including targeting large sized US corporations operating in China after the U.S. government announced it was preparing more tariffs on imports from China expanding to a ban on Chinese high-tech firm, Huawei. (Bolt et al., 2019; Strauss, 2019; Cong: 2019)

During the trade conflict, the U.S. government considered raising the tariffs on all imports of automobiles and auto parts that could impact on the global economy massively. It could raise the risk of spreading the trade conflict onto a global scale and escalating retaliation measures all over the world. However, the Trump Administration announced a delay of its final decision on whether to impose broad tariffs on automobile and auto part imports for about six months right after imposing the tariff of 25 percent on $200 billion of Chinese imports. (Salama& Mauldin, 2019) (See table 1)

Table 1: Category and content of US trade conflicts with major trading partners

Category	Content
Solar Panels and Washing Machine	Imposing safeguard tariffs on $8.5 billion in solar panels and $1.8 billion in washing machines
	Chinese preliminary tariffs on US sorghum & filing WTO dispute against US solar panels tariffs
	Korean filing WTO dispute against US solar panels and washing machines tariffs
Steel and aluminum as national security threat	Section 232 of Trade Expansion Act of 1962
	25 percent on steel & 10 percent on aluminum covering $48 billion of imports
Unfair trade practices for technology & intellectual property (IP)	Section 301 of Trade Act of 1974
	$50 billion of 1,333 Chinese products for 25 percent tariffs with two phases
	Identifying $200 billion for 10 percent tariffs in Sep. 2018
	Raising tariff to 25 percent on $200 billion in May 2019
Auto vehicles as national security threat	Announcing to raise tariffs up to 25 percent and delay six months in 2019 mainly against the EU, Japan and South Korea

Source: Bown & Kolb, 2018; McLarty Associates, NG & Chung, 2018, 2018; USTR, 2018, Salama& Mauldin, 2019, Strauss, 2019

Reasons for the trade conflict between the two economic superpowers

There are many reasons for trade conflicts whenever these take place regardless of whether they are between nations or regions. Among these, the trade conflict between the two major economies can be explained by the following four reasons. Generally, these are regarded as trade imbalance between the two nations, US protectionism based on income inequality, China's unfair trade against intellectual property rights (IPR), technology transfer and innovation for US companies, and competition of hegemonic power in the 21st century.

Firstly, the U.S. trade deficit with China accounted for $419 billion in 2018, increasing from $376 billion in 2017 despite U.S. protectionism against China. The U.S. trade deficit with China in 2018 accounted for nearly 42 percent of the total U.S. trade deficit, a decline from 49 percent in 2015. The U.S. imported $540 billion from China in 2018, while it exported $120 billion to China in the same year. The three biggest categories of U.S. imports from China were computers and accessories, cell phones, and apparel and footwear, accounting for $77 billion, $70 billion, and $54 billion respectively. The three largest US exports to China were commercial aircraft, soybeans, and autos that accounted for $16 billion, $12 billion and $10 billion respectively. It means that the U.S. trade deficit with China is not a short term phenomenon, but a long term chronic trend due to the different industrial structures between the two nations. As a result, it increased from $273 billion in 2010 to $419 billion in 2018. (Amadeo, 2019; Park, 2018; United States Census Bureau, 2019) (See fig. 1)

Secondly, the U.S. as the largest economy in the world, has led protectionism since the GFC in general and the Trump Administration in particular that has negatively affected the global economies. U.S. protectionism impacts on the global economy seriously due to its powerful economic influence compared with other economies that result from the income inequality and distribution in the U.S. that has risen since the 2000s. However, many economists are not sure yet whether the free trade has created the income inequality or not. Some economists urged that the free trade affected only about

Figure 1: The U.S. Trade Deficit with China from 2010 to 2018 (As of USD billion)

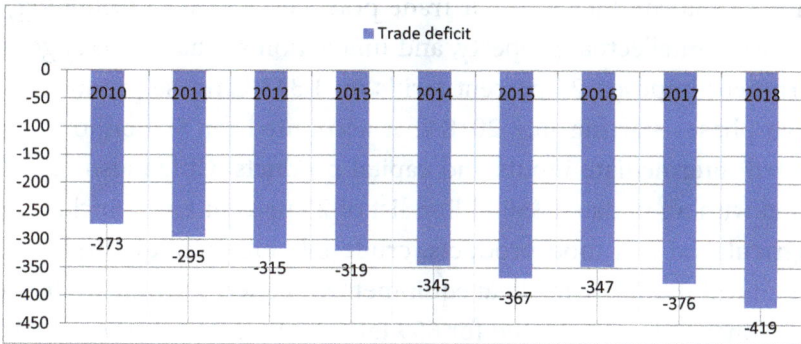

Source: United States Census Bureau, 2019

20 percent of the increase in inequality in the 1970s and 1980s when the U.S. trade was mostly North to North. With the shift of trade relations to North to South, a more negative impact on the wage of low skilled workers in the U.S. has taken place since the 1990s. Whatever the cause of the rise in inequality, the fact is that the average of real wage of production per hour has been stagnant since the 1980s. As a result, the wage increase in production has lagged behind the growth in real GDP per capita. Moreover, the share of pretax income held by the top one percent of the population's wealth-holders, increased from 10.5 percent in 1980 to over 20 percent in 2016, while the share of the bottom 50 percent declined from 20.5 percent to 13 percent during the same period. The U.S. is the most unequal nation among the advanced countries based on the Gini index that increased up to 0.41.5 in 2016. (Krugman, 2009; ERP, 2009;Hillebrand et al., 2010; OECD, 2014; Piketty, 2014; Alvaredo et al., 2017; World Bank, 2019)

Thirdly, President Trump asked the US Trade Representative (USTR) to investigate whether Chinese laws, policies, practices that may harm US intellectual property rights, innovation or technology development in August 2017 or not, and the USTR initiated investigation of China under Section 301 of the *Trade Act* of 1974. It found that China conducted unfair trade practices related to technology transfer, intellectual property, and innovation so that the U.S. government imposed 25 percent tariffs on 1,333 Chinese products in two phases starting July 2018 that accounted for $50 billion targeted intermediate inputs and capital products. China also retaliated with an updated $50 billion list of 25 percent tariffs including agricultural and food products, crude oil, automobiles, airplanes, chemical products, medical equipment and energy products etc. in two phases that accounted for 659 tariff lines. (NG & Chung, 2018; USTR, 2018)

Last, but not least the U.S.-China trade conflict is based on the competition to be the hegemonic power in the 21st century. Therefore, several scholars expect that it would take a long term instead of a short term. In the national security strategy report in 2017, the U.S. called China its strategic rival. Additionally, the U.S. government was particularly concerned about the Chinese national development strategy, the Made in China 2025 Program, as a national threat in terms of high tech development that plays the core role in strengthening Chinese future competitiveness. In line with such a strategic point of view on the high tech area, President Trump signed an executive order to ban the Chinese high tech firm, Huawei, one of the leading global telecommunication companies in 5G technology in the world in May 2019. The U.S. government has been suspicious about Huawei controlled by the Chinese Communist Party and asked its allies not to use Huawei's 5G technology due to national security reasons. Therefore, the key issue on the trade conflict between the U.S. and China is rather politics than economics that may escalate confrontation between the two nations in the future. (The White House, 2017; Chin et al., 2018; Jiming, 2018; Doffman, 2019)

Analysis on economic impacts of the trade conflict

Impacts on the U.S. and Chinese economy

Unfortunately impacts of the trade conflict can be not only bilateral, but also global. Particularly, the two largest economies in the world generate two fifths of global GDP and about a quarter of global trade. Therefore, the bilateral trade conflict between the U.S. and China is significantly worrisome for both the region and the world because the two nations are two of the three main hubs for global production chains along with the European Union (EU), with tight trade links in key industrial sectors such as electronics and high technology equipment. (Abiad et al., 2018)

Most of the products affected in the first two rounds of bilateral tariffs imposed on imports of Chinese goods for $50 billion are mainly capital and intermediate goods that are targeted for the Made in China 2025 Plan. In order to meet the target of the plan, China needs to import high tech products for its end-products that are deeply connected with global value chains (GVC). In contrast, China retaliated to impose tariffs mostly on imports of U.S. agricultural products, chemicals, medical and energy equipment that are rather homogeneous goods easily available in the global markets.

The second round of the trade conflict of $200 billion by the U.S. and $60 billion tariffs by China started in the middle of 2018 that affected to consumer goods because fewer supply chain lines were left to set the targets. The trade tension between the two nations escalated continuously, and the U.S. threatened to impose tariffs of another $267 billion on Chinese imports that were all goods imported from China in 2018. China also threatened to retaliate with similar tariffs on all imports from the U.S. and consider other measures for retaliation. In the global trade tension, the U.S. government has considered setting a tariff of 25 percent

191

on imports of automobiles and auto parts from all trading partners that would affect $350 billion worth of goods. (Abiad et al., 2018; Park, 2018)

The escalation of trade conflict and threats between the two nations caused a significant pressure on the outlook for global economic growth in general and the Chinese economy in particular. Chinese exports and sales started already weak in the third quarter of 2018. Additionally, the threats made investors be in a wait and see mode and accelerated restrictions of foreign direct investment (FDI) for the high tech areas from China and vice versa (Hanemann, 2018).

In order to analyse the impact of the trade conflict between the two nations on their economies, the implications of three scenarios are examined. The first scenario is a current scenario, including all trade measures implemented as of October 2018 with $200 billion of imports from China in 25 percent of tariffs. The second one is a bilateral escalation scenario intensifying to impose blanket tariffs of 25 percent on all merchandise imports from both countries. Finally, the last worst case scenario includes measures under the bilateral escalation scenario and a global escalation of trade conflict between the U.S. and other trading partners in automobiles and parts imposed by the U.S. on 25 percent tariffs of imports from other nations.(See table 2)

The immediate impact of these three scenarios will take time to fully materialise. The current scenario was affected fully in 2019, while the direct impact of the worst scenario will approach nearly a full effect in 2020 and will be completed in 2021. Moreover, the scenario modeling is used by the ADB Multiregional Input-Output Table (ADB MRIOT) for the year 2017 in order to quantify the impact of changes in tariffs working through local and production chains that provides advantages in individual economies and sec-

Table 2: Description and size of three modelled scenarios between the U.S. and China

Scenarios	US Tariff Actions and Size of Impact	Retaliatory Measures by China	Date of Implementation
Current Scenario (measures implemented as of Oct. 2018)	30% and 20% blanket tariffs on all imports of solar panels and wash machines worth $ 10.3 billion (0.4% of US imports)	China imposed 15% and 25% tariffs on $3 billion worth of US goods (2.3% of US exports to China)	First quarter 2018
	25% on $34 billion worth of Chinese goods (7% of Chinese exports to the US)	25% on $34 billion worth of US goods (26% of US exports to China)	6 July 2018
	25% on $16 billion worth of Chinese goods (3% of Chinese exports to the US)	25% on $16 billion worth of US goods (12.3% of US exports to China)	23 Aug. 2018
	10% on $200 billion worth of Chinese goods raised to 25% in 2019 (40% of Chinese exports to the US)	5%, 10%, 20% and 25% on $60 billion worth of US goods (46% of US exports to China)	Begins 24 Sep. 2018 and escalates 1 June 2019
Bilateral Escalation Scenario (add 25% tariffs on all bilateral US China imports)	US blanket tariffs of 25% on 100% of Chinese exports to the US worth $505.5 billion (an additional $267 billion from previous scenario)	Chinese blanket tariffs of 25% on 100% of US exports to China worth $ 130 billion (an additional $17 billion added from previous scenario) Chinese blanket tariffs of 25% on 100% of US exports to China worth $ 130 billion (an additional $17 billion added from previous scenario)	Model assumed first quarter 2019, but delayed after second quarter

Source: Author's own adaptation based on Abiad et al., 2018Abiad et al., 2018

tors as well as understanding the structure and evolution of GVC. The direct impact of the trade conflict is quantified at product level gathered by published lists of tariff affected commodities for all countries involved in the trade conflicts as of September 2018. Additionally, these commodities are matched with detailed trade data from BACI and the United States Census Bureau in 2017 that uses a 6- to 10-digit Harmonized System classification. (Abiad et al., 2018; Wang et al., 2018)

Given the ADB analysis, the trade conflict between the two economies will be affected negatively in all scenarios. Under the current scenario, the Chinese economy would only grow by 0.48 GDP, while the bilateral escalation scenario subtracts 0.55 percent GDP. In the worst case scenario, the Chinese economic growth could be less by 1.05 percent. In contrast, the U.S. economy could be affected by the trade conflict less than the Chinese economy. It could subtract 0.12 percent, 0.08 percent, and 0.24 percent respectively. It indicates that the trade conflict can impact on the two major economies rather more marginally than expected in the midterm period. (See fig. 2, 3)

Such marginal negative impacts of the trade conflicts on the U.S. and Chinese economies are also proven by the analysis of International Monetary Fund (IMF). Given the IMF analysis, the two economies had been affected least among advanced and emerging economies in 2019 and were expected to grow more than other economies in 2020. Among the advanced economies, the U.S. economy will generate higher economic growth than that of the EU and Japan, while the Chinese economy could perform the highest economic growth among emerging economies in 2019 and 2020. This estimation is more or less the same even in the COVID-19 Pandemic period. (IMF, 2019; 2020) (See fig. 4, 196)

Figure 2: Impact of the trade conflict on Chinese GDP by scenarios.

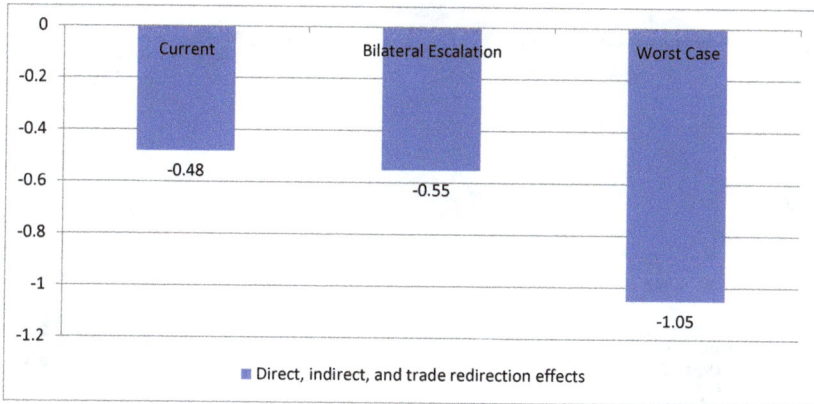

Source: Abiad et al., 2018.

Figure 3: Impact of the trade conflict on the U.S. GDP by scenarios.

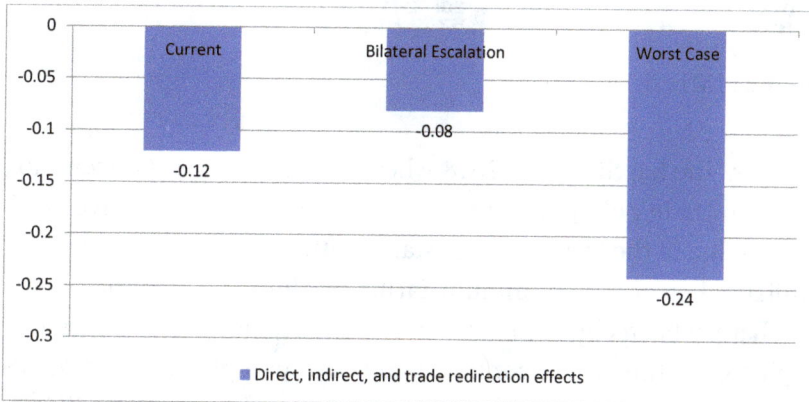

Source: Abiad et al., 2018.

Impacts on the EU economy

In order to analyse impacts of the trade conflicts on the EU economy, it is useful to adopt the World Scan simulations in the CPB's global CGE model. In the analysis, the macroeconomic results look

Figure 4: Half Yearly Growth Forecast in Advanced and Emerging Economies.

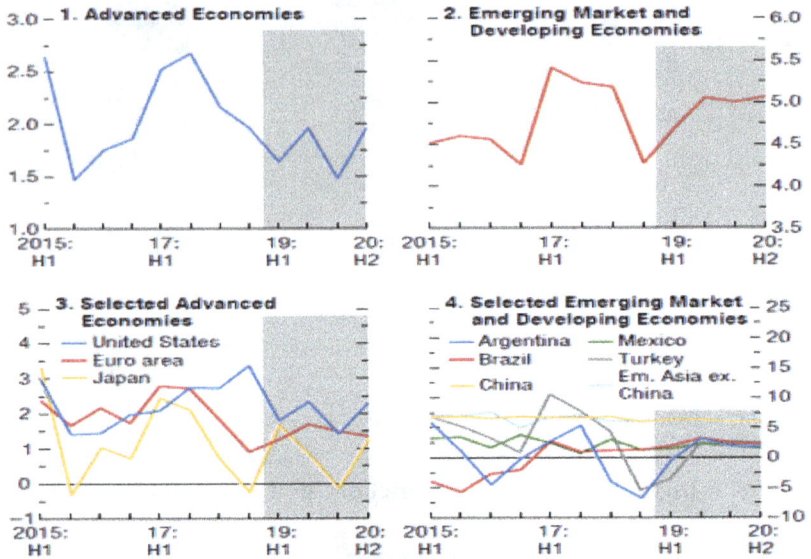

Source: IMF, 2019.

similar. The baseline is in 2018 when business is as usual scenarios with no trade policy change and a trade shock with negative GDP effects due to the tariff increase start in 2019. The four scenarios are unilateral steel and aluminum tariffs by the U.S., scenario 1 plus retaliatory tariffs by China, the EU, Canada, and Mexico, scenario 2 plus US-China trade conflict, and scenario 3 plus 25 percent US tariff increase on automobiles and parts imports from the EU. In these scenarios, the impact of the trade conflict on the two major economies results also in as marginal, and the U.S. economy is less vulnerable than the Chinese economy. The scenario 4 subtracts the former with -0.3 percent and the latter with -1.3 percent. (Bollen& Rojas-Romagosa, 2018)

The World Scan simulations as the CPB's global CGE model

also analysed the impact of the trade conflict on the EU that is rather positive impacts on the economic growth except the scenario 1 compared with the impacts on the U.S. and Chinese economies. The EU can even get economic benefits while the trade conflict between the two major economies is intensified unless the U.S. government does not impose tariffs on imports of EU goods in automobile and parts. Its economic growth ranges from -0.1 percent to 0.4 percent. Given the analysis, the EU economy can be vulnerable in the scenario 1 slightly and least affected by other scenarios among the major economies. (Bollen& Rojas-Romagosa, 2018) (See table 3, 198)

However, economic conditions in the EU have slowed down since the trade conflicts between the U.S. and China started. Among the major economies in the EU, the largest and second largest manufacturing nations, such as Germany and Italy, performed their manufacturing sectors with a downturn trend since 2018 that resulted in a manufacturing recession. As a result, economic outcomes in the EU have become worse since the trade conflict intensified in 2018.

First of all, the average economic growth in the EU declined from 2.8 percent in 2017 to 1.5 percent in 2018, that is nearly 50 percent less than in the previous year. Secondly the average unemployment rate in the EU increased to 6.4 percent in 2019 that is more than double higher than 3.1 percent in the U.S. The unemployment rate in the Euro zone in the same year was even higher than the average with 7.6 percent. Lastly, but not least, real household consumption in the major EU economies started to fall sharply since 2018. These indicate that the trade conflict between the two major global economies influenced the EU's economy negatively in the short term although the analysis on impacts of the trade conflict on the EU economy was predicted to be very marginal. (Eurostat, 2019) (See fig. 5, 6, 199)

Table 3: Main Macroeconomic Effects of the U.S. and China compared to the 2030 Baseline i

Scenarios	The U.S.	China	The EU
Scenario 1			
GDP (%)	0.0	0.0	-0.1
Export volume (%)	-1.6	0.0	-0.1
Import volume (%)	-1.0	0.0	-0.1
Scenario 2			
GDP (%)	-0.4	0.2	0.2
Export volume (%)	-6.3	-0.9	-0.1
Import volume (%)	-4.8	-0.9	-0.2
Scenario 3			
GDP (%)	-0.3	-1.2	0.4
Export volume (%)	-13.5	-8.2	0.0
Import volume (%)	-10.5	-8.4	0.0
Scenario 4			
GDP (%)	-0.3	-1.3	0.2
Export volume (%)	-14.0	-8.3	-0.5
Import volume (%)	-10.9	-8.4	-0.5

Source: Bollen & Rojas-Romagosa, 2018 based on World Scan simulations.

Figure 5: Trend of Manufacturing Sector in the EU Major Countries.

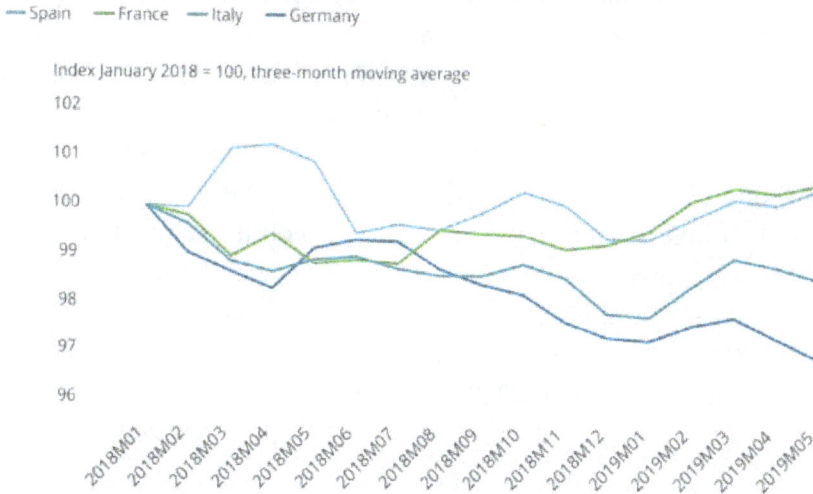

Source: Eurostat, 2019.

Figure 6: Real GDP Growth in the EU.

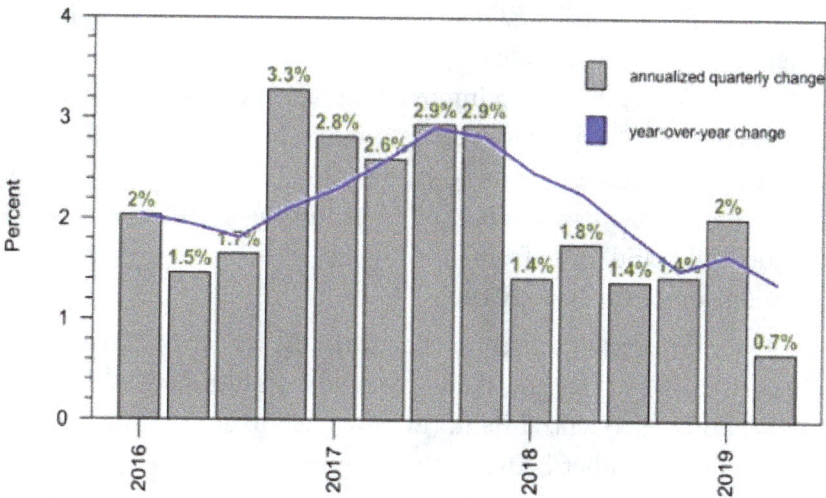

Source: Eurostat, 2019.

Conclusion

Trade conflict has always existed in the global economy as some trading partners gain more benefit than others. In economic history, our lesson is that there is no winner from the trade conflict if it is not solved by dialogue and trade agreements. We have already experienced the Great Depression in 1929/1930 that resulted in the Second World War. Unfortunately, we are again experiencing severe trade conflicts between the two major economies in the 21st century that may impact on the global economy negatively if it continues without any proper solution. Furthermore, we are experiencing the COVID-19 Pandemic since January 2020 that has resulted in the global recession. (IMF, 2020; World Bank, 2020)

First of all, ironically the trade conflict started from the U.S. pursuing trade protectionism particularly in the Trump Administration having various internal problems, such as trade imbalance with its trading partners, income inequality etc. The U.S. government imposed high tariffs on imports of solar panel and washing machine first and later steel and aluminum from imports of its trading partners. After revising KORUS FTA and NAFTA, the U.S. government focuses on the trade dispute with China that is still an ongoing process threatening to impose a 25 percent tariff on all import goods from China and vice versa although the two countries signed a preliminary agreement on 15 January 2020. Furthermore, the U.S. government plans to impose a 25 percent tariff on the import of automobiles and parts from all countries although it is delayed six months long from May 2019.

Since the severe trade conflict between the U.S. and China started in early 2018, several global and regional institutes such as the IMF, ADB, European Central Bank (ECB) started to analyse the impacts of the trade conflict between the two major economies as well as the EU economy. Additionally, individual nations' economic think tanks also joined this trend. For the impact of the trade conflict between G2 on their national economies in the midterm period, the analysis of ADB predicted a minor economic impact on the U.S. and China in the three scenarios although impact on China could be higher than that of the U.S. It may be the reason why the two major economies are not afraid of continuing the trade conflict because the trade conflict in all scenarios could impact on their economies marginally. Based on this reason, the trade conflict between the U.S. and China may continue despite the recent trade agreement between the two nations if the agreement is not fulfilled properly.

In the longer term perspective based on the World Scan simulations, the trade conflict between the two major economies could generate benefits of additional economic growth for the EU. However, the EU could also be affected negatively if the trade conflict between the two economies as well as the U.S. and the EU economies is escalated further. In fact, however, the real economic growth and the real household consumption growth in the major EU economies started to decline, while the EU's average unemployment rate started to increase since 2018. Therefore, the trade conflict between G2 influences the EU economy negatively. It is a serious challenge and a de facto threat for the EU economy at present instead of being regarded as an opportunity. Accordingly, the EU must react wisely in order to prevent its economic downturn from the trade conflict by urging for a free trade system based on multilateralism and reciprocity.

References

Abiad, A, Baris, K, Bernabe, JA, Bertulfo, DJ, Camingue-Romance, S, Feliciano, PN, Mariasingham, MJ & Mercer-Blackman, V (2018), The Impact of Trade Conflict on Developing Asia, Asian Development Bank Economics Working Paper Series, no. 566, ADB., Manila.

Acemoglu, D (2009) *Modern Economic Growth*, Princeton University Press, Princeton, NJ.

Alvaredo, F, Chancel L, Piketty, T, Saez, E & Zucman, G (2017), World Inequality Report 2018, https://wir2018.wid.world/files/download/wir2018-full-report-english.pdf.

Amadeo, KY (2019), US trade Deficit with China and Why It's So High, https://www.thebalance.com/u-s-china-trade-deficit-causes-effects-and-solutions-3306277.

Bezlova, A (2007), *China: Headed for Trade Wars with the U.S.*, Inter Press Service, 27 April.

Bhagwati, J (2009), 'Does the U.S Need a New Trade Policy?' *Journal of Policy Modeling*, vol. 31, no. 4, 509-514.

Bolt, W, Mavromatis, K & van Wijnbergen, S (2019), The Global Macroeconomics of Trade War: The EAGLE Model on the US-China Trade Conflict, https://www.dnb.nl/binaries/wp623_tcm46-381884.pdf.

Bollen, J & Rojas-Romagosa, H (2018), Trade Wars: Economic Impacts of US Tariff Increases and Retaliation, An International Perspective, CPB Background Document, CPB Netherlands Bureau for Economic Policy Analysis, Amsterdam.

Bown, CP & Kolb, M (2018), Trump's Trade War Timeline: An Up-to-date Guide, Peterson Institute for International Economics, https://piie.com/system/files/documents/trump-trade-war-timeline.pdf.

Bradford, S, Greico, P & Hufbauer, GC (2006), 'The Payoff to America from Globalisation', *The World Economy*, vol. 29, no. 7, 893-917.

Broda, C & Weinstein, DE (2006), 'Globalization and the Gains from Variety', *The Quarterly Journal of Economics*, vol. 121, no. 2, 541-585.

Cong, W (2019), 'Retaliation on American Firms Suggested After Huawei Ban', 17 May, *Global Times*, http://www.globaltimes.cn/content/1150422.shtml.

Doffman, Z (2019), *Trump signs Executive Order That Will Lead to U.S. Ban on Huawei*, 15 May, https://www.forbes.com/sites/zakdoffman/2019/05/15/trump-expected-to-sign-executive-order-leading-to-ban-on-huawei-this-week/#497d903168d9.

Economic Report of the President (ERP) (2009), Economic Report of the President Together with the Annual Report of the Council of Economic Advisers, U.S. Government Printing Office, Washington, DC.

European Commission (2019), *EU-China: A Strategic Outlook*, Strasbourg.

Eurostat (2019) Your Key to European Statistics, https://ec.europa.eu/eurostat/371.

Feenstra, RC, Mandel, BR, Reinsdorf, MB & Slaughter, M (2009), Effects of Terms of Trade Gains and Tariff Changes on the Measurement of U.S. Productivity Growth, NBER Working Paper No. 15592.

Genereux F (2017), 'Protectionism: A Brake on Economic Growth', *Economic Studies*, 17 February, https://www.desjardins.com/ressources/pdf/pv170217-e.pdf.

Gomory R, Baumol W (2009), 'Globalization: Country and Company Interests in Conflict', *Journal of Policy Modeling*, vol. 31, no. 3, 540–555.

Hanemann, T (2018), Arrested Development: Chinese FDI in the US in 1H 2018, 19 June, https://rhg.com/research/arrested-development-chinese-fdi-in-the-us-in-1h-2018/.

Hillebrand, EE, Lewer, JJ & Zagardo, JT (2010), 'Backtracking from Globalization', *Global Economy Journal*, vol. 10, no. 4, 1.

Hsieh, PL (2009), 'China-United States Trade Negotiations and Disputes: The WTO and Beyond', *Asian Journal of WTO and International Health Law and Policy*, vol. 4, no. 2, 386.

Hufbauer, GC & Schott, JJ (2008), 'What Should Leaders do to Stop the Spread of Protectionism?;, In Baldwin, R. and Evenett, S. (eds.), *What World Leaders Must Do to Halt the Spread of Protectionism*, Centre for Economic Policy Research (CEPR), London, https://voxeu.org/sites/default/files/file/protectionism.pdf

International Monetary Fund (IMF) (2015), IMF Executive Board Completes the 2015 Review of SDR Valuation, Press Release No. 15/543, https://www.imf.org/en/news/articles/2015/09/14/01/49/pr15543.

International Monetary Fund (IMF) (2019), World Economic Outlook: Growth Slow Down, Precarious Recovery, 2019 April, file:///C:/Users/user/Downloads/text.pdf,

International Monetary Fund (2020), World Economic Outlook Update, June, Washington DC.

Jiming, H (2018), China-US Trade Conflict: Causes and Impact, 2018 CF40-PIIE Joint Report, https://piie.com/system/files/documents/ha20180611ppt.pdf.

Kirton, J (2013), *G20 Governance for a Globalized World*, Ashgate, Farnham.

Krugman, P. R. (1997), 'Increasing Returns, Monopolistic Competition, and International Trade', *Journal of International Economics*, vol. 9, no. 4, 469-479.

Krugman, PR & Obstfeld, M (2009), *International Economics*, Pearson, Addison-Wesley, Boston.

Lewer, JJ & Van den Berg, H (2007), *International Trade and Economic Growth*, M.E. Sharpe, Armonk, NY.

Martin, MF (2018), What's the Difference? – Comparing U.S. and Chinese Trade Data, CRS Report, RS 22640, Washington DC.

Momani, B (2016), 'China at the IMF' In Lombardi, D & Wang, H-Y (eds.) *Enter the Dragon: China in the International Financial System*, McGill Queen's Press, Montreal & Kingston, 267-288.

NG, T & Chung, K (2018), *Trade Conflict between China and the United States and Its Impact on Hong Kong's Economy*, Hong Kong: Research Office, Legislative Council Secretariat, https://www.legco.gov.hk/research-publications/english/1718in14-trade-conflict-between-china-and-the-united-states-and-its-impact-on-hong-kongs-economy-20180717-e.pdf.

Organization for Economic Cooperation and Development (OECD) (2014), *Factbook* 2014, OECD, Paris.

O'Rourke, KH & Williamson, JG (2001), *Globalization and History: The Evolution of Nineteenth Century Atlantic Economy*, MIT Press, Cambridge.

Park, S-C (2017), 'Can Trade Help Overcome Economic Crisis? Implications for Northeast Asia Creating Regional FTA between Korea, China, and Japan and Mega FTAs such as RCEP and TPP', *International Organizations Research Journal*, vol. 12, no. 2, 104-128.

Park, S–C (2018), US Protectionism and Trade Imbalance between the U.S. and Northeast Asian Countries, *International Organizations Research Journal*, vol. 13, no. 2, 76-100.

Piketty, T (2014), *Capital in the Twenty First Century*, Belknap Press, Cambridge, MA.

Rosen, H (2008), Strengthening Trade Adjustment Assistance, Washington D. C.: Peterson Institute for International Economics Policy Brief, PD 09-2, January.

Salama, V & Mauldin, W (2019) 'Trump Administration Delays Decision on Car Tariffs', *The Wall Street Journal*, 15 May.

Samuelson P (2004) 'Where Ricardo and Mill Rebut and Confirm Arguments of Mainstream Economists Supporting Globalization', *Journal of Economic Perspectives*, vol. 18, no 3, 135-146.

Stewart, H (2006), 'US-China Trade War Looms', *The Observer*, 26 March.

Strauss, D (2019), 'Global Economy Counts Cost of Trade Dispute', *Financial Times*, 10 May.

The White House (2017), National Security Strategy of the United States of America, Washington D.C.: The White House, https://www.whitehouse.gov/wp-content/uploads/2017/12/NSS-Final-12-18-2017-0905.pdf.

United States Census Bureau (2019), Foreign Trade, https://www.census.gov/foreign-trade/balance/c5700.html.

US Trade Representative (USTR) USTR Finalizes Tariffs on $200 billion of Chinese Imports in Response to China's Unfair Trade Practices, https://ustr.gov/about-us/policy-offices/press-office/press-releases/2018/september/ustr-finalizes-tariffs-200.

Wang, Z, Wei, S-J & Zhu, K-F (2018), Quantifying International Production Sharing at the Bilateral and Sector Levels, National Bureau of Economic Research Working Paper No. 19677, https://www.nber.org/papers/w19677.pdf.

World Bank (2019), GINI Index, World Bank Estimate, https://data.worldbank.org/indicator/SI.POV.GINI?locations=US.

10

Aggressive Trilateralism?
The complexification of Australia's EU and UK Free Trade Agreements

Rémy Davison

Keywords: EU Integration, Australian Trade Policy, Free Trade Agreements, Brexit, Brussels Effect.

Abstract

The UK's decision to exit the European Union (EU) is of critical economic importance to Australia. The UK is Australia's second-largest investment partner and a key point of entry for Australian firms into the EU market. In 2018, Australia and the EU launched free trade agreement (FTA) negotiations, while in 2020, Australia-UK free trade talks commenced.

Following Brexit, the UK is unlikely to have privileged access to the EU Single Market, which will have an impact upon UK outward direct and portfolio investment flows to Australia, with consequential effects upon equity markets. This chapter argues that FTAs enhance EU 'regulatory power'. Australia also faces increasing competition as it negotiates a UK FTA. Trade competition renders FTA negotiations even more complex, as a prospective US-UK FTA not only reinforces the unpredictability of the AUKFTA outcomes, but also increases the probability of US exporters gaining preferential UK market access at the expense of Australian businesses.

Introduction

Brexit presents the most serious challenge to the Australia-UK trade and investment relationship since the UK acceded to the EU in 1973. Since Federation, Australia has been compelled to adjust to exogenous changes in the international trade environment. From the collapse of global trade in the wake of the 1929 Wall Street crash, to Britain's application for EC membership in 1961, every generation of decision makers has been forced to reorient trade policy as Australia's share of world exports experienced long-term decline by the 1970s. Despite Australia's strong support for the 1986–93 General Agreement on Tariffs and Trade (GATT) Uruguay round, Canberra found itself under attack by its American ally for industry subsidies. Both the Bush Sr. and the Clinton administrations employed the 1974 US *Trade Act* and the 1988 *Omnibus Foreign Trade and Competitiveness Act* to target US trade partners for unfair practices; this gave rise to the term 'aggressive unilateralism' (Bhagwati & Patrick 1990). In response, the Howard government's 1997 *White Paper on Foreign and Trade Policy* endorsed a more strategic approach to trade policy liberalisation, labelled 'aggressive bilateralism' (Capling 2001). In 2014, the Abbott government mounted an ambitious diplomatic effort to complete or commence a series of bilateral or plurilateral FTAs, including agreements with Japan and South Korea, the Trans-Pacific Partnership (TPP), and the resuscitation of the Australia-China FTA that had been abandoned by the Gillard government. However, Australia's FTA strategy has been criticised for undermining its trade agenda by prioritising political and security considerations over economic objectives (Capling & Ravenhill 2015).

In 2015, the EU and Australia's agreement to undertake pre-negotiation discussions was predicated upon a coterminous EU-28 with UK membership. However, the May government's 2016 decision to withdraw from the European Union (EU) after the Brexit referendum represented a critical juncture. The UK is Australia's most important economic partner in Europe and its second-largest investment partner (Austrade 2018; DFAT 2019c). It is also a key point of entry for Australian firms into the EU market. In 2017, the UK government published its Brexit White Paper, indicating a bilateral free trade agreement (FTA) with Australia was one policy option (HMG 2017a: 54–5). In January 2020, the UK formally exited the EU, with a deadline of December 2020 for the conclusion of a EU-UK trade agreement (BBC 2020b). The outcome of these negotiations could potentially jeopardise negotiation of an Australia-UK FTA (AUKFTA). A no-deal or suboptimal EU-UK deal could significantly affect Australia-UK negotiations and produce distortionary trade and investment outcomes at the regulatory level without discernible improvements in economic outcomes. This chapter analyses the stumbling blocks Australian policy makers face in negotiating discrete AEU and AUK FTAs. Moreover, the chapter concludes that the 'known unknowns' of a prospective US-UK FTA not only reinforces the unpredictability of the AUKFTA outcomes, but also increases the probability of US exporters gaining preferential UK market access, at the expense of Australian businesses.

From Brexit to Brussels: Canberra's 'European pivot'?

In 2015, Australia and the EU launched a FTA scoping study. Internally, the Abbott government was radical; the Prime Minister's office sought to circumvent bureaucratic objections to a EU FTA, as DFAT traditionally opposed an agreement in the absence of a comprehensive agricultural deal that overcame the bulwark of the Common Agricultural Policy (CAP). The AEUFTA pre-negotiation phase commenced prior to the 2016 Brexit referendum; consequently, DFAT's expectation was the conclusion of a bilateral agreement with the EU. However, the May government's decision to proceed with Brexit compelled the Australian Parliamentary

Trade Committee to launch an inquiry into the AUK trade and investment relationship (Parliament of Australia 2017a: 1.13). In July 2017, the Turnbull government announced that it would seek to negotiate FTAs with both the EU and UK, once the latter left the EU. In June 2018, the AEUFTA negotiations were launched formally. DFAT negotiators originally expected a rapid conclusion to an AEUFTA by the end of 2020 (DFAT 2018d). However, barring significant concessions on the part of the Australian government, the Commission's own documents, issued prior to the outbreak of the COVID-19 pandemic, signalled otherwise. Four negotiation rounds were conducted in 2020, with additional bilateral discussions scheduled on a range of chapters during 2021 (CEC 2019; DFAT 2020b).

The type and extent of inclusions and exclusions will heavily influence the economic impact of the AEUFTA. EU modelling predicts an increase in Australia-EU trade (two-way trade of $A11.2–$A17.9 billion). From 2021, the UK is unlikely to have privileged access to the EU Single Market (SM) in financial services; instead, it may be granted 'equivalence', similar to the access regimes granted to US and Japanese banks. As London has historically acted as a financial intermediary for EU capital and as a conduit for cross-border portfolio investment (Capie et al 2005: 305), a depreciated role for the City in EU financial markets will have a consequential impact upon UK outward direct and portfolio investment flows to Australia, with resultant impacts upon equity markets. In both the Australia-EU and Australia-UK FTAs, there is realisable growth potential, particularly in agricultural exports. The EU is Australia's second-largest partner in two-way merchandise trade (with or without the UK) and biggest partner in two-way services trade (DFAT 2018e). Without the UK, it remains the second-largest economic bloc in the world, behind the US-Mexico-Canada Agreement (USMCA) (World Bank 2020). The UK imports over 50% of its foodstuffs; after Brexit, it could provide a substantial opportunity for Australian farm exports. There are significant market opportunities on all sides, providing comprehensive FTAs are implemented that are 'living agreements', rather than static, minimalist, sector-specific agreements.

Theoretical context

Recent analyses focus upon the EU's increasing regulatory power, defined by Bradford (2012, 66) as the 'unilateral employment of tools of soft coercion that go against the preferences of its trading partners.' The 'Brussels effect' is similar to the repercussions of the 'California effect', where California's market power has effectively driven regulatory reform for decades across a wider range of policies, such as the *Clean Air Act* waiver and automotive passive and active safety (EPA 2014). Similarly, the EU has exported aspects of its competition regime utilising both EU anti-trust legislation and OECD roundtables (Davison 2002). Concomitantly, the EU and the G7 have implemented international banking regulation, anti-money laundering policy and countered terrorist financing under the rubric of the Financial Action Task Force since 1990 (Davison 2007). Within these frameworks, the EU has successfully exported governance aspects of the Single Market (SM) to foreign jurisdictions (Davison 2011, 10). As Bradford (2012, 3) notes, this has externalised EU law and regulations well beyond the territorial confines of the SM. Thus, the Brussels effect is market-driven, as the EU deploys its market power both to harmonise the regulations of its trade partners, as well to advance its own sectional interests through the protection of EU firms and their intellectual property. A key example is the EU's insistence upon the implementation of its geographical indications (GI) regime; for example, trade-marking the use of local European names to prevent their use by competing food and beverage products, which is designed to extend the commercial protection of specific products, particularly foodstuffs. In this chapter, the EU-Australia negotiations on the GI regime provide an apposite case study of the efficacy of the 'Brussels effect' in 'new trade agreements'.

Existing evidence demonstrates that FTAs that create more trade and investment than they divert tend to produce welfare-positive outcomes. This is the rationale behind 'new trade agreements', which include agricultural trade reform, regulatory harmonisation, liberalisation of services trade, investment and the elimination of customs 'red tape' at, and behind, borders under the landmark 2017 World Trade Organization (WTO) Trade Facilitation Agreement (TFA). The EU has responded to 'new trade' politics by advocating a 'deep' trade agenda, seeking multilateral agreements governing domestic regulations (Young 2006). 'New' trade agreements are also 'living agreements', subject to regular review, and amendable if all FTA parties agree. Australia is already party to 'living agreements', such as the Comprehensive and Progressive Agreement for Trans-Pacific Partnership (CPTPP) (2018). Consequently, any FTAs with the EU or UK are likely to be 'living agreements.' In the absence of a new WTO multilateral framework since 1994, states have relied increasingly upon bilateral, plurilateral and regional trade agreements (RTAs). Australia has adopted a 'networked FTA' approach, which, in some cases, results in overlapping and cross-cutting FTA agreements that collectively cover different market sectors, investment regimes and disciplines (DFAT 2018b). These include the Australia-NZ FTA (1984), the Australia-Singapore (2003) and Australia-Thailand (2007) FTAs, the CPTPP (2018) and the Regional Comprehensive Economic Partnership (2020). FTAs seek to lock in structural reforms, harmonise policy transfers and adjustments, facilitate technology transfer, foreign direct investment (FDI) and foreign portfolio investment (FPI), improve institutional capacity building and enhance macroeconomic stability via the minimisation of the impact of external shocks and exchange-rate volatility. Consequently, FTA implementation results necessarily in closer integration and greater macroeconomic cooperation (Plummer et al 2010).

The majority of studies have found empirical evidence supporting the positive effects FTAs have upon both two-way trade volumes, as well as services and investment flows. There is an integral connection between membership of an FTA and both horizontal and vertical investment flows (Thangavelu & Findlay 2011). A large number of studies examine the effect of RTAs at the country level in the context of how FTAs and cross-regional partnerships affect the flows of trade and FDI (Blomstrom & Kokko 1999; Park & Koo 2007). FTAs produce economies of scale; increased flows of FDI and FPI, more competitive and efficient firms and resource allocation, leading to higher long-run growth. For example, since the promulgation of the 2005 Australia-US FTA, two-way FDI and FPI volumes between Australia and the US had grown to $A1.47 trillion by 2016. US-Australia two-way trade volumes were more than $US7 billion higher in 2019 than in 2004 (US Census Bureau 2020). The ASEAN-Australia-New Zealand FTA (AANZFTA) saw Australia-ASEAN two-way FDI double to over $A220 billion between 2007 and 2016 (ABS 2016).

Thus, the dynamic and supply-side effects of FTAs are clear. The EU-South Korea FTA (2011) boosted EU exports by 35 per cent in its first three years. The North American Free Trade Agreement (NAFTA) quadrupled both goods and services trade between the US, Canada and Mexico between 1993 and 2015. The benefits also extend to investment. Utilising OECD datasets on 60 host countries, three economists found a 'huge' effect of FTAs upon FDI stocks. They found the direct effect of a regional integration agreement (such as the EU, NAFTA and ASEAN) increases the net FDI position by between 20 and 30 per cent (Yeyati et al 2003). Depending upon the size of the economies involved, this percentage could be much larger. A 2010 study showed that countries entering a preferential FTA are almost never affected negatively (Fernandez et al 2010). However, Bhagwati (1995) argues that cross-cutting FTAs militate against WTO multilateralism and instigate a 'spaghetti bowl effect' that produces trade and investment diversion, as well as discouraging firms from FTA utilisation due to cost and complexity.

The strategic shift to FTAs

A consequence of the collapse of the 2003 Doha WTO Ministerial conference has been the proliferation of bilateral, plurilateral and regional trade agreements. However, FTAs formed under the rubric of the 'New Trade Agenda', extend well beyond traditional issues such as tariff barriers (TBs) and non-tariff barriers (NTBs). 'New trade' agreements can incorporate behind the border (BtB) issues, services, mutual recognition agreements (MRA), intellectual property (IP), product standards, investment treaties, competition policy and public procurement. They are focused on global supply chains, services and FDI. As WTO multilateralism has declined, states have sought to address NTBs and technical barriers to trade in FTAs and regional trade agreements (RTAs).

The EU emphasised bilateral agreements in its 2006 'Global Europe' strategy, although it commenced signing bilateral FTAs well before the promulgation of the Doha Round, with partners such as Turkey (1995), Israel (1995) and Mexico (1997). The EU's FTA strategy has also targeted particular markets. For example, the 2019 EU-Singapore FTA (EUSFTA) emerged from the abortive EU-ASEAN FTA negotiations. Launched in 2009, the EUSFTA became the blueprint for the EU's penetration of Southeast Asian markets and the basis of any future ASEAN agreement. The EU-South Korea (EUROK) FTA (2011) and the EU-Japan Economic Partnership Agreement (2019) also demonstrated that Brussels was serious in expanding its trade and investment penetration of Northeast Asia. EUROK produced not only closer EU-ROK trade interdependence, but also negative externalities, such as financial volatility. The Euro-zone (EZ) crisis, particularly as the Greek crisis deepened in 2011, infiltrated ROK collateralised debt swap (CDS) markets and affect-ed won exchange rates. As the ROK's largest foreign investor, EU investment posed the most risk to ROK financial stability. However, the Bank of Korea conducted currency swaps with the US Fed, the Bank of Japan and the People's Bank of China but it did not resort to the Chiang Mai Initiative Multilateralisation (CMIM), the ASE-AN+3 swap arrangement that had been bolstered in the wake of the 2008 global financial crisis. In reality, the greater threat to South Korea's economy lay in its heavy trade exposure to China. Subse-quently, due largely to the EUROK FTA, ROK exports recovered rapidly once the ECB undertook market stabilisation measures in mid-2012, and grew strongly in 2013. The point here is that com-plex levels of interdependence via trade and investment agreements expose FTA partners to sensitivity and vulnerability interdepen-dence, as well as negative integration effects during periods of fi-nancial turbulence. Nevertheless, the EU's Asian FTAs have driven significant two-way trade and investment growth; consequently, it is scarcely surprising that post-Brexit Britain has sought to replicate the EU's Japan, South Korea and Singapore FTAs.

The UK's transition to a 'global FTA' strategy

In the wake of the 2016 Brexit referendum, the UK government an-nounced that it sought to become a global trade leader and sup-porter of WTO multilateralism. However, the May and Johnson governments also committed to utilising strategic bilateral and plu-rilateral FTAs to bolster UK trade and investment networks. The UK also aims to identify and remove NTBs to trade as part of its ef-forts to lay the groundwork for FTAs with 21 countries with which it conducted informal trade dialogues prior to January 2020. Given the commitments made by successive Conservative governments to multilateralism, two central goals are germane to the UK's FTA negotiations:

> Complete FTAs with key partners that focus on reducing NTBs that go beyond the WTO rules whilst continuing to support multilateral efforts to achieve trade liberalisation; and,
>
> Ensure WTO-plus FTAs will support and not hinder later efforts at multilateralism (Kenyon & van der Eng 2017: 257–8).

Australia and the UK committed to negotiate an AUKFTA in February 2020, with a focus upon services, investment, NTBs and digital economy. The UK is the source of approximately 50% of EU investment into Australia. In contrast, only a third of Australian investment in the EU is external to the UK. Consequently, the negotiation rounds of the AEUFTA have emphasised the removal of barriers to merchandise trade (Drake-Brockman 2017, 50–1). In comparing the prioritisation of the two potential FTAs, Treisman and Di Lieto (2017, 58–9) argue that Australia should prioritise an AEUFTA, due to lower intensity of competition in goods and services trade flows between Australia and the EU than between Australia and the UK. A range of intervening variables are likely to have a significant influence upon the negotiation of AEU and AUK agreements after 2020, including: exchange rates; the composition of AEUFTA and AUKFTA trade agreements; and the exogenous effects of third-country FTAs with the UK, such as a prospective US-UK FTA.

The revised UK tariff regime with third countries was not published until May 2020. The UK Global Tariff (UKGT) applies from January 2021 to all countries with which it does not have a FTA agreement. UKGT includes a 10% automotive tariff, while all tariffs below 2% will be abolished, increasing the proportion of zero-tariff goods to 60% (47% prior to 2021). However, UK agricultural and seafood tariffs will remain, and these sectors remain key areas of focus in the AUKFTA negotiation. Moreover, in November 2020, the UK *Internal Market Bill 2019-21*, which permits specific breaches of international and domestic law, was introduced into Parliament (UK Parliament 2020). The Bill sought to make it unlawful to impose trade controls between Northern Ireland and Great Britain, a piece of legislation that explicitly breaks the rule of law by abrogating UK undertakings made in the 2019 EU-UK Withdrawal Agreement. In response, the EU Commission stated it would commence legal action against the UK in the European Court of Justice, while the Irish government announced it would block any EU-UK trade deal if the UK did not withdraw the legislation (The Independent 2020). Throughout the 2020 EU-UK trade negotiations, the key obstacle to any clarity in UK trade policy was the uncertainty concerning the extent of EU-UK market integration from 2021. The breakdown of EU-UK negotiations in October 2020 compounded unpredictability for business and cast doubt over whether the UK would sign a comprehensive FTA or, conversely, adopt a 'hard', no-deal Brexit. Under a UKGT no-deal scenario, EU agribusiness would face food tariffs; conversely, under a AUKFTA, reduced or zero tariffs for Australian food products would thus gain a competitive advantage, although EU fresh food exports would maintain a proximity and green miles advantage. The UK also risked losing banking market share to competing EU capitals and New York in the absence of a UK-EU deal on financial services. An Ernst & Young survey in 2018 found that over 275 banking or finance firms had shifted operations to Dublin, Luxembourg, Paris, Frankfurt or Amsterdam. By 2019, over £1 trillion in UK assets had been shifted to the EU. In Switzerland, UBS moved $US36 billion from Britain to Germany (IG Group 2019). The European Council's guidelines of April 2017 and March 2018 reiterated the integrity of the Single Market and Customs Union; indivisibility of the Four Freedoms; and the prohibition of sector-by-sector participation in the Single Market (European Council 2018).

The context of the Council's guidelines and the Commission's EU-UK FTA negotiations working framework were largely uncontroversial and aimed to exceed WTO disciplines by adopting a WTO-Plus framework for technical barriers to trade (TBTs). However, obstacles emerged in relation to the EU's regulatory regimes, including state aid, product conformity, labelling (TBT) and regulation of sanitary and phytosanitary (SPS) products. In 2017, the May government introduced the Taxation (Cross-border Trade) Bill and the Trade Bill, foreshadowing the UK's own trade remedies regime after Brexit, where the EU Commission would no longer monitor unfair trade. Even the UK's own regime would involve EU regulatory transfer; the UK Trade White Paper notes the government would, 'identify which of the existing EU trade remedy measures are most relevant to the UK's industries.' The 2018 *Withdrawal Act* repealed the 1972 *European Communities Act* whilst confirming the transposition of the critical mass of EU law into UK legislation. From 2021, Westminster is not bound to retain harmonisation with the SM; instead, it allows Parliament to repeal or amend legislation on a case-by-case basis. The 2020 *European Union (Withdrawal Agreement) Act* did not provide enforceable undertakings regarding the types of trade and investment regimes the UK Parliament might implement following the expiry of the transition period at the end of 2020. In February 2020, Prime Minister Johnson stated the UK would accept no alignment and no jurisdiction of the European courts in any EU-UK FTA. Foreign Secretary Raab reiterated this point during his Australian visit in February 2020, arguing the UK would not align with EU rules (BBC 2020a).

This is problematic for an AUKFTA as some Australian disciplines and product standards are likely to be closely harmonised with EU regimes following the promulgation of the AEUFTA. Variance in UK standards or trade controls could effectively constitute technical barriers to trade faced by Australian exporters. In addition, the scope and timing of a UK-US FTA will also have a significant impact on the effectiveness of the AUKFTA. First, despite the AUK bilateral commitment to a comprehensive FTA, UK merchandise trade exports to the US exceeded $US64 billion in 2018, compared with only $US5 billion to Australia. Second, the US possesses a considerable advantage over Australia in terms of food miles from farm to plate. Third, leaked documents during the 2019 UK General Election revealed that the British government had covertly conducted six rounds of FTA negotiations with Washington since 2017 (BBC 2019).

For Britain, the Department for International Trade (2020) estimates a comprehensive UK-US FTA would deliver only modest gains of 0.16% of GDP within one year and £3.4 billion ($A6.2 billion) after 15 years. A less ambitious agreement would result in only 0.07% in GDP gains by the mid-2030s. The UK imports only small volumes of prepared foodstuffs, vegetable products, live animals and mineral products from the US. The 2019 US-China trade agreement saw significant opportunities emerge for US agricultural exporters; however, Australian and US producers do not compete directly in most farm export sectors. In contrast, Australian exporters seeking access to UK agricultural markets will still face significant competition from proximate products from the EU in market sectors such as wheat, poultry and dairy. A US-UK FTA would also give American exporters improved UK market access for these products, as well as beef, placing Australia in direct competition with US producers. However, with no UK-US FTA concluded in 2020, Canberra could obtain a first-mover advantage by concluding a UK FTA before Washington.

Europe: the 'missing link' in Australia's network of FTAs

Australia has no extant FTAs or bilateral investment treaties (BITs) with the EU or UK. An AEUFTA would incorporate traditional trade liberalisation precepts into a 'new trade agenda' model. This would include uniform regulations in mature markets, such as trade in services, intellectual property rights, geographical indications (GIs), digital economy, bilateral investment rules and the free movement of professional skilled labour.

Closer Australia-EU trade integration has been the focus of scholarly analysis for over 30 years (Davison 1991; Murray 2005; Mascitelli & Wilson 2019). The Rudd government transformed relations in 2008 with the EU-Australia Partnership Framework Agreement, which reinvigorated the impetus for deeper trade and investment relations. Australia undertook exploratory pre-negotiations with the EU prior to the UK Brexit vote. In 2018, Australia-UK two-way trade in goods and services totalled almost $A27 billion. (DFAT 2019b). In 2018, Australian firms had over $A400 billion invested in the UK, while two-way Australia-UK investment (FDI and portfolio) between 2010 and 2017 totalled A$815 billion, UK FDI represented almost 50 per cent of all Australian foreign direct investment (FDI) from the EU (Austrade 2018). In 2019, 16.4 percent of FDI and FPI originated from the UK, while the EU plus Switzerland accounted for over 17.7% (DFAT 2019c). In 2018, Australian combined direct and portfolio investment stock in the EU totalled $A713 billion, with EU outward investment in Australia totalling $1.22 billion (DFAT 2019d). The EU's scoping study modelling predicted an AEUFTA would increase Australian GDP by 0.13% under a conservative agreement, and by 0.2% under an 'increased liberalisation' model. This would result in EU GDP increases of 0.01% and 0.02%, respectively, equating to $A4.1–$A6.4 billion GDP gains for Australia through 2030 from an AEUFTA, depending on variables within the agreement. The type and extent of any inclusions and exclusions in any prospective AEUFTA will heavily influence trade and investment outcomes. Existing evidence demonstrates that FTAs that create more trade and investment than they divert tend to produce welfare-positive outcomes (Davison 2016, 2017). EU modelling predicts an increase in Australia-EU two-way trade of $A11.2–$A17.9 billion (CEC 2017).

The Australia-EU relationship has suffered from inadequate knowledge of the complexities of EU policy-making that has resulted in missed opportunities and negative consequences for Australia (Murray 2005; Winand et al 2015). Australia and the EU launched FTA negotiations in 2018, following a considerable volume of private sector and scholarly assessment that Australia should seek a comprehensive AEUFTA. Brexit only reinforces this view. In 2019, Australia-EU two-way trade totalled over $A85 billion, including approximately $A40 billion in services exports, where the EU has a comparative advantage (DFAT 2020a). The EU is the world's largest importer of commercial services, such as design, construction, tendering, outsourcing, legal services and telecommunication services. Australia has 4,000 services exporters, and 1,500 firms may no longer be able to utilise the UK as an offshore base for entry into the EU SM after 2019. 48 per cent of Australia's service exports to the EU entered Europe via the UK (Parliament of Australia 2017). This will no longer be possible, as the UK will not have automatic access to the four freedoms – freedom of movement of goods, services, labour and capital – throughout the EU. The EU is Australia's fifth-biggest export market and largest partner in two-way services trade. Minus the UK, it will remain the second-largest regional trade agreement (RTA) and market in the world, behind the USMCA.

Recent national business surveys indicate 46% of respondents are seeking new export markets facilitated by FTAs (CEC 2017). Australian corporations have identified benefits such as price competition, new customers and increased export sales as a direct consequence of new FTAs. Business has also identified government procurement, investment (FDI), market access, regulatory regimes, cross-border services, rules of origin (RoO) and NTB 'behind the border' (BtB) obstacles as the priorities in targeting FTA issues (PwC 2018).

Consequently, prospective EU and UK FTAs are viewed as considerable market opportunities. For example, Australian firms and policy makers regard agricultural market access to the EU and UK as a first-order trade issue. The UK imports over 50% of its food, and it exports 60% of its agricultural output to the EU. The 2020 COVID-19 pandemic compelled three UK food policy experts to call for rationing in the face of dependence upon Spanish and Italian food exports. UK food retailers carry no more than 24-36 hours stock. Concomitantly, a combination of Brexit and COVID-19 saw the UK face a severe seasonal farm labour shortage in early 2020. Consequently, the UK government's perspective is that there are clear incentives to diversify its food supplies from just-in-time EU sources to include major agricultural exporters, such as the US and Australia.

UK farmers have also relied upon EU subsidies for 50-60% of their income. In Scotland, Wales and Northern Ireland, the subsidies can comprise 75%-87% of farm incomes. Even highly profitable farms receive significant subsidies. Current UK Treasury policy envisages Common Agricultural Policy (CAP) subsidies will remain in place throughout the transition period. However, some studies envisage a post-Brexit shutdown of up to 25% of farms due to unprofitability (NIESR 2017). Australian policy makers regard a UK trade agreement as a major opportunity to secure free market access to UK food and beverage markets. The CAP farm support and complex EU tariff and quota systems will be eliminated from the UK at the end of the 2020 transition period. The UK is Australia's 15th-largest food market, with 2015 exports totalling $A700 million, comprising mainly wine and beef. The UK is also Australia's largest wine market by volume and third-largest by value. However, the EU-Australia Wine Agreement will no longer apply after 2021. The Department of Agriculture and Water Resources argues that, despite its small total share of Australian food exports, the UK is a high-value market. Peak groups such as Agribusiness Australia regard Britain as highly likely to diversify its food import sources from the EU to third countries after 2021 (Parliament of Australia 2017a: 41).

Equally, liberalisation of financial services in future AEUFTA and AUKFTA agreements are considered critical to Australia's investment, credit and equity markets. UK outward FDI is heavily concentrated in the financial services sector, with UK FDI and FPI representing a major part of the critical mass of both gross capital formation and capital markets liquidity in Australia. The vast majority of EU-sourced FDI and FPI flow through the City of London. However, depending on whether the EU and UK sign a services agreement after Brexit, London will otherwise lose its 'bank passport' access to the EU Single Market in financial services. All members of the EU Single Market possess 'passport' access, enabling all bank and non-bank financial institutions to offer services throughout the EU without restriction. Australian FDI and FPI, largely routed through London banks, would also lose access to EU markets and would be compelled to seek financial services access via an AEU agreement.

DFAT identified an AUKFTA as a priority early in the Brexit process. Over 1,500 Australian businesses are resident in the UK. Approximately 470 Australian-owned firms had 44,000 employees and total annual sales of $A22.3 billion in 2016. UK exit negotiations with the EU had 12 objectives. These included transposing the Acquis, the EU body of law, into domestic UK legislation; a comprehensive FTA with the EU; and forging global FTAs (HMG 2018a). The Trade Bill 2017-19 was introduced into UK Parliament in November 2017 to create the necessary powers to transpose FTAs signed by the EU into domestic UK law, and to allow the UK to implement the Agreement on Government Procurement (GPA) as an independent member, rather than through the EU (HMG 2017b). On 31 January, 2020, the UK entered a transition period during which the London can negotiate FTAs with third parties that can enter into force following the transition period. Current EU FTAs apply to the UK throughout the transition period (HMG 2018a). The 2018 'Global Britain' strategy identified the US, Europe and the Indo-Pacific as the UK's key relationships. It endorses an 'All of Asia' approach. In June 2020, the Australian and UK governments announced the commencement of negotiations for a comprehensive AUKFTA (DAWE 2020).

Aggressive bilateralism: Geographical indications and the 'Brussels effect'

The 'Brussels effect' of externalised EU law and regulations is well exemplified by the EU's strategic inclusion of GIs in its FTA negotiations. Australia and the EU agreed to include GIs in the FTA during the pre-negotiation process. The EU treats GI protection as central to its trade objectives and, consequently, GIs exist in all 'Global Europe' FTAs and GI or trademarked products typically command a 20-50% price premium over generic products (Moir 2017). There are three databases for EU GIs. The DOOR database for food and agricultural products; the E-Bacchus database for wine protections; and the e-Spirit-Drinks database for spirits (CEC 2020). EU FTA documents clearly view GIs as central, rather than side issues; the EU states that the public 'misperceptions' about GIs need to be addressed, noting that the protection of GIs is an important FTA issue aimed at securing market access for EU businesses which face 'unfair competition' in Australia and New Zealand. Moreover, the EU Commission states that 'robust protection of EU GIs through the FTA is essential for realising the potential gains for the EU processed food sector' (CEC 2019: 3).

GIs have proven a controversial policy area and a source of friction between the EU and Australia. Canberra has typically opposed the EU's attempts to introduce certain non-trade issues into the WTO. This includes the extension of GIs into new product areas and the EU's 'multifunctional' approach to agriculture. The EU has also considered extending GIs beyond agricultural products to include colours or symbols that may evoke the brand. The EU has generally sought to extend GIs to sui generis register systems and spread strong forms of protection for GIs beyond the wine and spirit protection in the WTO's Trade-Related Aspects of Intellectual Property Rights (TRIPS) agreement. This can allow for the clawback of some generic names, and the shifting of administrative enforcement onto taxpayers. In contrast, Australia's objectives for GIs are limited to IP, stating it will seek to 'maintain a balance between the interests of rights holders and users and the public interest', and 'address the protection of geographical indications in a mutually acceptable way' (DFAT 2018c).

The EU Commission's impact assessment on the AEUFTA noted that EU GIs have insufficient protection, specifically identifying the wine and spirit industries, as well as dairy, for further extensions of GI protection (CEC 2017: 8–29). In 2019, DFAT published the list of GIs for which the EU requested protection. The inclusion of feta, gruyère and scotch beef drew widespread opposition from the Australia farm and food and beverage sectors (DFAT 2019a). Gruyère remains on the 2019 AEUFTA list, despite the US Patent and Trademarks Office's declaration of its generic status in 2012 (International Dairy Foods Association 2012). However, most of the GIs listed are obscure products, although there are exceptions, such as

Prosecco, which the EU in 1994 labelled as a grape variety; it was also excluded in the 2008 Australia-EU Wine Agreement. However, the EU made an abortive attempt to register Prosecco as a GI in 2013, before once again including it on its GI list in 2019, in an apparent attempt to circumvent TRIPS Article 20. This would affect the $A60 million Australian Prosecco export industry (Consortium for Common Food Names 2019). DFAT has given no commitment to protect specific GIs, although consensus on the issue is a prerequisite for the finalisation of any AEUFTA. EU negotiators will likely horse-trade specific GIs, such as 'Prosecco' in return for other Australian market concessions. DFAT's clear strategy is to leverage GI protection into comprehensive market access, including agriculture, which the Australian government views as the most important aspect of the AEUFTA. The Department of Agriculture (2019) states this explicitly: 'Any commitments on GIs in the FTA will depend on what the EU is prepared to offer Australia, with regard to market access.' The Common Agricultural Policy's (CAP) complex system of subsidies, combined with high-tariff food markets, has rendered many Australian food exports uncompetitive in the EU market. In order to secure GI naming protection and other sectoral market access provisions in an AEUFTA, the EU is likely to allow Australian foodstuffs partial agricultural market access, most likely via reform of specific tariff-rate quota arrangements.

Brexit's variegated impacts include the UK's discrete development of a GI branding regime that will be independent from the EU. In its 2018 White Paper, the UK government announced its own GI scheme, with the stated objective of consistency with the WTO's TRIPS provisions. Following the UK's departure from the EU in 2020, the government planned to register all existing UK GIs automatically to ensure they retained legal protection. Although the White Paper contained few details, the scheme was open to new UK and non-UK applications; Australian producers are thus likely to seek new protections for agribusiness products under a UK GI regime. The White Paper stressed the importance of three protected UK products; Scotch whisky, Scottish farmed salmon and Welsh lamb and beef (HMG 2018b, 23–4). In a separate paper, the Commons' Scottish Affairs Committee noted the 'crucial importance' of the EU GI regime to the protection of Scottish products (HOC 2019). GIs remained a point of contention throughout the EU-UK withdrawal negotiations in 2016–18. In August 2019, the UK government published its own GI list of approximately 100 products. Under the October 2019 Withdrawal Agreement, London agreed to protect over 3,000 existing EU GIs under UK law, although such protections render any UK-US FTA negotiations more difficult. In 2019 the UK announced it would implement its own GI scheme from 1 January, 2021, which it states would 'mirror existing EU schemes' (HMG 2019b). Although it is unlikely the EU would renegotiate the GIs agreement, the British government maintains the existing regime would be challengeable in UK courts.

Agriculture has proven to be the major stumbling block in Australia-EU relations for over 40 years. Although agribusiness accounts for a diminishing proportion of GDP, Australia exports 75% of its produce, supplying 80–100 million international and domestic consumers. The farm lobby is well-funded and the National Party is influential within the Coalition government and dominates the Parliamentary Trade subcommittee, although the recent loss of its traditional trade portfolio in DFAT illustrates its diminishing influence over the FTA agenda. Since 1973, the CAP has proven the major obstacle to closer EU-Australia trade relations. While the 2015 Nairobi WTO ministerial largely extinguished farm export subsidies in developed countries, Brussels' multifunctional approach to agriculture has sought to broaden the agricultural policy agenda to include food quality, food safety, animal welfare, environmental protection, consumer protection and effects on rural communities.

In recently concluded FTAs, Brussels has retained its high-tariff food regime, while also leveraging its market power to extend GI protection. The EU Council's Directives for the AEUFTA negotiations indicate support for the highest possible level of merchandise trade liberalisation, but flags the agricultural sector for partial liberalisation only, reflecting the concerns of a number of agribusiness-intensive EU regions. The European Parliament (EP), will also need to approve an AEUFTA that maintains a delicate balance between maintaining protection of EU farmers and GIs, while assuaging the export-oriented Australian agribusiness sector with increased access to EU food markets.

Conclusion

Agriculture is the central issue in the AEUFTA and AUKFTA trade negotiations, and geographical indications are integral to the EU's strategic policy in the agricultural sector. This chapter illustrates some of the complex challenges associated with these two inter-related areas. The contested nature of agriculture and GIs also allows the larger policy implications of the dual-track negotiations to be considered. GI protection directly supports the CAP. Three thousand EU food products receive a major boost from the EU GI regime. This not only reduces direct competition in high-value sectors, such as dairy and wine, but also allows firms to charge higher prices for specifically-branded products.

The uncertainty surrounding the final Brexit outcome will limit the AUKFTA negotiations until London reaches an agreement with Brussels. A comprehensive EU-UK FTA may narrow the number of sector-specific negotiations that Canberra and London can undertake. No AUKFTA can be ratified until EU-UK negotiations are completed. In addition, if the Johnson government fails to negotiate a wide-ranging deal with the EU, the chances of the UK concluding a suboptimal FTA with Washington increase exponentially, in order to meet domestic political demands for a raft of agreements to act as ersatz substitutes to compensate for the loss of access to the EU SM.

As this chapter notes, a US-UK FTA would make Australia's EU and UK FTAs even more complex. A London-Washington agreement could adversely affect the chances of Australia securing improved access to the UK food markets. This leaves Canberra in an unpredictable position, amidst the uncertainty surrounding the level of SM access London may obtain from the EU. A US-UK FTA is also likely to amplify trade and investment diversion to Australia's disadvantage. This would further entrench the uncertainty Australian firms, which have traditionally utilised the UK as a EU operations base, have experienced since the Brexit vote. Consequently, the Australian government should seek the most comprehensive living agreement it can obtain via the AEUFTA, before negotiating the AUKFTA. Maximising market access in both the EU and UK for agriculture is desirable, but this must be weighed against the trade-off in NTBs in issue areas such as GIs. A successful balance of gaining agricultural access by granting GI concessions would mean Australia achieves its stated trade objectives, albeit at the expense of both its trade mark regime, as well as the considerable commercial losses faced by local industries, such as Prosecco exporters, if the AEUFTA were to concede well-known products to the EU under the rubric of GIs. In any event, Brussels' strategy is clear: the EU is leveraging FTAs and market access in exchange for GI concessions from partners.

The optimum outcome for Australia when it commenced the pre-negotiation talks with the EU was the *status quo*: for Britain to remain a EU member. However, the Brexit referendum compelled successive British governments to adopt a strategy that would effect a UK withdrawal from the world's most economically-integrated region with insufficient substitute market access regimes in place.

The lessons of Brexit are already clear: no country has ever exited a FTA, reduced its market access and increased its prosperity as a result.

References

https://www.austrade.gov.au/International/Invest/Importance-of-Foreign-Direct-Investment/UK-investment-in-Australia#:~:text=%E2%80%9CStrong%20Ties%2C%20Growing%20Stronger%E2%80%9D,all%20sectors%20of%20each%20economy.

Australian Bureau of Statistics (ABS) (2016), 'International Investment Position', ABS Catalogue No. 53520 Australia: Supplementary Statistics. 3.0%22http://www.abs.gov.au/ausstats/abs@.nsf/mf/5352.0.

BBC (2019), 'General election 2019: Source of UK-US trade document leak must be found – PM', 7 December.

BBC (2020a), 'Brexit: Raab in Australia at start of trade mission', 7 February. https://www.bbc.com/news/uk-politics-51399215.

BBC (2020b), 'Brexit: EU leaders call for UK trade talks to continue', 15 October.

Bhagwati, J (1995), 'Preferential Trade Agreements: The Wrong Road', *Law and Policy in International Business*, vol. 27.

Bhagwati, J & Patrick, H (eds) (1990), *Aggressive Unilateralism: America's 301 Trade Policy and the World Trading System*, University of Michigan Press, Ann Arbor.

Blomstrom, M & Kokko, A (1999), 'Regional integration and foreign direct investment', National Bureau for Economic Research, NEBR Working Paper No. 6019.

Bradford, A (2012), 'The Brussels Effect', *Northwestern University Law Review*, vol. 107 no, 1, 1-67.

Capling, A (2001), *Australia and the Global Trade System: from Havana to Seattle*, Cambridge University Press, Cambridge.

Capling, A & Ravenhill, J (2015), 'Australia's Flawed Approach to Trade Negotiations: and where do we sign?', *Australian Journal of International Affairs*, vol. 69, no. 5, 496-501.

Capie, F, Wood, G & Sensenbrenner, F (2005), 'Attitudes to foreign investment in the United Kingdom', in Huizinga, H. & Jonung, L. (eds) (2005) *The Internationalisation of Asset Ownership in Europe*, Cambridge University Press, Cambridge.

Commission of the European Union (CEC) (2017), 'Impact Assessment: Recommendation for a Council Decision authorising the opening of negotiations for a Free Trade Agreement with Australia', COM (2017) 472, 13 September.

Commission of the European Union (CEC) (2019), 'Support to EU-Australia & EU-New Zealand FTA Negotiations' FWC PSF 2019 – Lot 3, Ref. Ares (2020) 1148515, 24 February 2020.

Commission of the European Union (CEC) (2020), 'Quality products registers', 10 January. https://ec.europa.eu/info/food-farming-fisheries/food-safety-and-quality/certification/quality-labels/quality-products-registries_en.

Consortium for Common Food Names (2019), 'EU's Claim to Sparkling 'Prosecco' falls flat in Australia', 4 September. http://www.commonfoodnames.com/eus-claim-to-sparkling-prosecco-falls-flat-in-australia/.

Davison, R (1991), 'Between Europe and Asia: Australia's options in the world economy of the 1990s', *Melbourne Journal of Politics*, vol. 20, 40-67.

Davison, R (2002), 'Regulation or intervention? Australian and European Union policies on competition', *Law in Context*, vol. 20, no. 1, 63-100.

Davison, R (2007), "Soft law' regimes and European organisations' fight against terrorist financing and money-laundering', in L.T. Holmes (ed.), *Terrorism, Organised Crime and Corruption: Networks and Linkages*, Edward Elgar, Cheltenham, 61–85.

Davison, R (2011), *The Political Economy of Single Market Europe*, Lambert, Saarbrücken.

Davison, R (2016), 'Submission to the Inquiry into the Free Trade Negotiations between Australia and the European Union', Department of Foreign Affairs and Trade, Canberra. https://www.dfat.gov.au/sites/default/files/dr-remy-davison-monash-university-eufta-submission.PDF.

Davison, R (2017), 'Submission to the Parliamentary Joint Standing Committee on Foreign Affairs, Defence and Trade Inquiry into Australia's trade and investment relationship with the United Kingdom', Parliament of Australia, Canberra, https://www.aph.gov.au/DocumentStore. ashx?id=663a5004-ad9b-4e02-bd75-ee933f46dd17&subId=463922.

Davison, R (2018), 'The risks of a no-deal Brexit', Committee for the Economic Development of Australia (CEDA), 19 December.

Department of Agriculture, Water and the Environment (DAWE), Australia (2019), 'Free trade agreements signed or concluded (but not yet in force)', 13 November. https://www.agriculture.gov.au/market-access-trade/fta/ftas-signed-under-negotiation.

DAWE (2020), 'United Kingdom – Brexit and Australia-United Kingdom Free Trade Agreement', 18 June. https://www.agriculture.gov.au/market-access-trade/preparing-for-brexit.

Department of Foreign Affairs & Trade (DFAT) (2018a), 'Composition of Trade 2017', 9 July. https://dfat.gov.au/about-us/publications/Pages/composition-of-trade.aspx.

DFAT (2018b), 'China-Australia Free Trade Agreement', https://dfat.gov.au/trade/agreements/in-force/chafta/doing-business-with-china/Pages/guide-to-using-chafta-to-export-or-import.aspx.

DFAT (2018c), 'Australia-European Union Free Trade Agreement: Objectives', June. https://www.dfat.gov.au/trade/agreements/negotiations/aeufta/Pages/australia-european-union-fta-objectives.aspx.

DFAT (2018d), 'Australia-European Union Free Trade Agreement: Summary of negotiating aims and approach', https://www.dfat.gov.au/trade/agreements/negotiations/aeufta/Pages/summary-of-negotiating-aims-and-approach.

DFAT (2018e), 'European Union brief'. https://www.dfat.gov.au/geo/europe/european-union/Pages/european-union-brief .

DFAT (2019a), 'List of EU FTA Geographical Indications'. https://www.dfat.gov.au/trade/agreements/negotiations/aeufta/public-objections-gis/Pages/list-of-european-union-geographic-indications-gis.

DFAT (2019b), 'Prospective Australia-United Kingdom Free Trade Agreement', 19 June. https://www.dfat.gov.au/trade/agreements/prospective/aukfta/Pages/australia-uk-fta.

DFAT (2019c), 'Statistics on who invests in Australia', July. https://www.dfat.gov.au/trade/resources/investment-statistics/Pages/statistics-on-who-invests-in-australia.

DFAT (2019d), 'Australia-European Union Free Trade Agreement fact sheet', November. https://www.dfat.gov.au/trade/agreements/negotiations/aeufta/Pages/australia-european-union-fta-fact-sheet.

DFAT (2020a), 'Australia-European Union Free Trade Agreement'. https://www.dfat.gov.au/trade/agreements/negotiations/aeufta/Pages/default.

DFAT (2020b), 'Australia-EU FTA – Report on Negotiating Round Eight, 14-25 September 2020', https://www.dfat.gov.au/trade/agreements/negotiations/aeufta/news/australia-eu-fta-report-negotiating-round-eight-14-25-september-2020.

Department of International Trade (2020), *UK-US Free Trade Agreement*, https://assets.publishing.service.gov.uk/government/uploads/system/uploads/attachment_data/file/869592/UK_US_FTA_negotiations.pdf.

Drake-Brockman, J (2017), 'Trade and Investment Between the EU and Australia' in A. Mochan & M. Conley Tyler (eds), *The EU and Australia: Shared Opportunities and Common Challenges*, Australian Institute of International Affairs, Canberra 50-51.

Elijah, A-M, Kenyon, D, Hussey, K & van der Eng, P (eds) (2017), *Australia, the European Union and the New Trade Agenda*, ANU Press, Canberra.

Environmental Protection Agency (EPA), United States (2014), 'History of Reducing Air Pollution from Transportation in the United States'. https://www.epa.gov/transportation-air-pollution-and-climate-change/accomplishments-and-success-air-pollution-transportation.

European Council (2018), *Negotiating Directives for a Free Trade Agreement with Australia*, Brussels: Council of the European Union, 2-6. http://www.consilium.europa.eu/media/35794/st07663-ad01dc01-en18.pdf.

Fernandez, A, Arribas, I & Tortosa-Ausina, E (2010), 'Testing the trade diversion hypothesis: the case of the European Union', paper delivered to the Ivie-FBBVA Workshop, July.

HMG (2017a), 'The United Kingdom's exit from and new partnership with the European Union', White Paper presented to Parliament by the Prime Minister, February.

HMG (2017b), 'Policy Paper: Information about the Trade Bill', 7 November. http://gov.uk.

HMG (2018a), 'Statement on a New Partnership with the EU: Statement to the House of Commons by David Davis, Secretary of State for Exiting the European Union', 17 January. http://gov.uk.

HMG (2018b), The Future Relationship Between the United Kingdom and the European Union, July.

HMG (2019a), 'UK and Australia agree continuity of Mutual Recognition Agreement', 18 January. http://gov.uk.

HMG (2019b), 'Protecting food and drink names from 1 January 2021', 5 February. http://gov.uk.

House of Commons (HOC) (2019), *Scotland, Trade and Brexit: Seventh Report of Session 2017-19 Report*, Scottish Affairs Committee, 7 March. https://publications.parliament.uk/pa/cm201719/cmselect/cmscotaf/903/903.pdf.

IG Group (2019), 'How will Brexit impact UK financial services?', 11 April. https://www.ig.com/au/trading-strategies/how-will-brexit-impact-uk-financial-services-181114.

Independent, The (2020), 'Ireland says it will block Brexit trade deal unless Boris Johnson backs down on Internal Market Bill', 15 November.

International Dairy Foods Association (2012), 'US Patent and Trademark Office Affirms Generic Status of 'Gruyere'', 9 May.

Kenyon, D & van der Eng, P (2017), 'Australia and the EU: Partners in the New Trade Agenda', in A-M. Elijah, D. Kenyon, K. Hussey, K. & P. van der Eng (eds) (2017) *Australia, the European Union and the New Trade Agenda*, ANU Press, Canberra 257-76.

Kerneis, P (2018), 'EU-Australia Free Trade Talks: Services Essential', in *The EU and Australia: towards a new era*, Australia-EU Leadership Forum, Brussels, 52-55.

Mascitelli, B & Wilson, B (2019), 'From protectionism to 'Free Trade'. Australia's long road to a trade rules based order: The Free Trade Agreement with the European Union', *Asia-Pacific Journal of EU Studies*, vol. 17, no. 2, 1-20.

Moir, H (2017), 'Geographical Indications: An Assessment of EU Treaty Demands', in A-M Elijah, D Kenyon, K Hussey, K & P van der Eng (eds) (2017) *Australia, the European Union and the New Trade Agenda*, ANU Press, Canberra, 121-38.

Murray, P (2005), *Australia and the European Superpower*. Melbourne University Press, Carlton.

National Institute of Economic & Social Research (NIESR) (2017), Agriculture in the UK, NIESR General Election 2017, Briefing no. 4, 26 May.

Park, SH & Koo, MG (2007), 'Forming a Cross-Regional Partnership: The South Korea-Chile FTA and its implications', *Pacific Affairs*, vol. 80, no. 2, 259-78.

Parliament of Australia (2017a), Inquiry into Australia's trade and investment relationship with the United Kingdom: Interim Report, Joint Standing Committee on Foreign Affairs, Defence and Trade, Commonwealth of Australia, Canberra, October.

Parliament of Australia (2017b), Possible implications of 'Brexit' for Australia's trade with the UK and the EU: Interim Report on Australia's trade and investment relationship with the UK, Joint Parliamentary Standing Committee on Foreign Affairs, Defence & Trade, Commonwealth of Australia, Canberra.

Plummer, M, Cheong, D & Hamanka, S (2010), *Methodology for impact assessment of free trade agreements*, Asian Development Bank, Manila.

Price Waterhouse Coopers (PwC) (2018), *Free Trade Agreement Utilisation Study*, PWC, Melbourne.

Thangavelu, SM & Findlay, C (2011), 'Foreign Direct Investment in the Asia-Pacific region', in C. Findlay, (ed.), *ASEAN+1 FTAs and Global Value Chains in East Asia*. ERIA Research Project Report 2010-29, Jakarta, ERIA, 112-131.

Treisman, D & Di Lieto, G (2017), 'Trade Data Shows Australia Can Get More Out of A Deal with the EU than the UK', in A Mochan & M Conley Tyler (eds), *The EU and Australia: Shared Opportunities and Common Challenges*, Australian Institute of International Affairs, Canberra, 55-6.

UK Parliament (2020), 'United Kingdom Internal Market Bill – Hansard', Parliamentary Hansard, Bill 177. https://services.parliament.uk/bills/2019-21/unitedkingdominternalmarket.html.

US Census Bureau (2020), 'Trade in goods with Australia'. https://www.census.gov/foreign-trade/balance/c6021.html.

Winand, P, Kalfadellis, P & Witzleb, N (2015), 'European and EU Studies and research in Australia through thick and thin: public policy and higher education mismatch?', *Australian Journal of Politics and History*, vol. 61 no. 1, 67-81.

World Bank (2020) 'GDP (current US$) – European Union, United States, China', World Bank national accounts data and OECD national account data files. https://data.worldbank.org/indicator/NY.GDP.MKTP.CD?locations=EU-US-CN

Yetati, EL, Stein, E & Daude, C (2003) *Regional Integration and the Location of FDI*, Working Paper, No. 492, Inter-American Development Bank, Research Department, Washington, DC.

11

CONTINUITY BEYOND BREXIT? EU JURIDIFICATION AND THE PROTECTION OF RIGHTS

Russell Solomon and John Erik Fossum

Keywords: Brexit, European law, Juridification, Human Rights, Path Dependence

Abstract

Brexit, now achieved, is, in general terms, identified as a de-juridification exercise (removing the UK from EU legal control and influence) as the UK seeks to 'take back control' and place the UK parliament at Westminster, if not the government itself, in the 'driver's seat'. As the antithesis of EU integration and enlargement, it can be considered to be a revolutionary policy change. However, Brexit is more than just about EU membership and the ongoing Brexit process and outcome is likely to be shaped by the history of the UK's EU entanglement. In discussing EU juridification through its various dimensions, this chapter examines the influence of EU juridification upon the UK's relationship with the EU with reference to its possible impact on rights protection. Applying an institutional approach to assess the complexity of the relationship, the chapter will argue that the likely enduring influence of EU juridification on rights, as in other UK policy areas, can be explained through path dependence theory.

Introduction

Brexit is both a process and an outcome, as well as the ultimate and opposite expression to the EU integration project. Those advocating Brexit in the UK are seeking to effect both policy and institutional change and are the latest of those who, over time, have sought to disentangle the UK from the EU legal embeddedness found within UK law. With a particular focus on rights, this chapter asks how much of a path dependent thrust will such embedding exert on the UK post-Brexit. Those advocating leaving without a deal had sought a dramatic break with the past. In effect, they were advocating the need for replacing law, as the main action coordination mechanism, with that of politics in the UK's relations with the rest of Europe. Prime Minister Johnson in threatening a no deal Brexit as he negotiated an amended deal, appeared to envision future EU-UK relations only in political terms and for these to be determined almost exclusively between political actors. Those seeking a softer Brexit, on the other hand, wanted to retain a substantial portion of EU law. Nevertheless, the fact that the UK through its 46 years of EU membership has become heavily Europeanised testifies to the need to acknowledge some form of norm and rule continuity post-Brexit as is already apparent in the UK's *European Union (Withdrawal) Act 2018* (EUWA).

This chapter's analysis is not about seeing the Brexit process and outcome as a direct product of the asymmetrical power positions of the EU and the UK. Rather, it is about understanding how the nature and extent of the EU's legal embedding within the UK will impact the UK after Brexit and, in particular, assist in protecting rights. The closer the UK's Brexit deal is to the current single market arrangements with the EU, the greater will be the EU's legal regime's influence. However, this chapter argues that even without a deal, the juridified nature of EU-UK relations would have seen EU law continue to have a major, if not a dominant, influence over UK law.

Juridification and path dependence in the EU

Juridification is about law and law's expansion. The literature on juridification presents it as a complex and composite notion and may
be said to consist in at least five related dimensions: a) constitutive
juridification; b) law's expansion and differentiation; c) increased
conflict solving by reference to law; d) increased judicial power; and
e) legal framing (Blichner & Molander 2008; Blichner 2011). This
framework helps to assess the nature and impact of Brexit because
the UK's present EU membership affiliation is shaped by all five juridification dimensions.

Brexit aims at de-juridification seeking a reversal of these dimensions. It has been promoted as a significant break with a past that
was seen as involving the ever-increasing UK legal entanglement
with the EU through the years of its EU membership. Brexit can
also be construed as the antithesis of the EU's trajectory of consolidation (and possible enlargement) and is unique in being the first-
time the EU-membership and its policy implications have been rejected by a member state. The debate on Brexit thus far shows that
this is much more than a binary issue of EU membership though
the Brexit debate has not revealed clear distinctions between the
different dimensions of (de)juridification involved. The Brexit process has, itself, been shaped by the history of the EU's entanglement
despite proponents of Brexit wishing for a 'clean break'.

It matters to our understanding of legally entrenched path dependence which dimension(s) of (de)juridification gets activated;
how this happens; and how the juridification dimensions interact.
Importantly, this chapter does not claim that de-juridification is
about replacing law with politics and the relationship between politics and law is far from binary: there are different modes of politics (steeped in different action logics: instrumental, strategic and
norm-based) and these vary in terms of how they relate to law, with
the main distinction between those forms/conceptions of politics

that are norms/rules based and those that are not (power-based). The distinction between juridification/de-juridification as presence or absence of law is used here while acknowledging that different types of politics can emerge under conditions of de-juridification.

Path dependence is understood here to mean that once a political entity takes a particular path, the costs of reversal are very high and, while there may be a number of other 'choice points', as Margaret Levi tells us, 'the entrenchment of certain institutional arrangements obstruct an easy reversal of the initial choice' (Levi 1997, 28). If we consider juridification as being about the law and law-expansion, and that law is an institution (MacCormick 2007), then we can also understand both concepts together and see path dependence in relation to the specific action logics embedded in law.

This chapter briefly considers how the UK's pre-Brexit relationship with the EU has been structured with reference to the five juridification dimensions while taking account of the UK's special EU arrangements, its opt-outs and opt-ins (Adler-Nissen 2014). These arrangements have contributed to the UK being more of a marginal player and unable to influence the EU through its recent crises and challenges (Hughes 2019, 18). The Brexit process thus far will then be assessed with reference to the types and shapes of path dependence, the relative salience of law versus politics, and the sense to which juridification embodies path dependence as a built-in trait and whether juridification of the political space offers some protection for rights-holders in the UK.

How EU-juridified was the UK pre-Brexit?

3.1 Constitutive juridification

Constitutive juridification is a process where norms constitutive for a political order are established or changed to the effect of adding to the competencies of the legal system. This is the most profound of the various dimensions of juridification. While EU law has its origins in international rather than constitutional law, EU law is now considered as something qualitatively different from each and while the EU is without a formal constitution, it is widely acknowledged to have a material constitution (Fossum and Menéndez 2011). With EU membership has come the EU law's principles of supremacy and direct effect enabling EU law to overwhelm UK law on matters affecting EU law, much to the annoyance of many in the UK political class and the tabloid press.

In terms of constitutive principles, EU membership can be seen as a direct affront to the core UK constitutional principle of parliamentary sovereignty, in at least three key senses. For one, the UK's constitutional order was incorporated into the EU constitutional order causing UK law to be harmonised or rendered compatible with the constitutive principles of the European legal-constitutional order. When the UK entered the EU in 1972 it was not well understood in the UK that this amounted to a significant re-constitutive event that would effectively set the UK upon a different constitutional path (Bogdanor 2018). Secondly, EU membership upset the horizontal fusion of power as reflected in British parliamentary government and replaced it with an arrangement wherein courts would play a far more important role. Finally, the UK's incorporation in the EU legal-constitutional order upset vertical relations by superimposing the EU and EU law on the UK, as well as helping to give impetus to internal UK federalisation through devolution.

This legal transformation is amplified by the fact that EU law is constitutive of a European community of citizens as rights-holders because EU law establishes European citizenship and grants rights to individuals. In the UK, with the Charter of Fundamental Rights of the European Union (the Charter), judges were empowered to disapply legislation that contravened the human rights it guaranteed. That clearly surpassed the UK's *Human Rights Act 1998* (HRA) which, while not giving UK courts the power to disapply, had effectively brought the 'language of rights into the British constitution' (Bogdanor 2018, 136). The enactment of legal rights of citizens against the state, an indication of the effects of EU constitutive juridification, was a fundamental change for the UK which, since its 1689 English Bill of Rights, had been more concerned with the sovereignty of parliament.

The European Court of Justice's (CJEU) interpretations, along with the Treaty on European Union (TEU), have had constitutional status in the UK and the UK has both implemented EU secondary law and abided by the CJEU's interpretations of the TEU (Schmidt 2018, 3). The impact of European case law has been profound and remained immune from domestic political change despite the UK's doctrine of parliamentary sovereignty. Until Brexit, it continued to add to the EU constitution and case law, in particular through precedent, thereby creating a path dependency in terms of the future interpretation of the law. The EU integration process has long been presented as 'integration through law' and viewed as having 'progressed as a politics of de-politicisation' (Priban 2009, 44) resulting in the legal entrenchment and enforced curtailment of majoritarian rule within states.

The UK, through the involvement of its lawyers and the close relationships between EU and UK judicial officers, has had a major influence over the development of EU law and with some notable exceptions, UK courts have been willing to adopt and apply judgments of the CJEU. In determining a question related to a European Convention on Human Rights (ECHR) right, UK courts must 'take into account' but not necessarily follow existing law from the European Court of Human Rights (ECtHR) (Dickson 2011, 351). In doing so, this compliance has been tempered by the exercise of a 'margin of appreciation' by which states express their differences

(Weiler 1995, 54). Despite the activist and creative role given the CJEU, it should be noted that the EU member states have not explicitly granted EU law supremacy or what is often referred to as *Kompetenz-Kompetenz*. In addition, rather than conferring sovereignty on the EU, the member states have instead pooled sovereignty in a set of EU institutions that they largely control, notably the European Council and the Council configurations.

The legally entrenched exit procedure of Article 50 of the Lisbon Treaty does not preserve the constitutive juridification dimension of EU law. However, the more these provisions commit the exiting state as to its future relations with the EU, the more we see exit as a *reconstitution* of EU law's role rather than its outright removal. EU law shapes interstate and internal state relations in Europe such as through the Good Friday Agreement (GFA), with the EU as a guarantor, including its oversight over the protection of civil and political rights (European Commission, 2017; Gormley-Heenan & Aughey 2017, 499).

3.2 Juridification as law's expansion and differentiation

The second dimension, being about law's expansion and differentiation, is that which relates to the increased use of the law with juridification being a process through which law comes to regulate an increasing number of different activities. This may mean subjecting activities to legal regulation when they were previously not so regulated or subjecting other activities to even more detailed legal regulation when rules were already in place. Considered as both horizontal and vertical expansion and horizontal and vertical differentiation, the dimension on law's expansion and differentiation assists us to understand the UK – EU legal relations and patterns of path dependence.

EU law has consistently expanded its realm of action, including into so-called core state powers (such as foreign and security policy, tax and fiscal policy and border control) even if the European Court of Justice's role is weakly established in the latter areas (Genschel and Jachtenfuchs 2014). In addition, we see significant differentiation from the Rome Treaty's general legal provisions to today's *Acquis*, with its very detailed provisions. Even while the UK has obtained exemptions from significant bodies of EU law, the UK has become thoroughly Europeanised in a legal sense. The UK has shown a high degree of compliance with not only EU decisions but also with the embedding of EU law through recognition, if not strict adherence, to the jurisprudence of the European Court of Justice, something supported by UK courts. The UK's political constitutionalism and the common law's focus on individual and negative rights have been at odds with the EU's legal constitutionalism and, while its entrenched rights have been grounded differently (Bellamy 2007), rights were not considered any less important in the UK. With over 40 years of close alignment as well as the EU's economic importance to the UK, as well as in other policy areas, there will be strong pressure on the UK to align, if not necessarily be congruent, with the EU post-Brexit. This would have been regardless of the nature of the deal or even if there had been no deal.

EU law is both comprehensive in scope and range, and has also become deeply embedded in the UK's devolved legislation, applying, in particular, to the so-called common frameworks. These policy areas, where EU laws intersect with devolved legislative competence in at least one of the UK's devolved regions, require compatibility with EU law and regulatory consistency across the UK (Paun 2018, 4). Just as EU law was incorporated into UK law through the EUWA and the question became one of reallocating power and responsibility in the UK post-Brexit, so the extent of rights protection was also raised in the parliamentary debates in Westminster (Bogdanor 2018; Doward 2018).

3.3 Juridification as increased conflict solving by reference to law

The third dimension of juridification refers to a process whereby conflicts are increasingly being solved by or with reference to law. This is about law's expansion as a conflict solving device. In this section, attention is given to the role of courts in conflict solving/handling, whether or not the judiciary is involved. The EU's own development is closely associated with and to a large extent driven by legal activism, and an important aspect pertains to the dynamic interaction between the courts (Weiler 1994). European law, and the central role of the CJEU in upholding it, has become entrenched, while providing a framework for handling conflicts between levels of governing across states and between states, markets and civil society actors and complementing and reinforcing the role of courts as conflict handlers in member states. Decision-making around rights issues is affected by EU legal activism both indirectly through the operation of the CJEU, as it applies the ECHR through the HRA, and more directly through the application of the Charter. It places constraints on majoritarianism and in the case of the UK, bypasses the principle of parliamentary sovereignty (Bogdanor 2019, 138; Jay 2017, 850).

3.4 Juridification as increased judicial power and as legal framing

Juridification, as increased judicial power, can be partly explained in terms of the law's indeterminacy and to law's lack of transparency. The EU legal system has seen its reach expanded over time. Increased judicial power is in no little measure the result of the expansionist role of the European Court of Justice, the close interaction among EU and domestic courts and the legal community's role as an epistemic community. Judicial power also increases as and to the extent that judges, lawyers (and politicians) declare a political question as a 'technical question' thus placing it within the jurisdictional domain of the legal profession (Rehder 2010, 117-8).

Constitutional identity within the EU has served the process of self-empowering national constitutional courts that has, in turn, limited politicisation (Faraguna 2017, 1640). While the UK's tradition of parliamentary sovereignty implies that domestic courts are unlikely to challenge parliamentary decisions (Schmidt 2018, 28), judges' common law legal principles are, themselves, also treated as law. These developments in both the EU and the UK form part of a global trend towards enhanced juridification.

Juridification as legal framing is the process by which people increasingly tend to think of themselves and others as legal persons (such as citizens and rights holders) and attach meaning to the particular social practice called law. Legal framing has much to do with culture and mind-frames and relates to how a legal orientation to the world, including handling matters by legal means, influences people's thinking. Legal human rights dominate the field of human rights and encourage juridification. The EU has undoubtedly given impetus to this development with legal framing being intrinsic to the way in which EU-driven juridification empowered civil society groups and various types of public actors.

Juridification in a post-Brexit UK

4.1 Diminished constitutive juridification?

Brexit means the UK is no longer formally subject to the EU legal order but, as the *EU(Withdrawal) Act 2018* has revealed, while Brexit may end EU law's role in shaping UK constitutive juridification, the EU's constitutive influence on the UK legal order cannot be entirely undone by the UK's exit. Many of the vestiges of the way EU law reconfigured the UK constitution will remain and become embedded in UK law, albeit not necessarily in the same shape or form or with the same constitutional salience. Brexit can be expected to inject further constitutional uncertainty that can only be resolved by a codified British constitution (Bogdanor 2018, 261) while the process itself has already exposed three such sources of uncertainty relating to referendums, rights protection, and devolution. Rights protection in the UK, in a post-Brexit world, would become reliant on the HRA, an ordinary Act of Parliament that can be easily amended or repealed while, with devolution, uncertainty results from the Sewel convention having been largely ignored in UK parliamentary debates.

The Charter was targeted as alien law by some UK politicians and controversially exempted from inclusion in the EUWA. This was significant in that the Charter not only provided more extensive protection than the UK's *Human Rights Act* of 1998 but, under the Charter, judges could also disapply legislation that contravened rights guaranteed in it (Bogdanor 2018, 135). In exposing the 'nakedness of our unprotected constitution', Brexit might mean that 'taking back control' will come to be seen not as a return to parliamentary sovereignty, but rather 'a paradise for an overweening executive' (Bogdanor 2018, 274). Given the European Court of Justice retains power, albeit more limited, to adjudicate post-Brexit disputes involving EU law and with other panels to resolve other disputes under the EU-UK's Brexit deal, it remains questionable whether there can be de-juridification in a constitutive sense. With this dimension both framing and being the source of all other dimensions, can it be said that de-juridification exists in any sense. The Court's interpretations, along with the TEU, have constitutional status in UK and European case law and have been immune from domestic political change. They will continue to add to the EU constitution and case law, particularly through precedent, creating a path dependency for future interpretations of the law, even within the UK.

Interestingly, the Brexit process reveals that the EU's legal regulation of the process of a state's sovereign decision to terminate its EU membership and sever the umbilical cord of EU constitutive juridification is done through a set of rules whose status may be considered constitutive of interstate relations. As such, these rules guide the process and outcome of one part of EU's separation from the rest. In doing so, they guide not only the exit process but also affect the future of EU – UK relations, as in Northern Ireland where, with Northern Ireland now likely to be de jure in the UK but de facto in the EU customs union, the CJEU will be the body to adjudicate any disputes. The Brexit negotiating process thus far has undoubtedly proceeded along the EU's prescribed lines with the EU's constitutive rule-based approach prevailing over the UK's favoured politically-determined approach. As *Miller* decided, these negotiations involved the need to amend laws and the then UK government had to suffer the indignity of having to try, unsuccessfully, to secure a parliamentary majority for its agreement with the EU.

The UK's effort to open parallel, and political, negotiations reveals its failure to recognise path dependencies of the EU27 flowing from their previous decisions within the EU and, curiously, its own 1973 decision to integrate into the EU. This failure results from the UK government's politically constructed view, a 'sovereigntist' view focused on its internal processes, that its EU relationship is fundamentally a political one and not a legal-constitutional one (Patberg 2018, 1). A member state's exit from the EU, towards a form of EU disintegration, must be seen as no less juridified than the process of integration itself and not capable of political determination. Without a codified constitution it remains an open question as to what institutional framework is required for Brexit to produce the Brexiteer's de-juridification in a constitutive sense.

4.2 Brexit as detraction from law (de-regulation?)

Insofar as Brexit is about de-juridification, we should also expect a process whereby there is a clear detraction of EU-law. The UK government has decided not to transpose the Charter into UK law through the EUWA, igniting considerable opposition given the Charter is more than a consolidation of rights and protects rights against Parliament when it has legislated on EU matters. The Charter, while not applying in purely national situations, is seen by the CJEU and the ECtHR as binding where disputes have involved EU law and been recognised as the main source of fundamental human rights for EU purposes (De Burca 2013, 54). A retained Charter would need to be revised for the post-Brexit context, but to protect rights a revision would still be preferable to its wholesale deletion. The influence of the ECHR will remain given the repeal of the HRA now looks to be off the table, at least for the early post-Brexit period.

Protecting citizen rights has been an essential feature of EU constitutionalism with identity as a European citizen a mechanism by which the EU sought to reach over the member state and connect with people. Not surprisingly, their protection became an EU 'red line' in negotiations and path dependence helps to explain this bargaining imperative given the legal protection of citizen rights by EU institutions. The agreed right to settled status for resident EU citizens within the UK and for UK citizens living in the EU27 will both require statutory attention.

How devolution has developed also reveals the embeddedness of, and compliance with, EU law. With the incorporation of EU law into UK law, concerns have been raised about how power and responsibility will be reallocated post-Brexit. In particular, the Scottish government has referred to possible negative implications for devolved competences due to possible UK government legislative and regulatory changes (McKerrell 2018; McEwen 2019). Supplementary local regulations can be expected and given the differential treatment across the regions and their own historical engagements with the EU, sensitive constitutional issues will require devolution legislation regardless of the outcome (Gordon 2016). EU integration has facilitated bringing the 'genie out of the bottle' in terms of devolution and any UK government will not find it easy to 'put it back in the bottle' in any post-Brexit scenario.

The GFA, as much about the rights of those north and south of the border as about a common travel zone, recognizes the important sustaining role played by the EU. Prime Minister Johnson was willing to compromise over a hard border between Northern Ireland and Eire to secure his October 2019 deal though both Northern Ireland and Eire remain concerned that this deal does not work to sacrifice rights or otherwise undermine the GFA. Human rights bodies across the border, while satisfied with this deal's safeguards, have sought to have a special committee provide oversight of the Northern Ireland protocol, that the region retains EU law rights, and that UK immigration and nationality laws be made compatible with the GFA (Irish Legal News 2019). In effect, insofar as the Ireland/Northern Ireland Protocol involves the European Court of Justice and insofar as there is an open border between Ireland and Northern Ireland post-Brexit, the Northern Ireland issue is bound up in constitutive juridification.

The reintroduced European Union (Withdrawal Agreement) Bill, that became law on 23 January 2020, removed additional procedural protections for workers' rights that currently form part of EU law, opening the way for possible changes to UK laws. The new Act has also removed the previous obligation as to unaccompanied children coming from the EU seeking asylum with family members in the UK. While Brexiteers remain interested in using Brexit as a de-juridification exercise to remove the UK from a number of EU regulations (including as to employment, environmental, and rights issues) (Jolly 2019), this process of disentanglement from EU laws and regulations is more likely to result in just a different, and local, form of regulation as signalled by the EUWA. In whatever form, this would be a testament to juridification. On the other hand, Brexit may also result not simply in a different type of regulation coming out of Westminster but rather the UK having a diminished capacity to resume sovereignty or 'control' given much is now regulated supranationally (Rogers 2018).

A post-Brexit deregulatory thrust remains a possibility with a recent UK *Department for Exiting the EU* document about workers' rights and environmental standards alluding to differing interpretations from the EU as to UK commitments in the October 2019 deal and approaches to future bargaining (Merrick 2019). However, even the final Brexit trade deal, where it is focused on a 'level playing field', provides for arbitration where, for example, workers' rights are reduced below the current level. The Brexiteers' view seems to not appreciate that sovereign power is rule-based with political sovereignty legitimated and exercised through domestic and international law (Bellamy 2003, 172-3) and the UK may soon find that future foreign political and commercial relationships are subject to regulation, some externally determined.

4.3 Law's diminished role in conflict solving?

Brexit as de-juridification presumes that there is less recourse to the law as a means for conflict solving. The Northern Ireland Protocol of the deal agreed between Prime Minister Johnson and the EU prescribes that the European Court of Justice will adjudicate any disputes that arise from its implementation, despite the UK having preferred otherwise. This Court's retention of power over dispute settlement relating to both the negotiated deal and during the period of the post-Brexit transition is important and heralds a 'normative interpretation, reason-giving and the application of legal norms to facts in the course of resolving disputes' (Stone Sweet 2010, 7).

This second Withdrawal Agreement appears to endorse the previous Agreement which saw the parties attach importance, in terms of governance arrangements, to providing 'legal certainty and clarity to citizens, businesses and organisations and respect the autonomy and integrity of both the UK's and the EU's legal orders.' The *European Union (Withdrawal Agreement) Act 2020* (UK) has included legal and technical provisions relating to the key issues of citizen rights (of the EU citizens in the UK and the UK citizens in the EU27) and the Northern Ireland arrangements. Importantly, an Independent Monitoring Authority (IMA) is to be established to monitor compliance with these arrangements and the implementation of Citizens Rights Agreements. While having regard to EU law and how the European Commission exercises its functions in relation to citizen rights, the IMA's functions may now be delegated or transferred by regulation.

The UK government sought to use Brexit against its own parliament and as a convenient device to centralise power in Westminster and away from the regions (Magnussen 2013, 303). Parliamentary sovereignty has, on the other hand, been bolstered by recourse to the law with its constitutional position reaffirmed by the UK Supreme Court in declaring unlawful Johnson's September 2019 prorogation of parliament. The Supreme Court in *R (Miller) v The Prime Minister* (2019) held that the prorogation prevented parliament from holding the government to account. Even the parliamentary debate between the Conservative and Labour parties over the customs union, a legal and technical provision, can itself be interpreted as showing juridification of this aspect of the UK/EU economic relationship and the path dependency created by the customs union determining positions taken within the political arena.

4.4 Reduced judicial power & legal framing?

Brexit, as full-fledged de-juridification, would, of course, also entail an overall reduction in judicial power. A soft Brexit would arguably continue to subject the UK to the jurisdiction of the CJEU, while a hard Brexit would, at least at the outset, mean less EU judicial power over the UK. Given the broad omnibus nature of the EUWA, the Act foreshadowed delegated legislation which effectively enhances executive power and diminishes parliamentary scrutiny. These 'Henry VIII clauses', allowing legislation to be impliedly or expressly amended by subordinate legislation or executive action, meant government could choose which elements of EU law to keep without opening this up to parliamentary scrutiny. This increased delegated legislation and the powers they give administrative agencies will increase judicial review of the exercise of these powers (including any breaches of rights), thereby enhancing juridification. A House of Lords committee has recently warned against assuming that the transposing of EU powers into UK laws will not have equivalent effect (Weale 2018, 34) while the interpretation of transposed laws impacting regions and territories differently will likely result in court disputes.

Concluding comments

This chapter has sought to assess how legally embedded in EU law the UK will be post-Brexit and what this might mean for maintaining the protection of rights. It has examined the nature and extent of path dependence through considering five dimensions of juridification. The insertion of an EU-level legal order on top of the UK one has had re-constitutive effects for the latter as the UK institutional system was redirected from parliamentary sovereignty to some version of multilevel (deficient) constitutional democracy. Brexit thus directly questions the resilience of this type of arrangement.

Path dependence adds to juridification the important dimensions of timing and sequence: de-juridification as proposed by the Brexiteers suggests a return to the pre-EU past, whereas path dependence underlines that the UK cannot simply go back to the pre-EU situation because when it joined the EU it set off on a different path that through juridification-spurred increasing returns has taken the UK to a different place. It is returning to a different world from 1972 and, while removing the EU level takes away the justifi-cation and continued EU-based sustenance for the current arrange-ment, it does not easily do away with the remainder of EU program-ming. De-juridification cannot be assumed to be Brexit's outcome. Reality is more complex and there will be tendencies towards both more and less juridification, and these will vary depending on the particular juridification dimension.

5.1 Juridification and the likely post-Brexit options

With the Johnson government's success at the 2019 General Elec-tion, remaining in the EU is no longer a viable option for the UK. However, the path dependent processes involving the developed 'complementary configurations' of the EU and the UK (Pierson 2000, 255) cannot be ignored, and the juridification of the relation-ship prior to Brexit can be expected to constrain attempts by politi-cal forces within the UK to drive EU/UK relations on to a different path. The no deal option was until December 2020 a live one despite the October 2019 deal as passed by the UK parliament because, in debates for the *European Union (Withdrawal Agreement) Act 2020*, the UK government had indicated that it will not seek an extension beyond the transition period that ends on 31 December 2020. This raised concerns both in the EU and the UK that 11 months is insuf-ficient to negotiate their future relationship.

Upon Brexit, now realised, the UK will certainly no longer be subject to the EU's legal order and the constitutive dimension, at least formally, would no longer be in play. While the UK's incorpo-ration of much existing EU law in its domestic legal order through the EUWA testifies to considerable norm and rule correspondence, how much this has a path dependent pull remains uncertain as this will hinge on the extent to which the UK modifies its laws to foster greater divergence. Much depends on whether and how much in-creased judicial power results through enhanced judicial oversight of the increased administrative decision-making, the EU's responses themselves, how accommodating the EU will be, and whether the minimal deal finally agreed in December 2020 prompts significant centrifugal pressures from the UK's Remain regions.

Brexiteers had argued that the UK should opt for either free trade deals or otherwise become a member of the World Trade Organisation (WTO) and rely on its rules. As to rights and as to the status of EU citizens in the UK and vice versa, this has not been completely settled and much depends on which bilateral agreements the UK has with which countries and how these agreements are established. For other rights issues, the main issue is whether the UK proceeds to repeal the HRA to remove this formal link to the ECHR.

Johnson's withdrawal agreement was substantially the same as that previously agreed between the UK and the EU though it places Northern Ireland de facto in the EU customs union. In the *European Union (Withdrawal Agreement) Act 2020*, workers' rights, consumer rights and environmental commitments have been removed. The EU's own 'red lines' on the financial settlement, citizen rights as well as the Ireland/Northern Ireland Protocol have remained though the revised version inhibits parliament's ability to scrutinise. The impasse previously reached in the UK parliament was not over attempts at de-juridification but rather was due to differing political interpretations. The final 'thin' Brexit trade and cooperation agreement, particularly in regard to the 'level playing field', follows a juridified model reflecting, at least in part, the path dependency of the EU/UK historical and legal relationship. The agreement's 'non-regression clauses' to maintain certain current rights do not make up for the earlier removal of certain rights protecting commitments and concerns remain as to how commitments on citizen rights will be implemented. However, any breaches of the current levels of protection will be subject to forms of arbitration. Together with these not particularly strong arbitral provisions, the path dependency created by the juridified nature of the EU/UK relationship, with its historical attention to legal rights, could result in any moves by a UK government to diminish rights facing various forms of institutional resistance.

Brexit is, without doubt, a critical juncture for both the UK and the EU. It has been interpreted mainly through the prism of the often-febrile UK politics, made more so by Johnson's 'raising of the stakes' in promoting the possibility of a no deal exit. Not surprisingly, much of the analysis and commentary on Brexit has focused on the referendum and the external and domestic UK negotiations in terms of the rupture that it represents from continued EU membership. As important as this continues to be, the phenomenon that is Brexit is also an opportunity to consider the path dependencies that have developed from the UK's 46 years as an EU member, how difficult and costly they make reversals and the likely increased returns they produce from policy continuance.

The juridified nature of the developed relationship between the EU and the UK has created its own path dependencies. While these vary in both the nature and level of their intensity across the dimensions of juridification and in how they have protected rights, the influence of juridification can be expected to remain important regardless of the UK's post-Brexit scenario. The juridified nature of the relationship, and the necessary focus of the EU on citizen rights in particular, has not only made legal rights a target for removal by the Brexiteers but also given rights a salience in the Brexit negotiations. There are implications here for rights in that alongside the push by hard Brexiteers to de-juridify their relations with the EU, Brexit has also acted as a stimulus to integration elsewhere in the EU.

References

Adler-Nissen, R (2014), *Opting Out of the European Union*, Cambridge University Press, Cambridge.

Bellamy, R (2007), *Political Constitutionalism: A Republican Defence of the Constitutionality of Democracy*, Cambridge University Press, Cambridge.

Bellamy, R (2003), 'Sovereignty, Post-Sovereignty and Pre-Sovereignty: Three Models of the State, Democracy and Rights within the EU', in N Walker (ed.), *Sovereignty in Transition*, Hart Publishing, Portland, pp.167-190.

Blichner, L & Molander, A (2008). 'Mapping Juridification', *European Law Journal*, vol. 14, no. 1 (January 2008), 36-54.

Bogdanor, V (2018), *Beyond Brexit: Towards a British Constitution*, I.B. Tauris, London.

Caldeira, GA, Kelemen, RD & Whittington, KE (eds) (2008), *The Judicialization of Politics, The Oxford Handbook of Law and Politics*, Oxford University Press, Oxford.

Coppel, J (2018), *European Union (Withdrawal) Bill – EU Charter of Fundamental Rights*, Legal Opinion, Equality and Human Rights Commission, London, https://www.equalityhumanrights.com/sites/default/files/eu-with-drawal-bill-legal-advice-jason-coppel-qc.pdf.

Choukroune, L (2019), 'Human Rights are getting Cut from Britain's post-Brexit Trade Negotiations', *Global Policy Opinion*, 26 November 2019, https://www.globalpolicyjournal.com/blog/26/11/2019/human-rights-are-getting-cut-britains-post-brexit-trade-deal-negotiations.

De Burca, G (2003), 'The Development of European Constitutionalism and the Role of the EU Charter of Fundamental Rights', *Columbia Journal of European Law*, vol. 9, 355-82.

De Burca, G (2013), 'The Domestic Impact of the EU Charter of Fundamental Rights', *The Irish Jurist*, vol. 49, 49-64.

Dickson, B (2011), 'The Influence of European Law on the Protection of Fundamental Human Rights in United Kingdom Law', in P Popelier, C Van de Heyning & P Van Nuffel (eds), *Human Rights Protection in the European Legal Order: the Interaction between the European and the National Courts*, Intersentia, Cambridge, 343-363.

Douglas-Scott, S (2019), 'Citizenship, Identity and the EU', in K Hughes (ed.), *The Future of Europe: Disruption, Continuity and Change*, SCER Report, Scottish Centre on European Relations, Edinburgh, 34-41.

Doward, J (2018), 'Brexit bill leaves a hole in UK human rights', Guardian online, 14 January 2018, https://www.theguardian.com/law/2018/jan/13/brexit-eu-human-rights-act-european-charter.

Eeckhout, P (2018), 'The Emperor has no clothes: Brexit and the UK constitution', in B Martill & U Staiger (eds), *Brexit and Beyond*, UCL Press, London, 165-172.

European Commission (2020), *Trade and Cooperation Agreement between the European Union and the European Atomic Energy Community and the United Kingdom of Great Britain and Northern Ireland*. European Commission, Brussels, 24 December 2020, https://eur-lex.europa.eu/legal-content/EN/TXT/PDF/?uri=CELEX:22020A1231(01)&from=EN.

European Commission (2017), *Guiding Principles for the Dialogue on Ireland/Northern Ireland*, European Commission, Brussels, 20 September, 2017, https://ec.europa.eu/commission/sites/beta-political/files/dialogue_ie-ni.pdf.

Faraguna, P (2017), 'Constitutional Identity in the EU – A Shield or a Sword?' Special Issue, *German Law Journal*. vol. 18, 1617-1640.

Fossum, JE & HP Graver (2018), *Squaring the Circle on Brexit – Could the Norway Model Work?* Bristol University Press, Bristol.

Fossum, JE & Menéndez, AJ (2011), *The Constitution's Gift: A Constitutional Theory for the European Union*, Rowman and Littlefield, Lanham, Maryland.

Gearty, C (2016), *On Fantasy Island – Britain, Europe and Human Rights*, Oxford University Press, Oxford.

Genschel, P & Jachtenfuchs, M (eds) (2014), *Beyond the Regulatory Polity? The European Integration of Core State Powers*, Oxford University Press, Oxford.

Gordon, M (2019), 'Q + A: Supreme Court rules Boris Johnson's prorogation of UK parliament was unlawful – so what happens now?' *The Conversation*, 25 September 2019, https://theconversation.com/q-a-supreme-court-rules-boris-johnsons-prorogation-of-uk-parliament-was-unlawful-so-what-happens-now-124119.

Gordon, M (2016), 'Brexit: a challenge for the UK constitution, of the UK constitution?', *European Constitutional Law Review*, vol. 12, 409-444.

Gormley-Heenan, C & Aughey, A (2017), 'Northern Ireland and Brexit: Three Effects on 'the Border in the Mind', *British Journal of Politics and International Relations*, vol. 19, no. 3, 497-511.

Harvey, C (2018), 'Brexit, human rights and the constitutional future of these islands', *European Human Rights Law Review*, vol. 1, 10-12.

House of Lords Delegated Powers and Regulatory Reform Select Committee (2018), *European Union (Withdrawal Agreement) Bill*, HL Paper 73, 12th Report of Session 2017-19, House of Lords, London.

Hughes, K (2019), 'Europe's Future in the Face of Systemic Changes', in K Hughes (ed.), *The Future of Europe: Disruption, Continuity and Change*, SCER Report, Scottish Centre on European Relations, Edinburgh, 14-24.

Irish Legal News (2019), 'Human rights watchdogs meet to examine draft Brexit deal', 24 October 2019, https://irishlegal.com/article/human-rights-watchdogs-meet-to-examine-draft-brexit-deal.

Jay, Z (2017), 'Keeping rights at home: British conceptions of rights and compliance with the European Court of Human Rights', *The British Journal of Politics and International Relations*, vol. 19, no. 4, 842-860.

Jolly, S (2019), 'Brexit is necessarily a project of deregulation- how contemptuous that Labour still supports it', *Prospect*, 1 May 2019, https://www.prospectmagazine.co.uk/politics/brexit-is-necessarily-a-project-of-deregulation-how-contemptuous-that-labour-still-supports-it.

Kelemen, RD (2012), 'Eurolegalism and Democracy', *Journal of Common Market Studies*, vol. 50, no. S1, 55-71.

Levi, M (1997), 'A Model, a Method, and a Map: Rational Choice in Comparative and Historical Analysis', in MI Lichbach & AS Zuckerman (eds), *Comparative Politics: Rationality, Culture, and Structure*, Cambridge University Press, Cambridge, 19-41.

Lord, C (2019), 'Integration through Differentiation and Segmentation: The Case of One Member State from 1950 to Brexit (and Beyond)', in J Batora & JE Fossum (eds), *Towards a Segmented European Political Order: The European Union's Post-Crises Conundrum*, Routledge, London, 289-314.

MacCormick, N (2007), *Institutions of Law: An Essay in Legal Theory*, Oxford University Press, Oxford.

Magnussen, A-M & Banasiak, A (2013), 'Juridification: Disrupting the Relationship between Law and Politics?', *European Law Journal*, vol.19, no. 3 (May 2013), 325-339.

March, JG & JP Olsen (1989), *Rediscovering Institutions: The Organizational Basis of Politics*, The Free Press, New York.

Masterman, R (2009), 'Juridification, Sovereignty and Separation of Powers', *Parliamentary Affairs*, vol. 62, no. 3, 499-502.

McEwen, N (2019), 'Brexit and its implications for Scottish Devolution', Centre on Constitutional Change, Blog, 1 March 2019, https://www.centreonconstitutionalchange.ac.uk/opinions/brexit-and-its-implications-scottish-devolution.

McKerrell, N (2018), 'How Westminster raised the stakes on Scottish devolution with the Brexit bill', *The Conversation*, 15 June 2018, https://theconversation.com/how-westminster-raised-the-stakes-on-scottish-devolution-with-the-brexit-bill-98280.

Merrick, R (2019), '"This confirms our worst fears": Brexit will allow Boris Johnson to cut workers' rights, leak reveals', *The Independent*, 26 October 2019, https://www.independent.co.uk/news/uk/politics/brexit-deal-boris-johnson-eu-workers-rights-environment-leak-labour-a9171961.html.

Patberg, M (2018), 'Brexit demonstrates the need for a normative theory of political disintegration', *Europp*, LSE blog, 29 March 2018, https://blogs.lse.ac.uk/eurppblog/2018/03/29/brexit-demonstrates-the-need-for-a-normative-theory-political-disintegration/mative-theory-political-disintegration/.

Paun, A (2018), 'Common UK Frameworks after Brexit', SPICe Briefing, 18-19.

Pernice, I (2017), European Constitutionalism and the National Constitutions of the Member States, WHI-Paper 01/2017, Humboldt University, Berlin.

Pierson, P (2000), 'Increasing Returns, Path Dependence, and the Study of Politics', *The American Political Science Review*, vol. 94, no. 2, 251-267.

Priban, J (2009), 'The Juridification of European Identity, its limitations and the search for EU democratic politics', *Constellations*, vol. 16, no. 1, 44-58.

Rehder, B (2010), 'What is Political about Jurisprudence? Courts, Politics and Political Science in Europe and the United States', *Contemporary Readings in Law and Social Justice*, vol. 2, no. 1, 100-129.

Rogers, I (2018), *Brexit as a Revolution*, Lecture at Trinity College, Cambridge, 10 October 2018.

Schmidt, S (2018), *The European Court of Justice and the Policy Process*, Oxford University Press, Oxford.

Shapiro, M & Stone Sweet, A (eds) (2002), *On Law, Politics and Judicialisation*, Oxford University Press, Oxford.

Stone Sweet, A (2007), 'The Juridical Coup d'État and the Problem of Authority', Faculty Scholarship Series, no. 78, https://digitalcommons.law.yale.edu/fss_papers/78.

Stone Sweet, A (2010), 'The European Court of Justice and the Judicialization of EU Governance', *Living Reviews in European Governance*, vol. 5, no. 2, 1-50.

Tate, CN & Torbjørn V (eds) (1995), *The Global Expansion of Judicial Power*, New York University Press, New York.

The Institute for Government (2020), *Explainers. Sewel convention*, 7 September 2020, https://www.instituteforgovernment.org.uk/explainers/sewel-convention.

UK Government (2018), 'The Future Relationship Between the United Kingdom and the European Union', https://assets.publishing.service.gov.uk/government/uploads/system/uploads/attachment_data/file/724982/The_future_relationship_between_the_United_Kingdom_and_the_European_Union_WEB_VERSION.pdf.

UK Government (1998), *The Belfast Agreement*, 10 April 1998, https://assets.publishing.service.gov.uk/government/uploads/system/uploads/attachment_data/file/136652/agreement.pdf.

Walker, P (2019), 'What does Boris Johnson's withdrawal bill actually say?' *Guardian online*, 22 October 2019, https://www.theguardian.com/politics/2019/oct/21/what-does-boris-johnsons-withdrawal-bill-actually-say.

Weale, A (2018), 'Brexit and the improvised constitution', in B Martill & U Staiger (eds), *Brexit and Beyond*, UCL Press, London, 28-36.

Weiler, JHH (1994), 'A Quiet Revolution - the European Court of Justice and Its Interlocutors', *Comparative Political Studies*, vol. 26, no. 4, 510-534.

12

Brexit's Reshaping of Multinationals' Regionalisation Strategies across Europe and Australia

Gabriele Suder and André Sammartino

Keywords: Regionalisation, Multinational Enterprises, De-globalisation, Brexit

Abstract

While the world watches the continued crafting and consequences of Brexit, the EU has shown a slow, yet rather formidable, capacity and patience to support its remaining members as much as it accommodates the Brexiter. That is, the EU is demonstrating an ability to not only integrate but also de-integrate constructively and peacefully. In this chapter we argue this experience is an important example of globalisation's propensity for 'slow-balisation', and, furthermore, should be viewed through the lens of how multinational enterprises ('multinationals') navigate 'regionalisation' as both an institution and a strategic choice. By using examples of various multinationals' business activities across Australia and Europe, including the UK, we explore the challenges and implications of Brexit for their strategic choices.

Multinationals in a Regionalised World

In a post-globalisation world, and increasingly so over the past decade, regions such as the European Union have become crucial dimensions of most multinationals' strategies and structures (Flores and Aguilera, 2007; Rugman and Verbeke, 2004). While a small number of exceptions may have global aspirations, multinationals typically organise and strategise regionally, whether that be with a bi-regional or home-region focus (Osegowitsch & Sammartino, 2008; Sammartino and Osegowitsch, 2013). That is, their internationalisation, and strategic attention, rarely stretches beyond their geographic home-region, i.e., their neighbouring countries or economies that have an institutional proximity, even if distant in miles or kilometres, by means of comprehensive free trade agreements (FTAs) (Suder 2018).

The multinationals' regional focus can be explained by any or all of the following four key factors:

Geographic proximity makes for greater ease and lower additional costs of doing business simply from a logistics perspective; for example, whilst global value chains remain resolutely international, their value-adding core is regionally focused (Lee and Gereffi 2015; Suder et al 2015);

Despite usually overstated perceptions of differences with neighbouring countries, for most nations the least culturally and administratively different nations are those very close in distance (such as Australia and the rest of Asia-Pacific) or historically and institutionally close (such as Australia and the UK) (Flores et al 2013);

Explicit efforts to lower barriers to trade and investment, the increased harmonisation of standards, norms and reduction of red tape, especially through FTAs, have tended to be most concentrated at the regional level, with the EU as an example of possibly 'best practice' in the context of how many countries and people are involved. The EU continues to represent the most integrated market of sovereign countries in the world and has shown to serve as a highly effective geopolitical stabiliser of a region previously torn by the most frequent and deadly wars in history (Lorenz, 1992; Oh & Rugman 2012).

The cross-border facilitation mechanisms of regionalisation allow business and people to play a major part in influencing an otherwise highly complex geopolitical organisation that consists of many varying and often divergent interests.

In sum, there are strong incentives in seeking to leverage home-country advantages within the home region. Put simply, home regions (i.e., markets outside the boundaries of the home country but within an FTA or further integrated market) will, over time, typically become increasingly aligned to home-market conditions, and hence can be treated as similar to the home-country itself (Proff, 2002).

The pursuit of region-level advantages will often involve building distributed supply chains within the home region, and the development of local-then-regional brands. Such strategies rely on the relatively hassle-free mobility of people, capital, products and services within the region. A key tenet of international business (IB) is that multinationals must overcome liabilities of foreignness – stemming from knowledge deficits about business practices and norms, from maladapted processes and products, from limited or poor reputations, and from greater costs of operating across borders – relative to domestic firms in host markets (Nachum, 2003; Zaheer, 1995; Zhou & Guillen, 2016). Relative to multinationals from outside the region, home-region multinationals will face a lower liability of foreignness in regional host-markets, not only with regard to distances, but also regulations, compliance, and other knowledge elements (Qian et al 2013). Such multinationals have greater scope to pursue a 'region-specific advantage' (RSAs). This augments the traditional IB view that argued simply that a multinational succeeds when effectively and productively combining unique 'firm -specific advantages' (FSAs) and 'country-specific advantages' (CSAs) within an international business environment, such that:

Effective contemporary multinational strategy = FSAs + CSAs + RSAs

When multinationals do venture beyond their home region, they face considerable organisational challenges. As Zobel and Ambos (2018: 29) explain, multinationals often still strategise regionally, as, due to the 'limited scalability of their operations,... regional management [is] a way to better manage a global organisation'. One domain where this is apparent is the knowledge transfer that underpins current and future internationalisation (Riviere et al., 2017).

Multinationals operating bi-regionally or globally often still rely on region-level adaptation or concentration, in parallel to bilaterally sourced advantages. This can manifest as regional-level strategies, such as a portfolio of products or brands tailored for the region instead of each individual market, or designated mandates for one region within the global structure – such as a product or design hub (Ghemawat 2001, 2005).

Even if the firm favours some level of global standardisation, it is still typical to mandate a regional HQ role (Nell et al. 2011), so as to reduce some of the diseconomies of managerial complexity by delegating monitoring, service provision, and strategic leadership to the subsidiary in one core country in the region that oversees the rest of the region. In a nutshell, a regional focus seeks a balance between the boundaries of a corporation's scale, scope and manageable capabilities.

Regional HQs are often in the most important country or market in a region, and/or in 'global cities', financial service hubs, or, sometimes, those countries perceived as least distant culturally, linguistically and/or administratively from the home country of the

MNE (Goerzen et al 2013). In Australia's regional context, this typically includes a regional HQ in Hong Kong, Singapore or Japan; in Europe, this would traditionally be located in the UK, Germany or France. The selection of other subsidiary locations in the region and beyond, is then correlated with the MNE's goal, mainly represented by market-seeking, resource-, asset-seeking, efficiency-seeking motives, or various combinations thereof (Dunning, 2000). The selection of its entry and investment mode into the given locations, whether through import, export, FDI or forms of international collaborative ventures, are to leverage capabilities and enhance firm competitiveness in and through its marketplace.

For example, a number of major foreign-owned multinationals operating in Australia distinctly utilise the country as a testing ground (Kim & Gray, 2017: 685; Suder, Tsai, & Varma, 2021). The reasoning is that the market is mature enough to compare with other highly developed and exigent markets yet distant enough so challenges are less visible and can get fixed before going regional or global. There is also potential to generate advantages from Australia's Asia-capability, Furthermore, Australia can serve as a launchpad for building cultural and economic linkages and understanding before venturing into high-potential yet less predictable neighbouring markets such as Indonesia or Malaysia (Suder, Tsai & Varma 2021). The selection of what to design, innovate, produce, market, and/or sell in any of those markets within the Asian region, that is the scope of its activities and their scale, is dependent on these multinationals' global strategies as well as their global, regional and local capabilities to create value within their organisational structures.

The EU, of course, makes Europe a much more integrated region than Asia. The sovereign members have negotiated policies and initiatives across a wide range of domains. In doing so, domestic social, economic, and political ambitions have often converged, or at least been surfaced in a way that makes differences more apparent to keen observers. The effects of several decades of integration are reduced geographical, administrative, institutional, economic and cultural distance between the member states. Multinationals are active participants in this regional integration contributing to both trade creation and diversion, shaping and responding to initiative such as environmental standards, product and service standardisation and the like. Indeed, it has been reported frequently since the 1990s that multinationals operating within the EU benefit considerably from significant knowledge base, industry-specific and cluster-based spillovers (Zobel & Ambos 2018, 354).

Brexit: How de-regionalisation impacts multinationals

As in all contexts, where there is integration there is scope for de-integration. Brexit, the UK's exit from the EU, is certainly not a first, yet has become a unique example of this counter-phenomenon, and one that may affect the business relations between Australia and Europe, including the EU and the UK, in an unprecedented way. Also, this case of de-integration with its lengthy periods in the making, can serve as a case at hand to potentially expand IB theory around regionalisation strategies of multinationals.

Whilst some effects are indirect and not visible to consumers or discussed in the popular press, studying Brexit effects today – and again once Brexit has been accomplished – provides a significant opportunity to better comprehend the macro-environment that impacts the most international of all firms. Applying core IB theories, and using publicly available data and case examples to date, we offer our prognoses on the question: what will de-regionalisation and the post-Brexit setting mean for the strategies of multinationals operating within and between Europe and Australia?

Let us look at what Brexit means for multinationals and their regional status. British firms shift from being home-region multinationals in Europe to host-region multinationals in Europe. Operations of any foreign multinational within the UK now sit outside the European region. EU-based firms and subsidiaries become extra-regional partners to these operations. Australian multinationals need to rethink both their bi-and multi-country strategy in Europe, as they would now effectively be adding an additional region into their portfolio of operations. This can be summarised in a 'two-legged' approach that requires additional resources and efficiencies if strategic objectives are to be maintained.

Breaking this down further, we can look at this through several different lenses. If we make the reasonable assumption that the UK is undergoing a moderately 'hard' Brexit, yet with some transition period attached to it, it is likely we will soon see the following:

- increasing divergence of regulations and standards in the UK from those in the EU,
- a reduction in administrative and digital coherence,
- and a reduction in, and increased costs associated with, mobility of people, capitals and goods. This will affect
- expatriation, foreign direct investment (FDI), trade with Europe (especially in intermediate goods), and also a potential loss or reshuffle of key service functions across EU and non-EU locations.

Impacts are expected to increase over time. For example, the transport and financial hub roles of the City of London, Heathrow, and British ports are likely to diminish.

This hard-ish Brexit preparation includes, for cross-border business, a need for increasing agility of businesses especially regarding

- future of border preparations,
- supply chains,
- financial services and funding,

- contracts and commercial business continuity planning
- digital adequacy including post- transition period, and
- people issues.

The ongoing uncertainties about transitional arrangements as well as post-transition trade and investment conditions between the UK and the EU have brought multinationals to engage additional resources into de-regionalisation impact tracking, mitigation and contingency planning (Roscoe et al, 2020).

2.1 Australian multinationals, EU, the UK and Brexit

Taking the perspective of Australian multinationals, the EU-28 (the EU including 28 members before Brexit) has been Australia's largest economic partner for more than 25 years. It is Australia's largest trading partner in services, Australia's third-largest merchandise trading partner, its second-largest source of imports (17 percent of total Australian imports) and fifth-largest market for exports. The relationship between the EU and Australia is politically and economically significant, and the Free Trade Agreement that is being finalised will crucially shape the bilateral business environment in which multinationals will be continuing their strategic engagement. Many Australian companies (around 1500) have traditionally used the UK as their launching pad into mainland Europe, and the EU's 500 million-plus consumers. The EU with its focus on minimising red tape, and harmonised standards and product testing, offers a single market bloc of 28 countries. Multinationals can position themselves within global value chains while targeting economies at various stages of market development.

As we discuss further below, Brexit will change much of this appeal. The British Government has made attempts to compensate to some extent through its 'Get ready for Brexit' campaign although only short-termed. Contingency planning is hence required to mitigate any further surprises or undesirable outcomes of the Brexit transition, and the following negotiation of the new relationship that the UK will have post-Brexit with the EU. Consulting firm PricewaterhouseCoopers (PwC) has reported that those firms that had prepared mitigation plans for March yet not for October 2019 nor January 2020 mostly need to revise their plans (PwC 2019), yet again. As a consequence, given that investment provides more certainty than trade relations only, more firms have relocated at least some of their assets into the remaining EU.

2.2 Europe as a region for Australian (and other third-country) multinationals

As noted above, the UK's departure from the Single Market including its customs union and various initiatives around political and social integration, will make transactions between EU and British parties more costly and burdensome, and this is likely to reduce such activity. Coupled with Britain's departure, this will make the EU region smaller economically. They are the affected in that their strategies must be revised to handle potential transaction and other associated costs arising from Brexit. Some have taken to reduce investments in the UK to additionally open facilities in the remaining EU; others continue with a wait-and-see strategy, confident that institutional proximity will not lead to excessive hurdles in the near-to medium-term future.

Yet those dependent on smooth supply chain flows between the UK and the EU have not been sitting on their hands. The delays in arriving at a Brexit deal plays a part here. Many existing physical supply chains were forecast to be severed already, and this perception has led to repair-and-adaptation strategies. Consider, the contingencies and uncertainties facing subsidiaries that previously interacted with relative ease, in terms of flow of products and people, have faced over the past few years of Brexit negotiations. A subsidiary based in the UK now needs to be ready to meet new data requirements for selling to the EU and third countries, to prove origin of products and adhere to rules of origin requirements, be able to handle increases in duty and additional red-tape, and/or to counterbalance changes to current facilitated customs programmes and schemes.

Consider the financial services sector. Many of the main actors have sought, and found, alternative or additional venues for their activities. This industry is highly regulated and requires often-lengthy regulatory assessments and approvals to function smoothly across borders. Large firms in the financial sector have been shifting the business and contracts of EU-based customers into new EU-based business hubs, also relocating their key staff functions to those remaining EU locations. This is, of course, much more challenging for the smaller and medium-sized players. These relocation moves are also costly and tend not to be reversed easily.

London's financial market's high liquidity is an important source of price and product advantages. An even-partial relocation of functions by big players is expected to disperse the concentration of crucial high-level skills and expertise from the City. This can only be mitigated by quick favourable steps in regard to migration and mobility, perhaps specifically in this sector of the labour market. The consulting industry has reported that UK financial services suppliers have been facing recent reductions in their EU customer relationships.

2.3 Brexit and UK multinationals

British multinationals are those most likely to be affected by Brexit. As luck would have it, large British multinationals are the least Europe-oriented of the large European MNEs, so they will not be as 'cut-off' as we might think. It will affect exporters more, and hence, small and medium-sized enterprises in particular, as they typically have had a European supply chain orientation. The more complex issue is the interaction between British firms and other MNEs within the UK. If European MNEs reduce their UK operations, and multinationals from outside Europe move their regional HQs and/or substantive aspects of their European supply chains into the remaining EU locations, there will be disruptions to the activities of British firms within the UK. This will include any instance where the British firms played a role within broader supply chains driven by multinationals from these various home countries/regions. It will also extend to any situation where British firms relied upon such supply chains for their inputs. Put differently, the flow of crucial inputs could be substantially stymied, as may key markets. UK multinationals hence are also pivoting their attention, and looking to build and deepen their non-European foci. This may, eventually, be assisted by post-Brexit free trade agreements, bilateral or multilateral, with nations in North America and the Asia Pacific, for example. British firms, and those dependent on the British market, are warehousing extensively, and are relocating the non-essential assets offshore in mainland Europe as much as possible. Examples have already been reported (Woodman, 2019), of major British multinational delaying or cancelling new domestic investments (e.g., Dyson), or setting aside very significant budgets to deal with the expected short- and medium-term consequences (e.g., British Steel)

2.4 Brexit and mainland European multinationals:

It is not as clear cut what will happen with multinationals from within the remaining EU. Substitution benefits, whereby activities previously undertaken in the UK move to mainland Europe, will most likely trump disruption to supply chains. What is most illustrative of multinationals' adaptation to the UK's Brexit period, is that specific countries in Europe have already won out as new business hubs. For example, the Netherlands have gained from shifts in the location for finance, Germany for production and, especially Berlin for innovation, and the Scandinavian countries report R&D inflow that was traditionally located into the UK. Ireland is also benefiting from its cultural and linguistic proximity yet solid Single Market membership.

How multinationals from outside Europe, including Australia are responding to Brexit

A number of multinationals from outside Europe who had their regional HQs in the UK have already signalled their new regional strategies for the EU, knowing that the transition period will be brief in business terms. Most reshuffles have focused on diversifying operations into the remaining EU whilst keeping a footprint in the UK. Such firms are clearly neither waiting for a specific Brexit date, nor are they paralysed by uncertainty. Rather, they are taking the steps necessary to prepare their supply chains for this eventuality.

Let us look again at Australian multinationals and their stance towards the UK. The UK is Australia's fifth largest trading partner, and it serves as a common conduit into the EU (DFAT 2020). Almost one half, 48 percent) of Australia's exports in services to the EU pass through the UK (Suder 2018). The bulk of these are in the finance and mineral sectors. British exports to the EU constitute 43-44 percent of the nation's total. Over half (55 percent) of the UK's imports are from the EU (House of Commons, 2020). Thus, simply stepping away from the UK is not easy for any multinational with aspirations in the EU. But the question becomes whether the UK is as attractive as a 'standalone' opportunity? Can the UK still adequately facilitate the multinationals' access to the vast, mature, stable yet diverse EU market, a market that keenly supports the creation of innovation internally and with third countries such as Australia?

For example, for universities, the access to ERASMUS + type funding for student mobility, research collaborations, and more needs to be rethought. Partnerships with UK universities would appear to be much less valuable as their access to EU funding ceases or diminishes considerably. Attention has quickly turned to partnering with tertiary institutions and research bodies in the remaining Member States, and to EU candidate countries.

Returning to the financial services example, this industry constituted 6,9 percent of the British economic output in 2018 (UK Parliament 2019) and the largest proportion of Australian exports to the EU. At the time of the Brexit vote, the UK held the very influential EU Commission portfolio in the financial services area, reflective of the nation's ability to influence the broader European policy and regulatory landscape in the sector. That role has since been lost. It has been reported that since the Brexit vote, Credit Suisse, Goldman Sachs, JP Morgan, Citigroup, and HSBC have all moved some staff and facilities to mainland EU locations. Among Australian banks, Commonwealth Bank of Australia (CBA) was reported to move major European assets to Amsterdam, and so has Macquarie -moving staff to Dublin-, Westpac and ANZ, who have also moved assets to continental Europe (Smythe, 2018; van Leeuwen, 2018).

Bloomberg, Panasonic have also strengthened their Amsterdam-based operations for Europe.

Those MNEs that had used the UK as a beachhead into Europe have been rethinking their location. It might be fair to maintain some administrative and finance functions in the UK, but physical production, logistics (and at times also R&D, given labour flow constraints and loss of EU funding opportunities) were less likely to stay. A mandate battle is likely in terms of relocations of regional HQ and other high-value roles. This was evidenced by Nissan's, Honda's, Toyota's, Airbus' and Sony's moves to reinforce their main EU-located offices onto the continent.

It must be noted that such substantial UK-into-EU locational moves are neither taken lightly nor quickly. This reflects both the costs and logistics of reshuffling activities and responsibilities, and the associated strategic rethinks required. The momentum comes for the rising likelihood of greater transaction costs post-Brexit, as well as backlogs and uncertainties about whether goods, services, capital and people can move goods across borders. This affects also the strategic thinking regarding a given company's pipeline of intermediary products and services, financial resources, digital protection, and talents and skills that it will require to satisfy its medium and long-term objectives in the region.

Multinationals' Regionalisation paradigm: what's new, what's changing?

There is ample evidence to date that Brexit has redefined the international business strategy of local and international multinational firms. Those concerned are mainly firms that have traditionally accessed the EU Single Market through or from the UK and are part of region-centric supply chain efficiencies. In this way, Brexit provides an illustrative case to study the future of regionalisation, in which market integration is not seen as permanent and inevitably wider and deeper, but rather, as a mutating phenomenon that alters the traditional regionalisation paradigm.

We have identified some of the main direct and visible impacts that Brexit has on multinational enterprises. From a strategic viewpoint, de-regionalisation or its modification clearly shapes the modalities in which a firm and its network can benefit from region-specific advantages. Adaptation capabilities and agility become more important advantages for multinationals to develop and hone. It is crucial for multinational enterprises in the EU, as home or host MNEs, in the UK and in Australia alike, to strategically reassess and modify as needed the deployment of their resources to obtain the advantages traditionally sought in the region. We must be very cautious of the common assumption that multinationals today are nimble and agile, and are both able and willing to make quick and easy investment and disinvestment decisions without incurring significant cost burdens. De-integration of a region, as evidenced by Brexit even before it happened, is in most cases a costly and burdensome matter (Suder, 2018).

Stakeholders continue to hope for as little administrative and transactional disruption as feasible. However, the time span and repetition of periods of uncertainty in the making of a Brexit agreement, to be followed by FTA negotiations for a future UK- EU relationship, has forced corporate actors into contingency planning of various types. We see the adoption of mitigation strategies, which may result in relocation or de-location, stockpiling and warehousing to cover logistic contingencies, and budgets set aside to cover fallow periods. These all represent considerable efficiency losses at a macroeconomic level.

Overall this substantial increase in pluri-lateral complexities within what constituted one particularly integrated region in the world (relative to other regions), can be viewed as a warning. In the same way that the assumption of multinationals formulating global strategies has been challenged by the empirical and practical reality of regional foci, we must acknowledge regional strategies too are fraught. De-regionalisation must also be incorporated into the paradigm.

References

Cummings, D & Zahra, S (2016), 'International Business and Entrepreneurship Implications of Brexit', *British Journal of Management*, vol. 27, no. 4, 687-692.

Department of Foreign Affairs & Trade (DFAT) 2020, Trade and Investment at a Glance, https://www.dfat.gov.au/sites/default/files/trade-investment-glance-2020.pdf.

Dunning, JH (2000), 'The eclectic paradigm as an envelope for economic and business theories of MNE activity', *International Business Review*, vol. 9, no. 2, pp.163-190.

Flores, RG & Aguilera, RV (2007), 'Globalization and location choice: An analysis of US multinational firms in 1980 and 2000', *Journal of International Business Studies*, vol. 38, 1187–1210.

Flores, R, Aguilera, RV, Mahdian, A & Vaaler, PM (2013), 'How well do supranational regional grouping schemes fit international business research models?', *Journal of International Business Studies*, vol. 44, no. 5, 451-474.

Ghemawat, P (2001), 'Distance still matters', *Harvard Business Review*, vol. 79, no. 8, 137-147.

Ghemawat, P (2005), 'Regional strategies for global leadership'. *Harvard Business Review*, vol. 83, no. 12, 98-108.

Goerzen, A, Asmussen, CG & Nielsen, BB (2013), 'Global cities and multinational enterprise location strategy', *Journal of International Business Studies*, vol. 44, no. 5, 427-450.

House of Commons (2020), Statistics on UK-EU trade, No 7851, 10 November 2020 (M. Ward), House of Commons library.

Kim, Y & Gray, SJ (2017), Internationalization strategy and the home-regionalization hypothesis: The case of Australian multinational enterprises, *Australian Journal of Management*, vol. 42, no. 4, 673-691

Lee, J & Gereffi, G (2015), 'Global value chains, rising power firms and economic and social upgrading'. *Critical Perspectives on International Business*, vol. 11, nos. 3-4, 319-339.

Lorenz, D (1992), 'Economic geography and the political economy of regionalization: the example of Western Europe'. *The American Economic Review*, vol. 82, no. 2, 84-87.

Nachum, L (2003), 'Liability of foreignness in global competition? Financial service affiliates in the city of London'. *Strategic Management Journal*, vol. 24, no. 12, 1187-1208.

Nell, PC, Ambos, B & Schlegelmilch, BB (2011), 'The benefits of hierarchy? – Exploring the effects of regional headquarters in multinational corporations', in: C. Asmussen, T. Pedersen, T. Devinney and L. Tihanyi (eds), *Dynamics of Globalization: Location-specific advantages or liabilities of foreignness*, Emerald Group, Bingley.

Proff, H (2002), 'Business unit strategies between regionalisation and globalisation'. *International Business Review*, vol. 11, no. 2, 231-250.

PwC (2019), *Beyond Brexit - my view from the bridge*, Andrew Gray, 6 September, https://www.pwc.co.uk/the-eu-referendum/beyond-brexit-insights/beyond-brexit-my-view-from-the-bridge.html .

Oh, CH & Rugman, AM (2012), 'Regional integration and the international strategies of large European firms'. *International Business Review*, vol. 21, no. 3, 493-507.

Osegowitsch, T & Sammartino, A (2008), 'Reassessing (home-) regionalisation', *Journal of International Business Studies*, vol. 39, no. 2, 184-196.

Qian, G, Li, L & Rugman, AM (2013), 'Liability of country foreignness and liability of regional foreignness: Their effects on geographic diversification and firm performance'. *Journal of International Business Studies*, vol. 44, no. 6, 635-647.

Roscoe, S, Skipworth, H, Aktas, E & Habib, F (2020), 'Managing supply chain uncertainty arising from geopolitical disruptions: evidence from the pharmaceutical industry and brexit'. *International Journal of Operations & Production Management.*

Rugman, AM & Verbeke, A (2004), 'A perspective on regional and global strategies of multinational enterprises'. *Journal of International Business Studies*, vol. 35, no. 1, 3-18.

Sammartino, A & Osegowitsch, T (2013), 'Dissecting home regionalization: how large does the region loom?', *Multinational Business Review*, vol. 21, no. 1, 45-64.

Smythe, J (2018), 'Australia's banks begin relocating functions from London'. *Financial Times*, 29 October, https://www.ft.com/content/fa65bbce-db1d-11e8-9f04-38d397e6661c38d397e6661c.

Suder, G & Lindeque, J (2018), *Doing Business in Europe*, Sage Publications, London.

Suder, G (2018), 'The business case for a Free Trade Agreement', *Australian Journal of International Affairs*, vol. 72, no.3, 272-286. https://www.tandfonline.com/doi/full/10.1080/10357718.2018.1453481.

Suder, G, Liesch, PW, Inomata, S, Mihailova, I, & Meng, B (2015), 'The evolving geography of production hubs and regional value chains across East Asia: Trade in value-added'. *Journal of World Business*, vol. 50, no. 3, 404-416.

Suder, G, Tsai, T & Varma, S (2021), *Doing Business in Asia*, Sage Publications, London.

UK Parliament (2019), Financial services: contribution to the UK economy, published 31 July, 2019, https://commonslibrary.parliament.uk/research-briefings/sn06193/.

Van Leeuwen, H (2018), 'Macquarie awaits green light for Brexit push into Ireland', *Australian Financial Review*, 31 October, https://www.afr.com/companies/financial-services/macquarie-awaits-green-light-for-brexit-push-into-ireland-20181031-h17bdpinto-ireland-20181031-h17bdp.

Woodman, A (2019), 'Multinationals Brexit', *Global Finance* (08 April), https://www.gfmag.com/magazine/april-2019/multinationals-brexit.

Zaheer, S (1995), 'Overcoming the liability of foreignness'. *Academy of Management Journal*, vol. 38, no. 2, 341-363.

Zhou, N & Guillen, MF (2016), 'Categorizing the liability of foreignness: Ownership, location, and internalization-specific dimensions'. *Global Strategy Journal*, vol. 6, no. 4, 309-329.

Zobel, N & Ambos B (2018), 'European business research in perspective: The focus of regionalisation in the international business literature', Chapter 3 in: Gabriele Suder, Monica Riviere, Johan Lindeque, *The Routledge Companion to European Business*, Routledge, London.

13

ON REINVENTING THE WHEEL: RESPONSIBLE GOVERNMENT AND THE EUROPEAN UNION

Charles Richardson

Keywords: Responsible Government, Constitutionalism, Democracy, European Parliament, Spitzenkandidat

Abstract

Much commentary on the European Union depicts it as suffering from a 'democratic deficit.' I argue that this criticism is on the right track but that the terminology mislocates the problem. The EU already has a democratic parliament; its problem lies in the relationship between parliament and executive, and its failure to fully embrace parliamentary government.

The history of parliamentary government, as developed in Britain over the last 350 years and adapted in other democracies, demonstrates how an executive can gradually evolve into a position where it is subject to parliamentary control. I suggest that the EU has been too ready to 'reinvent the wheel' rather than take advantage of models that can be found in its member countries and lessons that can be learned from their experience.

I illustrate the argument by contrasting the recent installation of a new Commission in Brussels with the contemporaneous formation of new governments in Spain and in the United Kingdom. I argue that the debate over the Spitzenkandidat process at the last two elections, while relevant, has been to some extent a distraction from more necessary tasks of reform.

Introduction

There is general agreement that one of the key challenges facing the European Union is the threat of Euroscepticism, made manifest most recently in the departure of the United Kingdom. A key part of the Eurosceptic narrative depicts the EU as suffering from a 'democratic deficit.' According to this story the EU is unelected, unaccountable and opaque; its bureaucracy is remote from and hostile to national interests; and its institutions are artificial, lacking the authenticity of national governments. Anyone who has dealt with the EU can appreciate that this set of criticisms contains an element of truth. There is more than a hint here of problems that the EU needs to deal with if it is to prosper in the longer term. But I argue that the terminology of 'democratic deficit' risks mislocating the problem: 'democracy' is not the best word for what is missing.

The structure of this chapter is as follows. In the next section, I set up the problem with a brief look at the European Parliament and the relationship between democracy and parliamentary government. Then I look in more detail at the history of parliamentary government, mostly by way of a comparison between the United Kingdom and the United States. In the following two sections I discuss some recent cases that illuminate the relationship between parliament and executive in Europe: firstly at the level of the EU, and then in two of its member states (one of them now an ex-member). Finally, I draw on the preceding discussion to outline an agenda for reform of the European Parliament and associated institutions; some modest proposals, followed by a few that are slightly more ambitious.

The European Parliament

The EU already has a fully democratic institution in the form of the European Parliament. It has been democratically elected since 1979, with impeccably free elections using proportional representation. Its party groupings represent the broad range of European opinion, and it has genuine parliamentary powers: legislation requires its assent, it elects its own presiding officials, and it can force the resignation of the EU's executive, the European Commission, as it did in 1999. Its voter turnout has often been disappointing (although many national parliaments can say the same), but it is at least respectable, rising to 50.7% in the elections (European Parliament 2019). In most respects, the European Parliament looks a lot like a typical (if unduly large and bureaucratic – even without the United Kingdom it still has 705 members) national parliament.

The real problem for the EU lies in the relationship between parliament and executive, and its failure to fully embrace responsible government. Elections are not enough: the issue is not suffrage, or fair electoral procedures, or any of the other things that the term 'democracy' tends to point us to. The issue is about control.

For a simple comparison, recall the Democratic Peace Theory – the idea that democracies do not go to war against one another. The First World War is sometimes cited as a counter-example, on the basis that Germany in 1914 was a democracy just as much as Britain or France (White 2005). And indeed it was in the sense of having a parliament elected by adult male suffrage. But it lacked responsible government; ministers were answerable to the emperor, and parliament in practice was unable to force changes in either personnel or policy. If what the German Empire had is a democracy, then perhaps 'democracy' is not quite the right concept to be working with.

Conversely, the introduction of responsible government has sometimes predated anything that we would now recognise as democracy. For example, Britain prior to the Great Reform Act of 1832 had a parliament elected on a highly restricted and capricious franchise; the right to vote was confined to a small percentage of the population, of the order of one person in thirty. (Exact figures are endlessly debatable: see, for example, Cannon 1972: 290-2; Bentley 1996:53-5; Price 2007:320-1.) Yet by the 1820s the power of the House of Commons, unrepresentative though it was, to make and break governments was well established, and the influence of the crown was much reduced (Dodd 1956:ch. 9; Hill 1996:ch. 6). A government can be accountable, even if the constituency to which it is accountable is much less than the whole population.

And the parliamentary government is not some weird, exotic beast. This is something that we know how to do. Twenty-six of the EU's 27 states have parliamentary or semi-parliamentary regimes, the one exception being Cyprus. It is true, of course, that the EU is rather different from an ordinary nation state; at best it is a loose federation, and since its component national governments are unwilling to relinquish control it is likely to remain that way for the foreseeable future. But although parliamentary government has never taken hold in the most notable federal system, the United States, the roster of parliamentary governments includes several federal systems; federalism itself is clearly not an obstacle. That is true even for a very loose kind of federalism: Australia in the early twentieth century is a prime example. Most government powers were held by the several states, with a comparatively weak federal government, but that government was still responsible to its own elected parliament.

Parliamentary Government

We also know that parliamentary government can evolve; that it is not something that has to be introduced all at once. The history of responsible government, as developed in Britain over the last 350 years and adapted in many other democracies, demonstrates how an executive can gradually evolve into a position where it is subject to parliamentary control. The archetype of parliamentary government, the Westminster system, developed in very much this sort of gradual way.

Up to the end of the seventeenth century, England had a system not unlike the model of the separation of powers that we are used to in the United States. The monarch as head of state was also head of government; they appointed ministers and other officials as they chose, and directed the policy of their administration. There was a legislature that was needed to pass legislation and had considerable power to constrain or frustrate the administration (especially by its control over taxation), but it could not determine the administration's composition. The United States is a democracy and England of the 1690s was not, but neither is an example of responsible government.

In the early 1700s, that began to change, particularly after Queen Anne came to the throne in 1702. Embroiled in a major war with France she was constantly in need of parliamentary support, and she was less able than her predecessors to withstand pressure from the (male, of course) party leaders (Holmes 1967). Gradually they secured the upper hand; in 1706, the Whigs forced the queen, much against her will, to appoint one of their leaders as secretary of state (Somerset 2012:308-13). Previous monarchs had sometimes had to pay attention to the balance of opinion in parliament when choosing their ministers, but this was the first time a parliamentary group had been able to seize the initiative. Anne and a number of her successors resisted the trend, helped by the embryonic nature of the party system. Even in the late eighteenth century George III was able to insist at times on his right to choose his own ministers (Cannon 1969). But he was fighting a losing battle, and ultimately the situation was reached where parliamentary majorities completely determined the government, reducing the monarch to a figurehead.

So why did the United States, starting less than a century later in a similar position, not go the same way? How did its presidents not just preserve their powers but add to them? Three reasons suggest themselves. In Britain, there was a radical difference in status between the head of state, an anointed monarch, and the politicians; not so in America, where the president was always just first among equals, a politician among other politicians. Since American political leaders could (and did) aspire to be president themselves, they had less interest in weakening the office's power or prestige. British politicians could not hope to take the throne, so they were happy to curtail its powers. The growth in the size and complexity of government through the nineteenth and twentieth centuries produced a more powerful executive in both countries, but in the United States that power accrued to a president with their own democratic mandate. In Britain, only the parliament had such a mandate, and the executive became dependent upon it.

Another reason was that it had always been the norm in England for ministers to be members of parliament – usually the House of Lords, but sometimes the House of Commons. That created issues about royal influence over parliament, but it also left open the potential for a co-operative relationship between parliament and administration. The Americans, however – partly through fear of corruption, and partly through following Montesquieu's somewhat misleading model of the separation of legislative and executive powers (see Montesquieu 1748: Book XI, ch. 6) – inserted a constitutional provision to forbid members of Congress from holding government employment (US Constitution, article I, section 6.2). This was a measure that backbench members of parliament in Britain had often pushed for, but without success;it stopped the executive from using the distribution of jobs as a tool of parliamentary management, but it also blocked a pathway to responsible government.

The third reason also started as a feature designed to weaken executive power. The United States constitution took away the executive's ability to dissolve the legislature: instead, Congress would sit for fixed terms, with elections always held at regular intervals (article I, sections 2.1 and 3.1). On the face of it, that made Congress more powerful, since it could not be cowed by the threat of dissolution. But it also meant that disagreement between executive and legislature could become a permanent state of affairs. A deadlock could not be referred to the electorate for decision, as it could in Britain. Instead, presidents learnt to cope with the periodic lack of a Congressional majority.

Congress in the United States inherited most of the methods by which parliament in Britain had been able to hold the executive in check. It could deny it funding by refusing to approve taxes and spending; it could legislate in defiance of the executive; it could impeach recalcitrant officials. But the secret of modern parliamentary government is that these powers are there only as a last resort. In normal circumstances, they do not need to be used in parliamentary systems because the executive has become the creature of the legislature: their use, or even the threat of their use, is a sign of crisis. In the United States, however, it is precisely the mechanisms of co-operation that are missing. Executive and legislature have gone their separate ways. And because the United States operates under a written constitution that is difficult to amend, it may not be practically possible to alter the features that have driven its different path of development.

Contrast this with the way that parliamentary government works today in most of Europe (and much of the rest of the democratic world). Elections for parliament are elections for government as well: in form parties compete for seats in the legislature, but in substance also for a share in executive government. Voters are able to know what they are voting for in terms of both personnel and policy: if the party they support is successful, its leading members will sit in government and its platform will, at least to some extent, be implemented as state policy. Election results may not directly determine the composition of government, in the sense that complex inter-party negotiations are sometimes required, but those negotiations proceed on the basis of what the voters have determined as to the relative strength of the different parties.

In other words, resting the formation of government on the ability to legislate means resting it ultimately on popular support. But the representative mandate of the executive is not concentrated in a single figure such as a president; it is diffused among the members of the party or parties that support it in the legislature. This gives the executive flexibility; the composition of the government can change mid-term in response to shifts in party or public sentiment. Rogue individuals can be removed or shunted aside without overturning the whole government. And dissolution, with the holding of fresh elections, is available as a remedy if the relationship between legislature and executive breaks down irretrievably.

In the remainder of this chapter, I look at the current constitutional structure of the EU in the light of these desiderata of parliamentary government. Some of the features of parliamentary government, as developed in the United Kingdom and in other countries of the broad Westminster family, can be discerned in the relationship between the European Parliament and the European Commission. But some are present only in attenuated form, and others are absent altogether. While it would be unrealistic to suggest that the European Commission could be reconstituted overnight to work like a modern parliamentary executive, there are a number of steps that could usefully be taken to move it in that direction. Some of this gradual change has already been happening in recent years, but more needs to be done if the European Parliament is to fulfil its potential.

Spitzenkandidat

Consider, for example, the *Spitzenkandidat* process as it has operated over the last two cycles of election to the European Parliament. *Spitzenkandidat* is German for 'lead candidate': the idea is that the party groups contesting the election should nominate beforehand their preferred choice for President of the European Commission, who would then be proposed for the job if that party wins the election (we will return shortly to the question of what 'winning' means). This, of course, is how national elections usually work in countries with parliamentary government. Parties or coalitions go into elections with identifiable leaders who are expected to take office if that party or coalition is able to form a government. They may hold an official position elected by the members of some party, or they may be designated by a combination of parties as their chosen standard-bearer. Either way, the electorate knows what it is voting for.

But elections for the European Parliament had never looked like this. Prospective candidates to head the European Commission were rarely mentioned prior to an election, and were never the focus of the campaign. The *Spitzenkandidat* process, introduced to much fanfare in 2014, was intended as a remedy. Unfortunately, it did not work very well. It gave the election some of the trappings of a regular parliamentary election, but it did not do much to bring the result into line with voter sentiment. The voting showed a groundswell of public dissatisfaction with the EU; Eurosceptic parties topped the poll in France and the United Kingdom. But the centre-right European People's Party (EPP) won a plurality of seats, and it stuck with its *Spitzenkandidat*, Jean-Claude Juncker, despite the fact that his conservatism and business-as-usual approach seemed the reverse of what was called for. He was duly nominated by the European Council and confirmed by the parliament with obvious reluctance.

Then in 2019 the system broke down completely. The EPP again won a plurality, but its *Spitzenkandidat*, Manfred Weber, was unable to win the support of the other parties whose votes he would have needed in the parliament. Instead, the European Council, after extensive debate, settled on Ursula von der Leyen, who was also from the EPP but had not been a candidate in the election (and at the time was still a member of the German parliament). She was confirmed by the European Parliament, but only with a narrow majority, and many members expressed their discontent with the apparent backtracking on accountability (De La Baume and Herszenhorn 2019). Although the centre-left parliamentary group, the Progressive Alliance of Socialists and Democrats (S&D), officially supported her, up to a third of its members either voted against or abstained (voting is by secret ballot, so it is impossible to be precise about where von der Leyen's support came from).

Part of what's going on here is a familiar problem from national elections. There is a widespread misunderstanding of what it means to 'win' an election, often abetted by poor media coverage and by politicians who make unfounded claims. Winning a plurality of seats is not enough. If the goal is to control parliament, what is needed is a combination of parties that can jointly command a majority, regardless of their individual size. That might involve the largest party taking a subordinate place in a coalition as the price of building consensus, or being left out altogether if smaller parties can combine effectively against it.

The more general problem, however, is that the appointment of the President of the European Commission is not driven primarily by the need to command a parliamentary majority. The configuration of party groups in the parliament is almost an afterthought. In an ordinary national parliament, members know what will happen if they vote down a prime-minister-designate: the leader of the opposition will be invited to form a government, and if no alternative majority can be formed then parliament will be dissolved for a fresh election. But the European Parliament has no such position as leader of the opposition, and it cannot be dissolved mid term. If it rejects a nominee for President of the Commission, its members know only that the same opaque process that produced that nominee will be resorted to again to come up with a different name. It is perhaps not surprising, then, that it has never done it.

So while the introduction of the *Spitzenkandidat* can be described as a step in the right direction, it has been to some extent a distraction from more necessary tasks of reform. Even if it were to work as intended, its effects would be more cosmetic than real. What matters is the 'why' of appointment, not the 'how'. The European Commission has become a party-based executive – its members are mostly members of political parties and it depends on continued support from those parties in parliament – but the process of selecting it has not caught up with that reality. The 'why' of parliamentary government is lacking, inasmuch as the Commission is not primarily appointed for party reasons. In this respect, it resembles the ministries of eighteenth-century Britain, where the monarch's wishes were the primary consideration and securing parliamentary support was something of an afterthought. Because Commissioners are appointed in consultation with the governments of the member states, they tend to reflect more the party strength in the country they come from than the overall party balance in the European Parliament. And there is nothing the parliament can do about it other than reject a whole slate of Commissioners and send the process back to square one.

Countries with parliamentary government employ a variety of different methods for the nomination of their head of government: election by parliament, consultation by a constitutional monarch, inter-party negotiations led by an *informateur*, politically informed choice by an elected president; often subject to a vote of confidence in one or both houses of parliament, or simply to a potential veto by parliament, sometimes as to individual ministers or just to the whole government. What they hold in common is the shared understanding on all sides of the need for a parliamentary majority: that is the fundamental goal that the appointment process is driving at. The debate over the appointment of the European Commission needs to focus less on the detail of that process and more on an explicit embrace of that fundamental goal.

Two Recent Examples: Spain and the U.K.

To illustrate the contrast, consider the procedures followed by two of the EU's (then) largest member states at the same time as the von der Leyen Commission was being installed.

In Spain, a new government under Pedro Sánchez had taken office in the middle of 2018. It lacked a reliable majority, and called an early election in April 2019 after its budget had been rejected by parliament. The election returned a broad centre-left majority, but negotiations for a coalition government broke down and Sánchez sought to retain office at the head of minority government. He was duly proposed for the position by King Felipe VI, but failed to win an investiture vote, or vote of confidence, in parliament. With no other available option, the king dissolved parliament for a second election, held in November. It produced a similar result, but this time the parties concerned quickly reached an agreement to co-operate in forming a government. In January 2020 Sánchez narrowly won the investiture vote and was again sworn in as prime minister.

In the United Kingdom, the occasion for a change of prime minister came in June 2019, when Theresa May resigned as leader of the Conservative Party. The party elected Boris Johnson to replace her, and he was sworn in the following month. That was followed, however, by a number of defections from the party, and it soon became clear that he could not command a majority in parliament. But nor was there a majority for any alternative government, and the complexities associated with the negotiations for Britain's exit from the EU prevented an immediate dissolution of parliament. Only after parliament had forced him to secure an extension of time from the EU did Johnson push for an early election. This required an amendment to the *Fixed-Term Parliaments Act*, which the opposition parties eventually agreed to support. The election was held in December, and Johnson won a clear majority in his own right.

Both cases were abnormal. Each was described in terms of 'crisis', including features that were unprecedented in decades of political experience. (No coalition government had been formed in Spain since the 1930s; no British court had ever previously accepted jurisdiction over a purported prorogation of parliament.) Nonetheless, in each case the system worked. Both countries, in slightly different ways, have mechanisms that ensure accountability of the executive to the legislature, and ultimately to the electorate. In each case the rules were placed under an unusual degree of tension, but they did not break down. The electorate in each case had the final say, and all parties respected its decision, even if they did not agree with it.

A Reform Agenda

Not everyone will agree that the 'democratic deficit', leaving aside the question of whether that is the correct term for it, denotes a real problem. Evidently, there are powerful institutional interests that are broadly content with the EU the way that it is. Inertia is a powerful factor in any large organisation and it would be idle to deny that marshalling support for reform is a major task, even before the specifics of reform are addressed. Nor is this conservatism without theoretical support: almost two decades ago Andrew Moravcsik argued that the EU was as democratic as it needed to be, and that the idea of a crisis of legitimacy was without foundation (Moravcsik 2002).

On the other hand, the EU has not stood still in the face of the challenges of recent years. It is difficult to see its response to those challenges as anything other than a recognition (whether fully sincere or not is immaterial) that reform of some description is necessary, and that the complaints of the EU's critics are in some measure genuine. In any case, I do not propose to pursue that particular debate further. In what follows I assume that a more responsive EU is a desirable goal, and that, however remote the political prospects of it might be, it makes sense to think about the specific reform measures that might serve the purpose.

The central problem, it seems to me, is that the EU has been engaged in a process of 'reinventing the wheel' rather than taking advantage of models that can be found in its member countries and lessons that can be learned from their experience. As a result, its moves towards parliamentary government are clunky and half-hearted. They lack a natural constituency within the EU; those who would usually support taking power away from the bureaucracy in Brussels are opposed to anything that looks like a 'federal Europe'. On the other hand, even pro-European politicians are wary about shifting power away from the member states, while the institutional drivers that support greater integration are often only lukewarm about democracy. As I said on the occasion of the installation of the Juncker Commission:

The EU's opaque procedures are the product of something of an unholy alliance between national governments, who don't want European integration to get out of control, and EU bureaucrats, who like integration but don't much like democratic accountability. (Richardson 2014)

The peculiarities of the EU's structure are the products of its history, which is unlike that of any modern nation. Its institutions are less the product of organic growth and more of conscious design. The EU began as a mechanism for economic co-operation, and its progress has been shaped throughout by the need for compromise between the major national interests involved, especially those of France and Germany. It is no surprise that the results would often be complex and lacking in transparency. But all politics involves compromise, and the very artificiality of the EU can also be seen as an opportunity to learn from the experience of other countries and incorporate those lesson in institutional design.

To illustrate what I think could be done, what follows is an agenda for modest change in the workings of the European Parliament and its relationship with the executive. Some are things that may happen gradually given time, but they indicate the presence of roadblocks that need to be removed or circumvented for real parliamentary government to develop.

Provide for Commissioners to have a close and continuing relationship with the European Parliament. In most countries with parliamentary government, either all or most ministers are chosen from among members of parliament, and remain members while they are in office. By my count, only nine of the current 27 Commissioners have ever been members of the parliament. Continued membership of parliament is not essential (some countries manage without it), but Commissioners at least should appear regularly before parliament to answer questions, provide information and speak in debates. Existing provisions for this seem inadequate.

Abolish fixed parliamentary terms. A key ingredient of parliamentary government is the ability for parliament to be dissolved mid-term in the case of otherwise unresolvable deadlock between it and the executive. The precise mechanisms vary considerably, but the important thing is that gridlock, or irresponsible government, cannot become institutionalised. As the American example indicates, to guarantee the legislature against dissolution is not actually doing it any favours.

Introduce open voting for all votes of confidence. At present, the European Parliament votes on the final approval of the Commission in a normal open vote, but at the previous stage, when the President of the Commission is elected, voting is by secret ballot. It is difficult for any executive to be responsible to a parliamentary majority if it doesn't know exactly who that majority consists of. Secret voting potentially allows members of the parliament to deceive either their electorate or the Commission (or both) as to how they are voting, thus undermining accountability all round. It also undermines the already rather fragile coherence of the European political parties.

Rename positions to aid transparency. A number of offices and institutions bear titles that tend to obscure rather than reveal their function. The term 'president' is particularly overused: President of the European Council, President of the European Commission, Presidency (but not president!) of the Council of the EU, President of the European Parliament, President of the Court of Justice, and so on. Similarly the European Council is easily confused with the Council of the EU or the Council of Europe (the last of which is not even an EU institution).

Give the parliament power to initiate legislation. The fact that the parliament can only legislate at the initiative of the Commission has been a grievance for many of its members for some time. (Article 17:2 of the Treaty on European Union provides that 'legislative acts may only be adopted on the basis of a Commission proposal'.) It is possible that change would be of mostly symbolic importance; in most parliamentary systems it is rare for a parliament to pass legislation contrary to the wishes of the executive. But symbols matter, and this would be a useful step to push the Commission towards a more co-operative relationship with the parliament.

More ambitious change

For the medium term, a number of other structural reforms should be considered.

Provide for salaried post of Leader of the Opposition. Consensus is a fine thing, and it is no criticism of the European Parliament to say that it has generally tried to avoid an adversarial approach to issues. It's also true that not all parliamentary systems incorporate such a position as Leader of the Opposition. In particular, multi-party systems can produce parliamentary situations that offer more than just a binary choice, and more than one party may be a plausible contender for the role of opposition. But the concept is usually there even if the formal office is not. It's basic to parliamentary government that there are alternatives – parliament's power to force a government from office is all but meaningless if it knows that this will probably result in chaos. Provision for a Leader of the Opposition at least entails that someone has the ability to criticise a government from outside and provides a default option to form an alternative government.

Reconstitute the Council of the EU as a proper upper house. The Council of the EU, formerly and often still known as the Council of Ministers, is usually described as the upper house of the European Parliament, but it is a most unusual one. Its members represent the governments of the member states, and its composition varies depending on the subject being discussed, and in some circumstances it can legislate independently of the parliament. It appears more like an alternative to a parliamentary regime rather than a component of one. Instead, permanent delegates elected by the member states and enjoying parliamentary privileges could perform a valuable function as a house of review, as happens in many federal systems.

Limit the European Council's role to nomination of the head of state. The European Council, consisting of the heads of government of the member states, can provide valuable political impetus to the direction of the EU. But that fundamentally informal role is complicated by reserving official duties for it as well. Currently, in addition to appointing the President of the European Council, it also appoints the EU's foreign minister (the 'high representative') and the President of the European Central Bank, and nominates (for parliamentary approval) the President of the Commission. Its role should be confined to the first of those: once the President of the European Council – in effect, the EU's head of state – is in place, that person should be responsible for nominating the head of the executive government, the President of the Commission. Parliamentary government should put the formal task of appointing a government the hands of someone without a conflicting political stake in the process.

Reapportion seats in the parliament to reflect population, perhaps including cross-country seats. As noted earlier, parliamentary government can coexist with many 'undemocratic' features in the election of a parliament. It was established in many countries at times when the franchise was based on property, when women were unable to vote, or when the distribution of seats bore little relationship to population.

Nonetheless, the European Parliament would probably be more likely to act like a genuine parliament if the distribution of seats in it was not so obviously designed to protect the interests of member states as states, rather than the voters at large.

Conclusion

The purpose of this reform agenda is to align the EU's processes more with the canons of parliamentary government that have been demonstrated to work in its member countries and elsewhere. There they ensure – imperfectly, like all human institutions, but better than any other mechanism so far discovered – that executive government is kept in close touch with the wishes of its electorate, being held accountable while retaining an appropriate degree of flexibility.

Logically, that should meet many of the objections of the Eurosceptics who complain about the EU's lack of responsiveness and undemocratic nature. Unfortunately, even if the political will were there to enact such an agenda, it most probably would do nothing of the sort. Although, as remarked at the beginning, there is substance to a number of Eurosceptic complaints, the reality of Euroscepticism is that it is driven less by issues of process than by fundamental political disagreements. While its leaders may claim to want transparency and democracy, experience suggests that they will actually resist those things if they see them involving a drift towards 'federalism" – that is, towards the EU behaving like a real government. As Jonathan Freedland remarked (Freedland 2019), 'The Europhobes' demands can never be met because what they want – cake in both its having and eating modes – is impossible.'

But a more accountable governing structure in the EU, in addition to being a desirable goal in itself, does have the potential to diminish the constituency for Eurosceptic complaints. An EU that is governed more transparently and more democratically should be better placed to deal with the issues that fuel discontent and that have driven many voters into the arms of the discontented.

References

Bentley, Michael (1996), *Politics Without Democracy 1815-1914: Perception and Preoccupation in British Government* (1984), 2nd ed., Blackwell, Oxford.

Cannon, John (1969), *The Fox-North Coalition: Crisis of the Constitution 1782-4*, Cambridge University Press, London.

Cannon, John (1972), *Parliamentary Reform 1640-1832*, Cambridge University Press, London.

De La Baume, Maïa & Herszenhorn, David (2019) 'Ursula von der Leyen elected European Commission president,' *Politico*, 16 July, https://www.politico.eu/article/ursula-von-der-leyen-elected-european-commission-president/.

Díez, Anabel & Marcos, José (2019), 'Spain's acting PM wants constitutional change to prevent new stalemates,' *El País*, 12 July, https://english.elpais.com/elpais/2019/07/11/inenglish/ 1562859165 _143284.html

Dodd, A.H. (1956), *The Growth of Responsible Government from James the First to Victoria*, Routledge & Kegan Paul, London.

European Parliament (2019), '2019 European Election Results,' https://europarl.europa.eu/ election-results-2019/en/turnout/.

Freedland, Jonathan (2019), 'After this staggering defeat for May, our country is left lost and adrift,' *The Guardian*, 16 January, https://www.theguardian.com/commentisfree/2019/jan/15/defeat-may-errors.

Hill, Brian (1996), *The Early Parties and Politics in Britain, 1688-1832*, Macmillan, London.

Holmes, Geoffrey (1967), *British Politics in the Age of Anne*, Macmillan, London.

Montesquieu, Charles Louis de Secondat, Baron de 1748, *The Spirit of the Laws*, trans. T. Nugent (1750), https://oll.libertyfund.org/titles/montesquieu-complete-works-vol-1-the-spirit-of-laws.

Moravcsik, Andrew (2002), 'Reassessing Legitimacy in the European Union', *Journal of Common Market Studies*, vol. 40, no. 4, 603-624.

Price, Munro (2007), *The Perilous Crown: France Between Revolutions*, Pan Macmillan, London.

Richardson, Charles (2014), 'Change at the top in the EU', The World is Not Enough (blog), 1 September, https://worldisnotenough.org/2014/09/01/eu-president/.

Somerset, Anne (2012), *Queen Anne: The Politics of Passion*, HarperCollins, London.

Taylor, Simon (2013), 'Bettel to lead three-party "Gambia" coalition in Luxembourg', *Politico*, 4 December, https://www.politico.eu/article/bettel-to-lead-three-party-gambia-coalition-in-luxembourg/.

VoteWatch Europe (2019), 'Election of the Commission', https://www.votewatch.eu/en/term9-election-of-the-commission-appointment-of-the-von-der-leyen-commission-election.html#/##vote-tabs-list-2.

White, Matthew (2005), 'Democracies Do Not Make War on One Another. … or Do They?', https://web.archive.org/web/20051230112813/http://users.erols.com/mwhite28/demowar.ht.